AMERICAN VERNACULAR DESIGN

1870  1940

AN ILLUSTRATED GLOSSARY

AMERICAN VERNACULAR DESIGN

1870  1940

AN ILLUSTRATED GLOSSARY

HERBERT GOTTFRIED   JAN JENNINGS

VNR VAN NOSTRAND REINHOLD COMPANY
New York

For two of our favorite vernaculars, our son Jon
and our friend, Annetta Cheek.

Printed in the United States of America

Published by Van Nostrand Reinhold Company Inc.
135 West 50th Street
New York, New York 10020

Van Nostrand Reinhold Company Limited
Molly Millars Lane
Wokingham, Berkshire RG11 2PY, England

Van Nostrand Reinhold
480 La Trobe Street
Melbourne, Victoria 3000, Australia

Macmillan of Canada
Division of Gage Publishing Limited
164 Commander Boulevard
Agincourt, Ontario M1S 3C7, Canada

16 15 14 13 12 11 10 9 8 7 6 5 4 3 2 1

Library of Congress Cataloging in Publication Data
Gottfried, Herbert, 1940–
     American vernacular design, 1870–1940.

     Bibliography: p. 256
     Includes Index.
     1. Vernacular architecture—United States—Dictionaries. 2. Building
materials—United States—Dictionaries. I. Jennings, Jan., 1946–
     . II. Title.
NA710.G68 1985   720′.973   84-17240
ISBN 0-442-23067-2 c
ISBN 0-442-22739-6 pb

Acknowledgments

MANY PEOPLE HELPED US COMPLETE THIS HAND-book. When we were conducting historic surveys of Tulsa and Oklahoma City, Oklahoma; Cheyenne, Wyoming; and Council Bluffs, Iowa; local historians and librarians helped us relate local building traditions to national trends. We appreciated having had access to historic photograph collections in the Panhandle-Plains Museum of Canyon, Texas; in the Museums and Historical Department of the Wyoming State Archives at Cheyenne, Wyoming; and the Oklahoma State Historical Society of Oklahoma City, Oklahoma. We also examined trade catalogs and architectural pattern books in the collections of the Northwest Architectural Archive of the University of Minnesota at St. Paul, Minnesota; the Iowa State Historical Building Library at Des Moines, Iowa; the National Museum of American History, Smithsonian Institution, Washington, D.C.; and the Iowa State University Library at Ames, Iowa. We also appreciated having copies of the Bellows family's records on their Sears Roebuck house in Scotia, New York.

We wish to acknowledge as well the help of several individuals without whom we could not have realized our study: Forrest Wilson for his enthusiasm and belief in the idea, and for introducing us to Larry Hager of Van Nostrand Reinhold, who makes publishing easy; graduate assistant Jim Sipes for drafting the copy and illustration borders; landscape architect Jeff Benson for labeling the drawings; and Deb Arneson, who in her willing and reliable way typed the text.

Preface

THIS BOOK IS ABOUT DESIGN IN INDUSTRIAL VER-
nacular architecture. As a handbook it describes and illustrates the compositional elements and the design concepts
that have underwritten much vernacular building. The time
period under consideration, 1870–1940, is framed by the post–
Civil War era and the onset of World War II. *American Vernacular Design* is not a style manual. In our scheme of things,
style is the last question to be addressed in assessing vernacular design. This book, rather, is an extensive examination of
the industrially produced structural, cladding, and finish
materials that were assembled into prototypical vernacular
buildings. Vernacular buildings are broken down into their
component parts in the first section and reassembled into
cohesive and rational designs in the second.

Vernacular architecture, as referred to in this study, is the
traditional American architecture that was passed on to successive generations of builders and designers through the use
of materials, shapes, and textures, spatial organizations, proportions among elements, and systems of ornamentation.
Within the development of industrial vernacular design, the
industrial manufacturing system became the medium by
which the tradition was broadcast. The sharing of values that
characterizes folk vernacular architecture in other cultures
was subsumed by industrial development in America. Whereas architectural values were once transmitted by word of
mouth or by demonstration, in industrialized America they
were transmitted through manufacturing—the changing of
raw or finished materials into architectural products.

This transmission was facilitated by a developing distribution system and by communication media. Ultimately, the
kind of shared values and trust in materials and forms that
characterizes vernacular architecture developed across the
country. Seen in this way, the vernacular also reflected what
was popular. Pattern books from architectural offices, journals, and magazines such as *Carpentry and Building, The
Building Age, Pencil Points, The White Pine Series, House
Beautiful*; services such as the Architects Small House Bureau
(an architect-sponsored, Minnesota-based organization); pub-
lications such as the "how to build your own home" books, and

the trade catalogs of the hundreds of companies that produced or distributed building materials—such were the vernacular links among American social groups and cultures.

HISTORICAL BACKGROUND

The period 1870–1940 saw great development in manufactured building materials. Whereas some important machinery designed to produce building materials was developed before the Civil War, the twenty-year period after the war witnessed the invention and patenting of a great number of machines and manufacturing methods to work wood and metal, as well as the development of mills and factories to produce building products, finish goods, and furniture. Meanwhile new saws, planes, boring and sticking machines, and presses began to produce precise and reliable goods. Although standardization of components was not resolved nationally until the twentieth century, most millwork and conventional lumber fit together, and carpenters and joiners altered components to suit the job at hand.

The millwork or woodwork industry provides a good example of the development of vernacular components. Millwork includes moldings, door frames and entrances, blinds, shutters, sash and window units, doors, stairwork, kitchen cabinets, mantels, and china or corner cabinets. For this study the development of the lumber industry and the production of joists, sills, studs, plates, and rafters is equally important.

Woodworking machinery was developed in the late eighteenth century and throughout the nineteenth, with major breakthroughs in machinery design coming from the introduction of metal framing, the increasing specialization of machines, and the evolution of special blades and cutting knives. While there were pre–Civil War machines, such as the planer-matcher that produced tongue-and-groove flooring, the last quarter of the nineteenth century witnessed the development of new jointers, shapers, tenon-and-mortise machines, boring machines, lathes, and sanders.[1]

Millwork shops were established throughout the country. But the Mississippi Valley, from Minnesota to Louisiana, was the locus for mills that produced lumber and millwork from the white pine timber of Michigan, Wisconsin, and Minnesota. Although timber and finished lumber were transported by water, it was railroad expansion that facilitated the rapid and far-reaching distribution of building materials.

In its early stages, millwork manufacturing was tied to local resources and uses—that is, local timber was used to produce materials for area builders, and the need for standardization of materials was confined to the locality. As the railroads expanded millwork markets and as white pine began to give way to various species of yellow pine brought in from the West and South, the need for standardization became apparent.

National standardization of milled work, however, did not occur until the first decade of the twentieth century.

A second development in woodwork manufacturing that influenced vernacular design was the move by mills to break down elements—say a window—into constituent parts and ship the parts bundled. Thus the wholesale or retail millwork dealer could assemble any size of window from the bundles of rails and stiles on hand. This innovation lessened the need to order finished work from the mill. Custom work—fancy work, as it was called—was still done on a piece-by-piece basis. The change in the method of making windows typifies developments throughout the millwork industry: in the course of time, all elements were broken down into groups or single pieces and were assembled and finished by the seller or the builder. Focus shifted from the mill to the job site, and it put design in the hands of the carpenter and the designer.

But the drive toward standardization was not realized all at once. Prior to being able to order millwork from any geographic area, the builder could sometimes rely on regional organizations that promoted common sizing and common business practices. Moreover, individual mills produced pieces that were compatible with their entire line of stock work. To ensure proper fit and proper relationships among all pieces, builders often ordered all millwork from the same mill.

The production of woodwork in standard lengths, profiles, and thicknesses, coupled with railroad development, expanded the housing industry in all parts of the country. Not only was the distribution system altered from one in which jobbers and other middlemen added handling fees to the costs of materials to a streamlined system of mill-retailer-consumer, but the sheer volume of production facilitated the development of industrial vernacular design. For example, white-pine lumber production in the Chicago area increased from 1.2 billion feet in 1873 to 2.4 billion in 1890. Those figures demonstrate a steady growth in the housing industry. During the same time, however, production of shingles went from 3.9 million to 1.5 billion.[2] The latter figure indicates a change in the use of shingles for cladding and roofing, the extensive use of shingles for ornamentation, and a change in design.

Millwork and lumber production in Chicago serves as a microcosmic example of the kind of industrial development that supported vernacular design. Wood manufacture began in Chicago as early as 1839, and by 1857 there were some twenty planning mills and sash, door, and blind factories. In 1872 there were about twenty millwork shops and forty planning mills, and by 1889, approximately ninety mills of all kinds employing 4500 workers who produced 10 million dollars in goods.[3] Chicago was a one of several key cities that processed raw and finished lumber. The editors of *Industrial Chicago: The Building Interests* described in detail the production of one large millwork firm, Palmer, Fuller and Company:

This corporation's sash, door, and blind plant has an average daily capacity as at present operated [1891], of about six hundred doors, one thousand windows, and two hundred and fifty pairs of blinds, including a large amount of odd work. . . . In illustration of the scope of territory over which the output of the factory is distributed it is related that in one day thirteen car loads of sash, doors, and blinds were loaded each for a different state or territory.[4]

The Palmer, Fuller facility was modern in that it had a system of long sheds, all joined, so that a board entered the plant and remained "under cover" until it was finished and loaded in a rail car. Granting some exaggeration in the description, and granting also that the day's production was exceptional, if one multiplies only half the amount cited by the number of millwork shops in Chicago, the production level is significant. And if one includes the shops along the Mississippi River, around the Great Lakes, and in the South and Northwest, woodwork production by the turn of the century was enormous.

The impact of this production was the creation of the built environment as most of us know it. Industry gave us a building system that was the basis not only for vernacular design but for high style as well: the production of partial or whole millwork elements, of structural members and systems, and of cladding and other finish materials continues, although with fewer manufacturers. Over time, the elements have been modified by new design concepts or philosophies, but the manufactured element remains the basis for the vernacular system.

The significance of this development is harder to assess. On the one hand, it seems monumental when one considers how successfully the United States has developed a sophisticated building industry. We have managed to satisfy most human needs—social, economic, and cultural—with industrially produced materials. We have spawned a two-track parallel-design system—architect-designed high style, and vernacular—that embraces an entire society. We have generated what Amos Rapoport describes as a form of design that is both product and process. Seen this way, vernacular design had a "polythetic definition, that is, a multidimensional one based on a number of characteristics both as product and process. This then allows the classification and definition of various forms of design in terms of the presence or absence of a certain percentage of these characteristics."[5]

Rapoport is interested in integrating the total context of vernacular design, including life style, social and work activities, and any other ingredients that help uncover the vernacular in terms of experience and meaning. But that is not at issue in this work. Instead, we have started with the physical properties of the products and the design schemes that result from the fusion of elements. This aspect of the vernacular is seen as a ground for the figures known as "experience and meaning."

Industrial vernacular design was effected by the tension between the use of elements in generic concepts, such as the use of cottage-style windows in the design of cottages, and the desire to expand on their use, to push the cottage window into the bungalow or the Italianate villa. The system was so flexible, so enticing, that it encouraged experimentation and trial-and-error design until coherent forms emerged. This was not wholly a free-market environment in which each builder or designer was an entrepreneur, licensed to use anything in the catalog. There was a heritage of forms, some borrowed from other cultures, and others originating both in high-style design as well as in vernacular folk-based design. The vernacular design process had a bias rationality that was reflected in the detailing of elements—the way the arc in one section of a molding was reinforced by other curves on the same face or on adjacent pieces—and in the integration of units into systems—the way the front door integrated with the side-lights, porch, and steps so that, psychologically and aesthetically, entering a building became a meaningful act. Most small elements related to adjoining elements. Surfaces were integrated and profiles were finely wrought. Consumer preference and other factors, such as changes in materials or the development of better machinery, eliminated many unsatisfactory designs. Ultimately, the whole system was delivered to the consumer, or the consumer at least had access to it. The materials, tools, and distribution system gave the individual the opportunity to engage the process and to create a product.

SCOPE OF THE STUDY

This handbook attempts to contribute to the understanding of the continuum of vernacular design in the built environment, as described in its products and organizing principles. The characteristics of the products and principles have been limited to those that seem to have been most prevalent in vernacular design. Thus, this is not an encyclopedia of all the materials ever used in constructing a vernacular building. To the contrary, our first study of the literature of the period, academic studies on the subject, and extant buildings produced a set of elements and types found to be most popular from 1870 to 1940. To arrive at a conclusion about the use of elements, we developed a computer program to enable us to record elements during the survey of a city, then asked the program to calculate the frequency distribution of those elements. Our sample, therefore, listed summaries of the types of roof, window, entrance door, and the like for all structures, which gave us data about the overall character of any neighborhood as well as a profile of its primary building types.

At this point it cannot be stated unequivocally that every element illustrated was the most popular element in its class, but there was enough evidence of its use to assume significance. The same logic holds true for generic designs in the second section: the types illustrated were most evident throughout the period 1870–1940 and had proof of distribution throughout one or more regions of the United States. The historical basis of each design is not at stake here, but rather the design's active ingredients. In this sense the study leans toward design criticism as well as design history. For example, gabled cottages have a rich development throughout most of the building history of the country. As a form, gabled cottages have something in common with a folk vernacular house, the so-called I-house, which has been adequately described by cultural geographers and folklorists, and also with imported styles such as houses in the English medieval tradition. It was not our intent to research and to document the historical relationships among these influences on cottages with gable roofs. Rather, we are encouraging the on-site engagement of vernacular buildings. We hope to promote visual analysis of design properties and to put vernacular design within the perspective of the Industrial Revolution's impact on American life. Furthermore, we intend to celebrate the rationality and coherence of vernacular design. It is, after all, the system that most of us encounter as part of our human development; perceptually it embodies a large portion of our spatial system. The vernacular has proven to be a healthful environment. Although it may not have become the moral force that promoters of the modern home had hoped it would, it has certainly contributed to the foundation of significant social structures like the single-family house, the neighborhood, and the town.

Vernacular design, for better or for worse, has been closely tied to the economic system. It celebrates differences in property values, yet has always been scaled so as to be accessible to a range of income levels. But symbolically it has stood for much more than the prospective capital gains of our economic system. Alan Gowans sees vernacular buildings as visual metaphors in which social values and aesthetics are linked.[6] Gowans argues that the vernacular provides continuity with our history and beliefs. In making meaningful visual metaphors, the vernacular tradition has been eclectic, taking the best of the past and using it in the present. To our way of thinking, the industrialization of the vernacular tradition made it possible to express our convictions, our agreements about the "rightness" of forms and proportions. We see the process as having two dimensions: a personal dimension in which one can exercise one's inalienable rights by building within the vernacular, and a social dimension in which the past is appreciated and the social function—as Gowans puts it, "what buildings do in and for society"—is realized. Seen in this way, the vernacular is not historicism for its own sake, nor is it normative either, since it does not promise the good society. The vernacular is present-oriented, contemporary; it declares what the current state of civilization has to offer. Imagistically, the vernacular is direct. Vernacular design may wax sentimental in the hands of the overindulgent, or it may be brutal in registering the lack of adequate distribution of wealth in our society. But in the main the vernacular represents some of the best we have to offer, and it does so with conviction.

ORGANIZATION

The text is divided into two sections. The first is an inventory of components organized logically, following a procedure that can be used to analyze any vernacular building—building type, structure, cladding, roof form and roof elements, windows, porch and entrance systems, elements of walls, and ornamentation. Each of the illustrated elements has been defined on the left-hand side of the page. Taken together, the definitions constitute a vernacular design glossary. The glossary has been derived from historic and contemporary architecture or building dictionaries, all of which are listed in the Bibliography. Most of the entries in standard works address historic or high-style or commissioned design and are not always appropriate for the vernacular. As much as common sense would allow, traditional definitions have been broadened or focused to include vernacular design.

How the components were distributed throughout a structure, and how they were organized to produce a generic design, is the subject of the second section. While most of these buildings are house types, some attention has been given to commercial and public buildings. Only building types for which enough information existed to make a case have been included. Individual structures and categories of buildings, such as resort or vacation buildings or vernacular industrial buildings, did not provide enough evidence to develop a general statement about design; in time, these types may become better known. Specific names for building types derive from several sources: a significant design feature, a façade treatment, or occasionally a design concept. Primary design characteristics are listed for each building type, and if appropriate, characteristics of variations on the main form are included.

NOTES ON BUILDING TYPES

Most of the building types analyzed are house types, such as *gabled cottages* and *hipped cottages*. Both of these were wide-ranging types, and both were built throughout most of the period studied. By grouping these buildings under their dominant design feature, the roof form, we intend to make a case for continuity in design. The roof in both cases contributed greatly to the overall shape of the buildings, and at the same time provided limits and opportunities for design. These opportunities or variations are classified and listed, in approximate chronological order, as subsets of each general category. Chronology is not precise, because many of the building types overlap and on occasion influence one another.

The *mansard* and *gambrel cottages* are more clearly defined, because they had fewer variant developments over time. In each case the roof form was so distinctive that their designs became associated with historic styles, and as such, they were susceptible to the shifting sands of fashion.

The *organic cottage* is the most intuitive of the cottage types. The concept of organicism was based on the conceptual approach that designers and builders took toward a group of house types all characterized by a strong feeling for centrality. In some cases the centrality came from a central core, perhaps tied to circulation paths, or from a "living hall" or a stairway central fireplace configuration. This is true even with side-hall plans. The movement toward the center was often expressed vertically so that the houses seemed centripetal, yet there was also a centrifugal type that flowed out from the center. Both attitudes toward plan contributed to the development of the modern, open-plan building, a progression suggested by historian Vincent Scully in his study of the history and development of the shingle style.[7]

Bungalows are a special house type, in that they have had several translations into other idioms. Besides having a malleable façade, the bungalow also contributed to the evolution of open plan. As such, it deserves credit for inculcating modern sensibility, particularly modern perception of the continuity between inside and outside space. The bungalow has received mixed reviews in terms of its original intent to provide low-cost housing for middle-class families. Although it turned out to be more expensive to build than predicted, it delivered modern amenities within modest square footages. As today's housing market moves toward smaller houses and as family structure changes, the bungalow concept may return.

Multifamily buildings have been part of the vernacular tradition from 1870 to the present. Because of increases in land values, multifamily structures moved toward large-scale apartment buildings and away from the vernacular toward commissioned work in most cities. Throughout their development, multifamily buildings were consistently an integral part of neighborhoods, of working-class housing districts, and of commercial districts. They were especially successful in creating the illusion of the single-family residence on the inside as well as the outside.

There is another class of vernacular buildings that deserves mention—the mass-produced house or commercial building.

The kind of structures referred to are the houses that the Iowa Railroad Land Company advertised in its *Iowa Farming Lands* brochure of 1870. The company operated out of Cedar Rapids and sold "ready-made" houses of all sizes manufactured by Major Lyman Bridges of Chicago. Prices for such buildings included all materials and finish goods, and packaged houses were shipped by rail to the station closest to the buyer. Such activity was not new. People in Maine remember stories about houses being built, then taken apart, numbered, and lettered, and shipped on three-master schooners around Cape Horn to northern California. But the railroad was the real key to the distribution of vernacular goods. It was the railroad that permitted companies like Sears Roebuck, Montgomery Ward, and the Aladdin Company to build prefabricated houses and ship them across the country. The authors have copies of the records of a Sears house, model #16052, being built in upstate New York in 1926 from materials shipped from Sears mills in Newark, New Jersey; Philadelphia, Pennsylvania; and Dunkirk, New York. Elements were manufactured at different sites and assembled by a carpenter or by the owner. Besides the plants listed, Sears at the same time had facilities in at least five locations in Ohio, and more in West Virginia.

In examining the designs of industrially produced houses, we found that the elements of design and the building types had been included in the examples given in the handbook. This is because the industrial housing manufacturers, whether selling individual houses or entire towns, designed within the given vernacular tradition.

AUDIENCE

This handbook was written with several groups of readers in mind. The authors have spent considerable time training people with little or no architectural background to analyze the design of vernacular buildings. Some of these people were conducting surveys of historic structures to assess the significance of cultural resources in their built environment. Others were planners or design professionals who were developing design guidelines for historic preservation districts or conservation districts.

Readers may use the same method that underwrites the elements portion of the book to make an analysis of a given district. If the design elements of buildings in an area can be surveyed and a simple frequency distribution developed as to the occurrence of elements and building types, then one has a basis for design or conservation guidelines. How guidelines are to be addressed varies with each situation, but in general design guidelines should be generic: respect for scale, shape, materials, and significant design elements is more important than the replication of historic details.

This book is also written for real estate brokers who might like to describe the designs of buildings in their sales area. As advocates for good design, we encourage the use of referring to design values in assessing the significance of a building. As academics we have also directed the book toward those interested in the history of design. Through the glossary, through the discussions of the implications for design of manufactured elements, and through the classification of design types, we hope to make a contribution to the developing literature on American architecture and building. Finally, *American Vernacular Design* has been written for anyone who likes the physical properties of the built world. We hope to encourage visual literacy for vernacular environments.

TO THE READER

In conclusion, we note that vernacular buildings are composed of both arithmetic and geometric progressions of elements and concepts—that is, elements and ideas have been added to one another in single or multiple steps. To arrive at an assessment of the extent to which any building has used the vernacular vocabulary, one asks a series of questions. Starting with obvious ones such as what kind of building it is, and what kind of structure, roof, and cladding it has, the reader can begin to construct a framework for determining design. A second set of questions includes queries as to the relationships established among design elements, and the nature of proportional schemes, of tensions among large-scale elements, and of continuities among the elevations. As you refer to the handbook for answers to these questions, begin with the glossary, in which terms are underlined, and proceed to the illustrated elements and the discussions about their relevance for design.

To ascertain a building type, reassemble the elements visually, keeping some overall design concepts in mind, and work through the second section. It is also possible to start backward—that is, to locate a type and work back through the elements to understand its origins. Since not all the vernacular types ever built have been included in the handbook, readers will discover variations that have not been illustrated. Should the reader come upon one of these, it is the authors' hope that, with the aid of the handbook, the reader will be able to identify the building's salient features as the first step toward understanding its form and design.

NOTES

1. William B. Lloyd, *Millwork: Principles and Practices* (Chicago: Cahners Publishing, 1966), p. 6.
2. *Industrial Chicago: The Building Interests* (Chicago: Goodspeed Publishing, 1891), pp. 331–33.
3. *Ibid.*, p. 356.
4. *Ibid.*, p. 380.

5. Amos Rapoport, "An Approach to Vernacular Design," in *Shelter: Models of Native Ingenuity* (Katonah, NY: Katonah Gallery, 1982), p. 45.

6. Alan Gowans, *Learning to See: Historical Perspectives on Modern Popular/Commercial Arts* (Bowling Green, OH: Bowling Green State University, Popular Press, 1981), pp. 395–456.

7. Vincent J. Scully, Jr., *The Shingle Style and the Stick Style,* rev. ed. (New Haven: Yale University Press, 1955).

ELEMENTS

DETACHED HOUSES OCCUPY MOST OF THE AREA OF a platted lot and are the dominant vernacular building type in the United States. Most detached houses were built as single-family residences; they were built on open homestead land, on narrow railroad lots, on boulevards and crowded city streets. They were built individually as speculation houses or as commissions; in groups as small-, medium-, and large-scale developments; and as prefabricated buildings.

Detached single-family houses have been built in all shapes and styles. They have been constructed from almost every kind of manufactured construction material produced. These houses also reflect a wide range of socioeconomic factors, both public and private tastes, and numerous responses to climatic conditions.

The most common multiple of the single-family unit is the *semidetached house* that shares a common wall with another house. These buildings are usually of frame construction, with variety in cladding and with floor plans that mirror each other. A common porch may unify the façades, and both may have a common roof. Sometimes referred to as the *double house,* these structures usually have front and back yard space. They have been built in multiples, so that entire blocks may consist of double units. The two-family house or *duplex* is another kind of two-family building whose units usually have similar floor plans; it is arranged with a dwelling or an apartment on each floor. The upper level has either an exterior or interior access. While a duplex may share a wall and a roof, it does not share a porch.

Rowhouses are continuous houses with similar plans, fenestration, and ornamentation. A rowhouse shares a common or party wall with the adjoining house or houses. Usually constructed of masonry (at least veneer), rowhouses were built as single-family units. A row consists of three or more houses, and rowhouse structures cover entire blocks in eastern cities. Rowhouses range in height from two to four stories, with most making use of the attic space. The houses are seldom wider than 25 or narrower than 13 feet. Most rowhouses have no front yard, being built right to the sidewalk line, and most extend deep into the lot with a little space left for a back yard. Variety in style can be found in a particular row, because row groups were often built over an extended period of time. Basic composition, however, usually remained constant, which created uniformity and rhythm throughout the façades. An elegant version of the rowhouse that originated in England and was usually architect-designed was the *terrace*.

DETACHED HOUSE

1 FAMILY

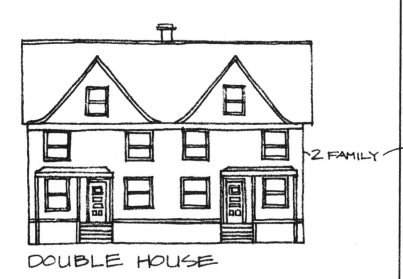

DOUBLE HOUSE

2 FAMILY

DUPLEX OR
TWO-FAMILY

ROWHOUSES

Specific design issues in residential and commercial buildings will be addressed in the sections dealing with prototypes, such as the bungalow or the arcaded business block. In most of these buildings, the façade is the primary elevation, but that does not mean that the entire design concept appears on the façade. Historical buildings were especially thought of as having four sides. Thus elevations relate to one another, and floor plan, fenestration, and the like may have continuous effects from one side of a building to another.

In house designs, large geometric units—rectangles, square, triangles, even circles—are integrated. In looking at vernacular houses, one should consider not only the wall planes but also the roof planes and the planes of any secondary elements such as dormers, back or side porches, and porte-cocheres. In a well-designed house, all these shapes will fit into a cohesive form. Windows, doors, and building materials will articulate the planes and their integration, through repeats or irregular placement, and reinforce the unity of the design.

THE MULTIFAMILY DWELLING HAS A RICH HISTORY. Structurally it is usually composed of three or more apartments, usually having common access, service systems, and use of land. Most multifamily buildings consist of rented living space in which families or individuals may live independent of one another and do their own cooking on the premises. Vernacular types in apartment buildings were built of masonry or with brick, wood, or metal cladding over frame construction. These buildings are rarely more than three stories in height and usually occupy an entire building site.

The *triple decker* is found primarily in New England, where it served as housing for millworkers and business personnel. It is most often of frame construction with either exterior or interior access and rear porches for each story. The *quadriplex* and *sixplex* are common arrangements in which apartment units are accessed through a central hall. Units are stacked over one another and usually repeat a basic floor plan, although occasionally there are differences in room arrangement and size between the apartments that face the street, which are larger, and those that face the back of the lot, which may face an alley.

TRIPLE DECKER

3-FAMILY

QUADRIPLEX

4-FAMILY

SIXPLEX

6-FAMILY

Multifamily buildings concentrate most of their design features on their façades. Depending upon siting, side elevations may also carry elements from the façades. Overall, symmetrical schemes predominate. The arrangements may use a central hall entrance as the center axis, or a side entrance may be balanced by a window grouping on the opposite side.

Most multifamily designs tend to spread out across the site and emphasize horizontal lines such as the foundation, the banding of windows by story, and a cornice. Vertical accents in these designs come from establishing bays, usually through the vertical alignment of windows, on the façade.

Some multifamily buildings will organize the façade into projecting and receding planes. For example, a common treatment includes projecting corner pavilions with a recessed entrance area. The converse can also be found, in which the entrance projects forward beyond the plane of the main wall. In multistoried buildings the entrance hall is carried through each floor and may be lighted by façade windows. The stacking of these lights over the entrance generates another vertical accent.

A *STORE* USUALLY OCCUPIED AN ENTIRE BUILD-ing, whereas a *shop* was part of a building. In vernacular buildings there are more extant stores than shops. While the tradition of using buildings in this way was imported, American business people changed the nature of stores in that goods, wares, and merchandise were offered for sale in American stores. Sales were both wholesale and retail, and most stores had space for display, sales, and storage. In sum, stores were eclectic both inside and out.

The *movie theater* took many shapes in the early years of the motion-picture industry. Early theaters were often shops or stores converted to the new use with little accommodation for the medium. As the motion picture became a significant force in American culture, the movie theater acquired architectural style. Opera houses were used as movie houses, and opera house design seems to have played a role in the evolution of the movie theater, especially the ability of the opera house to address the glamour and romance movies offered as entertainment.

The term *business block* is thought to be British in origin. The block was a business building with a pronounced design that was referred to by its proper name—say, the Van Zant Block. Such buildings were built in central business districts and featured combinations of shops, offices, and apartments. The corner block was a visual and financial anchor for many business districts. It often marked the edge or the heart of the commercial area.

STORE

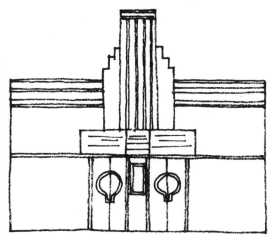

MOVIE THEATER

CORNER BUSINESS BLOCK

Early stores were deeper than their width, and in those areas where railroad surveyors platted the town sites, the lots were especially narrow and deep. Wealthy entrepreneurs bought two or three lots. Later stores lost lot depth to alleys and other commercial developments, and they tended to be developed on the horizontal. In both cases, the stores divided into levels; city stores used one or two stories for merchandise, and all stores had office or living space above the commercial area. On the exterior, store design balanced display space below against fenestration for the upper levels.

Movie theaters changed design motifs in the course of time, but most designs focused only on the façade, and most façades were designed to accent the vertical: the walls were built skyward from the corners toward the center, or the whole façade was projected high enough to enclose a balcony. A marquee, dramatically thrust toward the street, countered the vertical elements. A third major design feature included the ornamentation of the walls.

The corner block had to integrate two elevations and develop a strong entrance. Since profile was important, the cornice of each elevation received more detailing than other sections. The walls were integrated by various means including arcading, continuous sills and lintels, and belt courses. Quite often these buildings had different dimensions and one side would be longer, though rarely higher, than the other. A very popular entrance for these buildings was a canted one, set at 45 degrees to the intersection of the walls.

THE NAMES OF SOME VERNACULAR COMMERCIAL buildings vary according to their geographical location. *Café*, for instance, was, in vernacular design, the name of a midwestern and western restaurant that might be called a lunch room, luncheonette, or diner in other regions. Menus also vary in each of these businesses, but most are devoted to light meals and short-order cooking. Interior organization followed that of a store, in that most were deeper than they were wide, with kitchen and dishwashing at the back and a counter and tables parallel to the walls.

The *continuous business block* has been used in central business districts as well as in secondary commercial districts that service neighborhoods. Like many commercial buildings in the vernacular mode, these have domestic scale and support a variety of enterprises. Upper-story space in these buildings was also used for office space or apartments.

The vernacular *hotel* has often been built near a rail line or near the center of town to accommodate business traffic. These establishments frequently served as centers for commerce and social activity, and as temporary quarters for adventurers. Most hotels were sited to front a busy street. Corner lots were especially useful in providing the most entrances and one or more first-floor businesses. Stylistically, the vernacular hotel or inn had a domestic scale. It has often been replaced by an architect-designed high-rise building.

CAFÉ

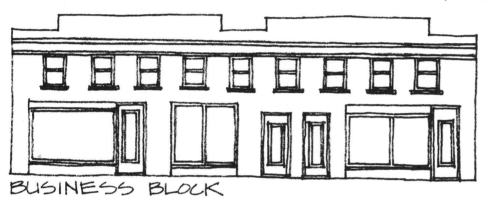

BUSINESS BLOCK

HOTEL

Café design is simple in that most buildings divide the façade into display space (perhaps based on the theory that watching people eat or prepare food encourages others to eat), signage, and an entrance. Cladding materials play a large role in design, because some materials such as metal panels may bind the façade into a neat, tight package, while brick or clapboard may understate the building's function and integrate it into other structures in the area.

The continuous business block relies on continuity of materials, most often brick, on a uniform profile, and on orderly fenestration.

Entrances service the stores or the upper-level spaces. These buildings were often built over an entire block so as to make their identity clear: they were the commercial center of the area. At times they were given special detailing, such as terra cotta cladding, that separated them visually from their context.

Hotels were built both on open spaces and as part of groupings. Their scale was residential, although many reached four or five stories. Design elements included a street level (for business area hotels) or a porch space, uniform wall treatment, and roof detail including a strong cornice or roof shape. They were compact buildings, but with additions they could become rambling.

WAREHOUSES ARE BY DEFINITION BUILDINGS USED to store wares, goods, and merchandise. They have been associated with wholesaling and with the assemblage of component parts. Warehouses have played an important part in the development of towns and cities linked by railroads, waterways, or interstate commerce highways. In many cities, warehouses are grouped or clustered. Because of their tendency toward uniform shape and uniform building materials, they define industrial districts.

In the vernacular tradition, *factories* are small- or medium-sized buildings, usually of masonry construction, in which component parts of products are made and assembled or in which special manufacturing processes are carried out. Designed to accommodate machinery, a factory is any building in which workers perform these tasks in a uniform fashion. The organization of the tasks—say, into assembly lines—sometimes determines the shape and size of the building.

A *mill* is a special kind of industrial building. Originally, mills chiefly ground grains for flour or oil. As textile and wood products developed, the mill changed in form and purpose. Mills came to rely on mechanical systems to alter the state of raw materials, and on significant amounts of energy, such as water power, to run the machinery. Vernacular mills that process scores of materials may be found in most regions of the United States, because the technology was transferable. Mills are of both masonry and frame construction.

WAREHOUSE

FACTORY

MILL

Warehouse design is quite uniform throughout the country. Most vernacular buildings are brick, with plain walls, orderly placement of windows, and modest ornamentation. Shipping and receiving areas have large openings for ease in transferring goods, and many utilize loading docks that mediate between transportation and storage. In warehouses that provide display space for goods, the ground level often has an office space and a well-marked entrance. Such entrances may be ornamented. As in most modest buildings in the vernacular, the cornice line is often the most architectural element on the building.

Factory design differs from warehouse design in the fenestration. Factories require much more light, so the proportion of window to wall increases dramatically in factories. Piers become more obvious on the elevations, and walls rely on window type, shape, and size as organizing elements.

Mill design is the most varied of these industrial buildings. Mills have been adapted for many uses and tend to be accretive: new manufacturing processes require additions to the old building. Mills too require light, and like the factory, the mill may expand window arrangements and/or add light through the roof. Skylights, monitor roofs, or roofs that trap light, such as the saw-tooth are common.

VERNACULAR PLACES OF WORSHIP COME IN ALL sizes and shapes, with variations in floor plan somewhat tied to theology and ritual. Christian—particularly Protestant—churches exhibit a remarkable flexibility, in that they are often recycled through several denominations. Vernacular *churches* are most often domestic in scale and are composed of simple, direct geometric forms. Massing is limited to the walls of the building and a tower or spire element. Most remaining vernacular churches are located in rural settings.

School buildings also tend to be rural buildings of one or two stories built of frame construction. Many were prefabricated structures. School buildings have much in common with rural churches in that scale, materials, and shape are often similar. Like churches in cities, schools outgrew the vernacular tradition; by the turn of the century most were architect-designed.

Railroad stations, both freight and passenger, usually were designed buildings: specific rail companies commissioned firms to design buildings that could be replicated throughout their system. Some companies had architectural divisions that produced any kind of structure. These designs used manufactured elements common to the industrial vernacular system. Stations were often designed and built in bays, so they could be adjusted to fit a town of any size. Most were domestic in scale, with low roofs and common cladding. Stylistically, these stations were modest structures intended to convey an image of confidence and service. Stations could, however, use local materials and absorb historic styles.

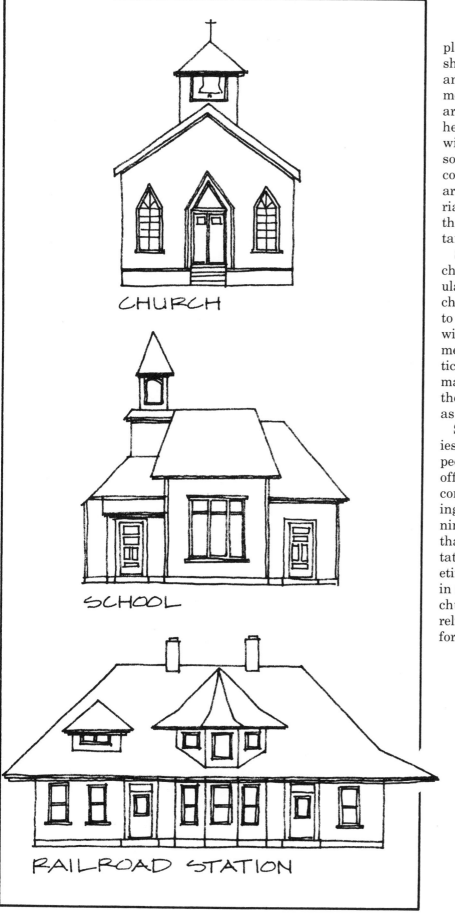

CHURCH

SCHOOL

RAILROAD STATION

Church design centers on the placement of the entrance, the shape of the congregational space, and the location of vertical elements. Most vernacular buildings are rarely over two stories in height and employ a modest window-to-wall ratio. Solid masonry, brick veneers, and frame construction with wood cladding are all common. Building materials play a major role in design: that is, the materials are as important as any other element.

School design is quite similar to church design, except that vernacular schools are larger than churches. Floor plans arrange one to four rooms on a single floor, with symmetrical window placement and a gesture toward the vertical. Whereas the church spire may extend toward sacred space, the schoolhouse bell simply serves as a landmark.

Station design consists of a series of bays meant to hold goods or people, with one bay serving as an office. Both frame and masonry construction are common. Buildings tend to be long and low, running parallel to the track, rather than tall and compact. Ornamentation is limited to trim and bracketing, with some lintel or sill work in masonry structures. Like the church and the school, the station relies on simple, direct geometry for effective design.

FRAMING IN VERNACULAR CONSTRUCTION IS DIrectly tied to the production of dimensioned lumber and the making of wire nails. The standardization of framing elements allowed for ease of framing and adaptation to a myriad of building styles. The *balloon frame*, the most common in the United States, has the vertical studs that make up the wall run in one piece from the foundation to the roof. All pieces in this framing, including intermediate pieces such as floor joists, are nailed to the studs.

The *platform frame,* also referred to as the Western frame, is a type of frame in which the wall, floor, and roof frames are independently built. For example, each floor is supported by studs that are only one story in height. To provide resistance, diagonal braces are often added to the floor, the external walls, and the roof. This kind of construction has also been called the braced frame.

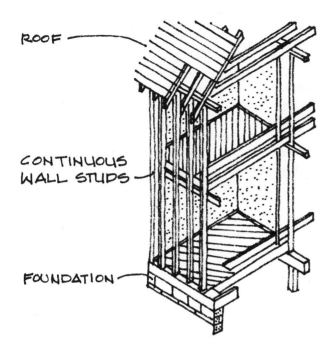

ROOF

CONTINUOUS
WALL STUDS

FOUNDATION

BALLOON FRAME

Wood-frame construction has played a role in overall design, especially light framing, which permitted the use of a wide variety of cladding materials. The light frame also provided opportunity for adding to or taking away from the body of the frame. One framing style, the Craftsman, exposed rafters and purlins that gave bungalows and cottages a unique stylistic quality. Light framing also allowed for the application of ornament or style systems so that house types in particular were more extensively developed than they might have been with masonry construction.

Other design features in wood framing include adaptation to climatic conditions as in the use of the platform frame in the midwest and west, and the universality of dimensioned lumber, which gave access to framing methods no matter what the species of wood or the geographical location.

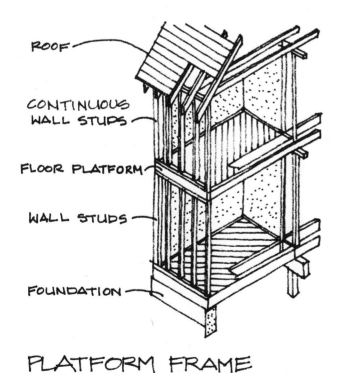

ROOF

CONTINUOUS
WALL STUDS

FLOOR PLATFORM

WALL STUDS

FOUNDATION

PLATFORM FRAME

STRUCTURE: MASONRY AND POST AND BEAM

MASONRY CONSTRUCTION REFERS TO THE BUILD-
ing of *load-bearing walls* of brick, stone, hollow tile, cast
block, or concrete. Such bearing walls carry their own
weight as well as other weights, such as that of the roof. In
brick construction, walls are at least two bricks thick; a
thickness of as many as four or six bricks is possible. In
some commercial or public buildings, walls may be thicker
on the first story than at upper levels.

Post-and-beam or *post-and-lintel construction*—the terms
are used interchangeably—is one of the oldest building systems known to man. It is a type of framing in which upright
supports or posts carry horizontal beams or lintels.

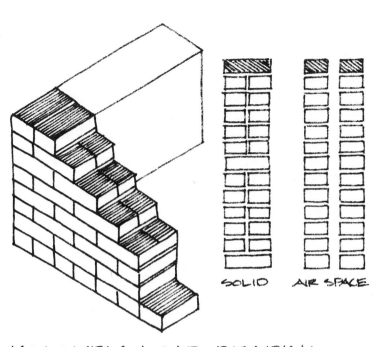

SOLID   AIR SPACE

MASONRY LOAD-BEARING

Load-bearing walls are difficult to discern from the outside, with stone being somewhat easier than brick. House construction has used this heavy wall construction, and many commercial buildings have it, particularly on the lower levels—the foundation and first floor. Sometimes the load-bearing wall will give a building a definitive shape and size, and the material used may affect the massing of elements and the texture of walls.

Post-and-beam construction is also hard to read, because the structure is covered. Exceptions include cast-iron store fronts and reinforced concrete piers and beams on industrial buildings. Post-and-beam framing in wood or metal may also be evident on interiors, where evenly spaced posts or columns organize interior space.

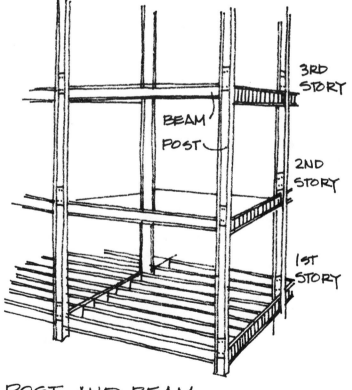

3RD STORY

BEAM
POST

2ND STORY

1ST STORY

POST AND BEAM
(WOOD OR METAL)

ALTHOUGH *SHINGLES* WERE ORIGINALLY ASSO-ciated with roofing and cladding for some types of folk housing, the vernacular tradition has incorporated them as cladding and ornamentation. As cladding, a shingle is a wedge-shaped piece of wood or a relatively flat piece of asbestos cement, molded to look like wood or an asphaltic material, used in overlapping courses to cover an outside wall surface. Wood shingles were at first split and shaved, and later sawn. Sawn shingles could have their exposed surface, the butt, shaped to create unusual patterns. In this way shingles added visual texture to building design.

Specific names for shingles seem to have come from trade catalogs. Shingle patterns shown here are standard types, but more ornamental shingles could be cut.

Most cladding materials contribute pattern to design. In the case of manufactured shingles, pattern may be determined by a combination of factors including the shape of the shingles, the surface texture, and the arrangement of the shingles in rows.

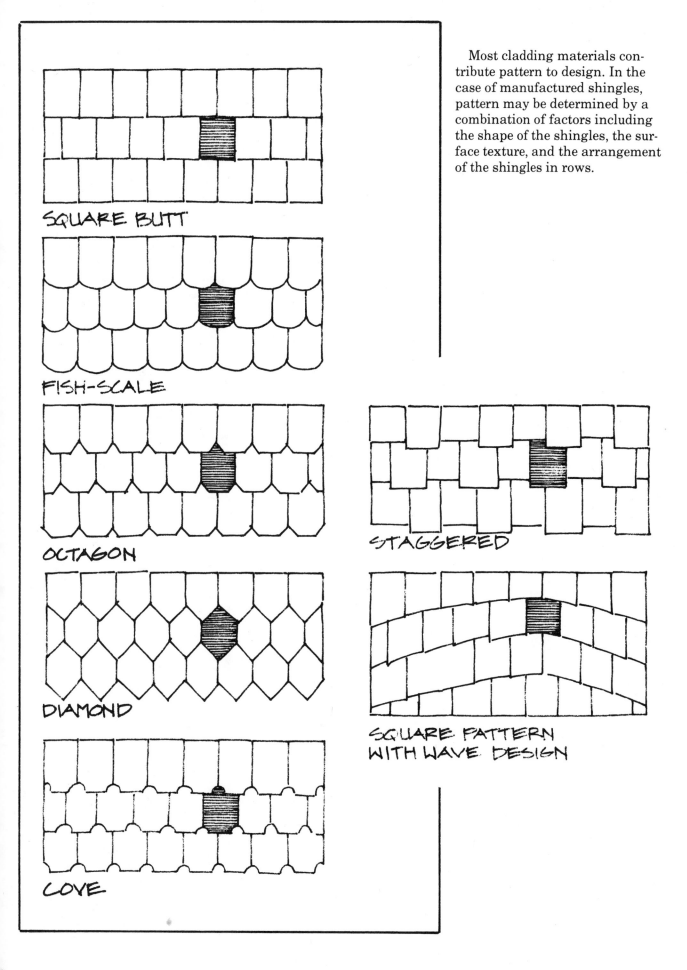

SQUARE BUTT

FISH-SCALE

OCTAGON

DIAMOND

COVE

STAGGERED

SQUARE PATTERN
WITH WAVE DESIGN

STANDARD *CLAPBOARD* SIDING IS COMPOSED OF long, relatively thin boards that vary in width and have a thick lower edge and a feathered upper edge. The shape of the boards permits them to be overlapped horizontally. Clapboards used in vernacular buildings have been made of pine, cedar, and cypress and are nailed, depending on width, with as little as two inches and as much as eight inches exposed to weather.

Weatherboard is usually wide, with rabbeted or lapped edges; it is laid on the horizontal with the edge of each board overlapped to prevent rain or other moisture from passing through the walls.

Beaded siding is a form of beveled siding, like clapboard, that features a bead on the lower edge. The bead is a molding with a convex circular section and a continuous cylindrical surface. Beaded siding is nailed the same way that clapboard is.

Board and batten siding consists of wide boards placed on walls in a vertical position with their joints covered by narrow battens. Alternatively, the battens are nailed on first and the cladding boards second, so that the battens are exposed.

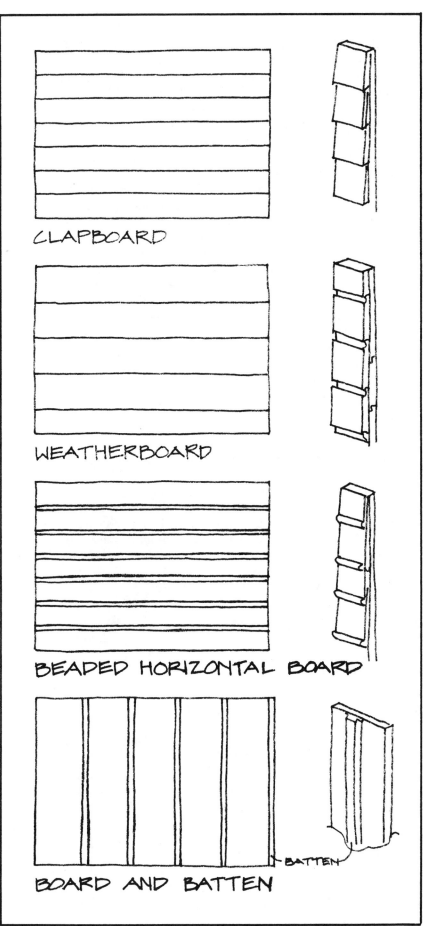

CLAPBOARD

WEATHERBOARD

BEADED HORIZONTAL BOARD

BOARD AND BATTEN

BATTEN

Design with clapboard is centered on the overall appearance that the continuous and integrated boards give to a building. Clapboard walls look solid, of one piece, which makes the fenestration an important design element, in that it relieves and punctuates the walls. Horizontal divisions are possible with clapboards by varying the width of the boards on selected portions of elevations. For example, the gable ends of a house may have narrower boards than those on the lower portions of the walls.

Wood siding also produces a shadow line in most of its applications, with weatherboard or any kind of lapped board producing the least shadow because of the tightly fitted joints.

Beaded siding is the most three-dimensional of these types. The bead molding diminishes slightly the seeming solidity of the walls, but it enlivens the wall surfaces.

Board and batten work is rhythmical and capable of casting shadows, and it is often tactile as well because it is made from rough-cut boards. This siding may be found on houses, but it has also been used on outbuildings and minor commercial and industrial buildings.

THE METHODS BY WHICH BRICKS OR STONES CAN be coursed constitute a system organized by patterns. Some coursing produces a stronger wall, and some produces more ornamental patterns. The key to all coursing lies in the placement of the unit, be it a brick, a block, or a stone. In brickwork, a *stretcher* is a brick placed lengthwise in a course. A *header* is laid across a wall to bond parts of the wall together, with its end toward the face of the wall. *Soldier bricks* stand on end with an edge to the front. *Shiner courses* are laid lengthwise with the wide face of the units exposed. A *rowlock* is a brick-on-edge course with the end of the bricks showing on the face of a wall in vertical position. The *sailor* is also vertical but has its wide face exposed.

The typical use of brick in vernacular design is as a veneer of single courses over a wood frame. Solid brick walls, built to carry wall and roof weight, are the next most prevalent type. Bricks are laid up in patterns that usually take their names from traditional forms of bonding. *Bonding* refers to the laying of bricks or stones regularly in a wall according to a recognized pattern usually designed for strength.

The *Flemish bond* pattern consists of headers and stretchers alternating in every course, laid up so as to break joints, each header being placed in the center of the stretchers in the course above and below.

Common bond, also referred to as American bond, consists of stretcher courses except that the fifth, sixth, or seventh course is composed of headers.

Running bond originally saw more use in interior walls or in party walls between adjoining buildings, but lately it has been employed on exterior walls. In this pattern each brick is laid as a stretcher, with each vertical joint lying between the center of the stretchers above and below.

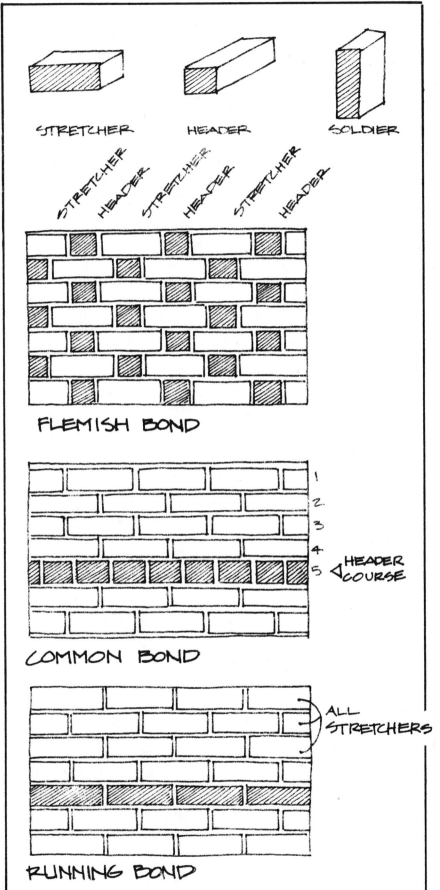

STRETCHER HEADER SOLDIER

SHINER

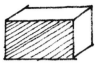
ROWLOCK

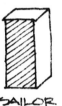
SAILOR

STRETCHER HEADER STRETCHER HEADER STRETCHER HEADER

FLEMISH BOND

COMMON BOND

1
2
3
4
5 ◁ HEADER COURSE

RUNNING BOND

) ALL STRETCHERS

Reading pattern in brickwork is a bit like translating Morse code, in that the stretchers resemble dashes and the headers, dots. These two placements far out-number all other placements of bricks in bonding patterns. Soldier, shiner, rowlock, and sailor courses are almost exclusively ornamental.

From a design point of view, the use of brick offers an opportunity to apply color, both monochromat-ically and polychromatically, and to have the mortar joints play a role in the visual scheme. Joints are thick or thin, and of a certain texture, color, consistency, and profile. Profile refers to the shape of the joint on section, how far it recedes or projects, and the outline of the shape.

Brick walls have a powerful presence, and the impact of bond-ing is often subtle. Look for alter-native coursing at the lower and upper portions of walls, above and below openings, and at corners.

ENGLISH BOND IS NOT USED IN VERNACULAR building as frequently as other patterns. It is a strong wall form in which one course is composed entirely of headers and the next course entirely of stretchers, the header and stretcher courses alternating throughout the wall.

In *English garden wall bond* the courses are put up like common bond, except that header courses occur in every fourth course.

English cross bond is also a less frequently used form of bonding. This pattern also employs alternate courses of headers and stretchers, with the stretcher course breaking joints with its neighboring stretcher courses.

Stack bond is a more contemporary pattern that requires "stacks" of stretchers, which generate a precise rectilinear wall.

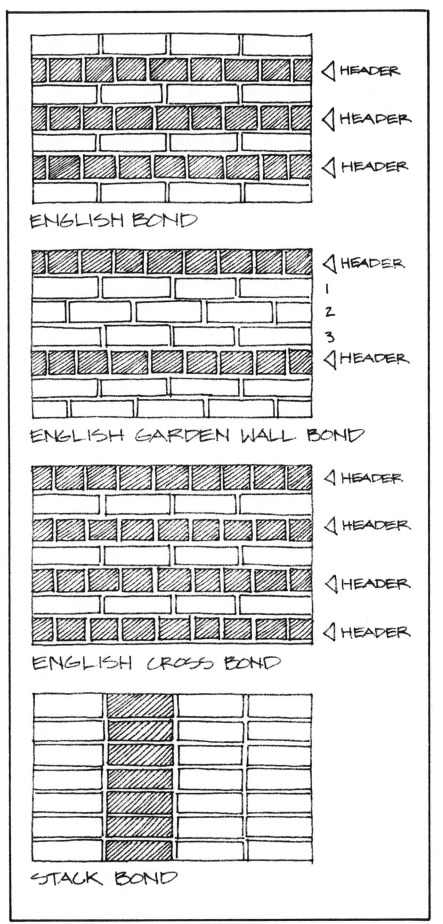

ENGLISH BOND

ENGLISH GARDEN WALL BOND

ENGLISH CROSS BOND

STACK BOND

The shape of a brick can affect the general appearance of walls. Visually, stretchers tend to pull the walls away from the center, while headers seem more centripetal. Brick is a hard-surface material, and when it is coursed in the manner of the English bonds, it appears to become even denser. Similarly, the infrequently used stack bond looks almost monolithic and impenetrable when compared to other patterns.

STONE MAY BE LAID UP IN COURSES AND PAT-
terned in ways similar to the brick bonds, but because of the
variety of cuts or natural shapes stone can take, it has
unique patterns of its own.

An *ashlar* wall has a face of square or rectangular stones.
In *coursed ashlar,* stones are of equal height on each course.
In some ashlar walls, the various blocks have been arranged
according to height, and there may be a progression from
larger to small sizes from bottom to top.

Rock-faced ashlar employs stones with natural faces or
faces left as they were received from the quarry. In *uncoursed ashlar*—sometimes referred to as broken-range
ashlar—the masonry is not laid up in layers but is irregularly or randomly placed.

So-called *random ashlar* is not as random as the name
implies. Stones are squared and assembled in a pattern that
is repeated again and again, but the pattern is not always
immediately discernible.

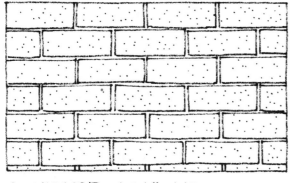

COURSED ASHLAR: SMOOTH FACED

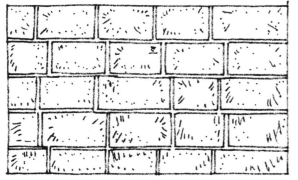

COURSED ASHLAR: ROCK FACED

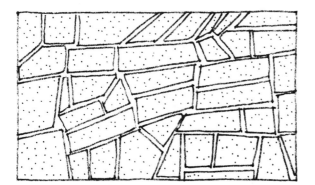

UNCOURSED ASHLAR: ROUGH CUT

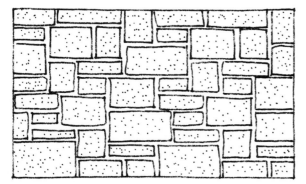

RANDOM ASHLAR

Bricks and stone blocks may be thought of as modules that systematically organize walls. Design in stone is generally related to design in brick in that coursing, color, and mortar are integral elements in any scheme. Texture, both visual and tactile, is more important in stone, because of the very nature of stone and the increase in size of each unit.

Stone has the ability to convey the feeling of durability better than any other cladding material. Likewise, one can infer something about its weight, whether imagined or literal, and one invariably responds to its pronounced mass.

Stone encourages both restrained and vigorous design. Generally, the more the stone is dressed—that is, cut or shaped— the more restrained the design becomes. Some blocks, such as rock-faced ashlar, generate a fine tension between the dressed and mortared edges and the raw rock face.

RIVER ROCK IS PRECISELY WHAT IT SOUNDS LIKE— stone found in and along streams and rivers that has taken on rounded and organic shapes because of erosion. In glaciated areas glacial till has the same properties. This kind of stone is used in specialty walls to take advantage of its shapes.

Coursed rubble consists of broken pieces of masonry that may be roughly dressed but are still built up in courses. As is often the case in river rock, spaces between the rubble blocks can be filled with smaller pieces.

Cobweb and *puzzle-type rubble* are novelty walls in which the builder takes advantage of the broken quality of the stone to generate one large form, the cobweb or puzzle. Such work is usually reserved for houses or outbuildings.

Random rubble includes almost any kind of stone, regardless of its shape and size, with all blocks irregularly placed so that there is no suggestion of coursing.

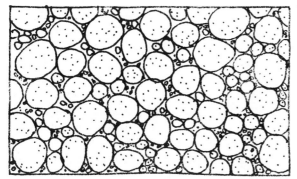

RIVER ROCK (COBBLESTONE)

COURSED RUBBLE

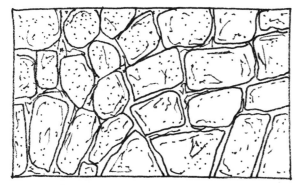

COBWEB OR PUZZLE RUBBLE

RANDOM OR UNCOURSED RUBBLE

The use of stone in its natural state, or with very little cutting, has been associated with the desire to create rustic effects in design. In this sense such use is part of the picturesque tradition. To find river rock and rubble applications, one looks in rural areas.

Texture is very much at stake in using these materials, but so is the placement of units. Most of the design in this idiom wants the stone to look "found," to suggest that the rock has a natural relationship with the site, as if it had been found there. It may also suggest that the building in question is part of the folk tradition in building. In industrially inspired vernacular design, such appearances on bungalows or cottages are illusions, because the stonework is a veneer over a wood frame.

STUCCO REFERS TO THE PLASTERING OF EXTERIOR walls. The stucco mixture is composed of cement, lime, and sand, and the mix is applied wet. When dry, it is exceedingly hard and durable. Stucco is placed over masonry walls or frame walls to which furring or wire mesh has been added.

Cement that is thrown or sprayed on walls has a different finish from traditional stucco. Compositionally, the base plaster may be similar to stucco, but coloring may be added, and pebbles, chips, or flecks are thrown on the top coat. A rough but plain thrown surface has often been called rough-cast, while a surface with embedded pebbles has been called pebble dash.

In commercial vernacular buildings, *terra cotta* panels could accent a plain masonry building or completely sheath and thereby enliven a plain shape. Terra cotta is cast and fired clay units, usually larger and more intricately molded than brick. Most terra cotta was glazed, and some was finely colored.

Ceramic veneers were also built with thin glazed or un-glazed tiles that were hand-molded or machine-extruded with a very wide color range. Favorite shapes were square and hexagonal units.

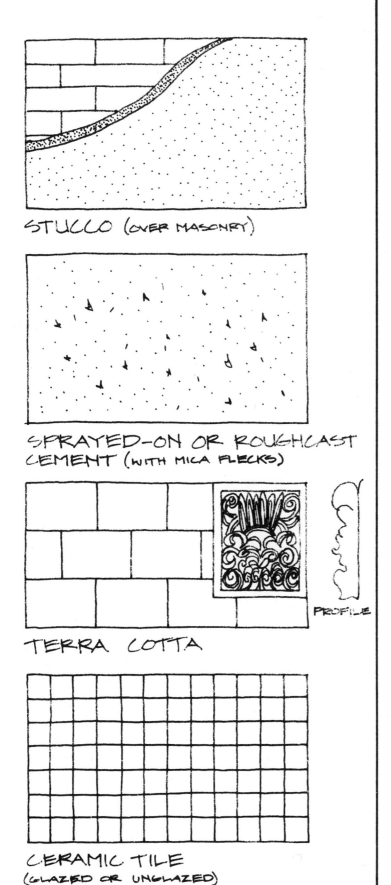

STUCCO (OVER MASONRY)

SPRAYED-ON OR ROUGHCAST
CEMENT (WITH MICA FLECKS)

TERRA COTTA

PROFILE

CERAMIC TILE
(GLAZED OR UNGLAZED)

Both stucco and cement walls tend to appear monolithic. Both materials are rarely finished flat, so that the rough texture helps to bind the wall visually and mask the irregularities that occur in troweling or spraying the material. Both materials rely on color, which is embedded in the plaster mix in stucco, and may be in the mix or added to the top coat in cement.

While cement and stucco are plastic, almost fluid media, terra cotta blocks and ceramic tiles are static and precise. Their design strengths derive from their overall continuity, the shape of their units, and the use of color. Terra cotta uses color as punctuation, to form edges or to cap a wall or a section of a wall. Tile relies on patterning, on geometric more than naturalistic figures. Both materials may be used to create horizontal bands or vertical strips, which can delineate the general design scheme.

CONCRETE HAS BEEN A POPULAR VERNACULAR building material for over a hundred years. Its use has expanded greatly during that same time period. Depending on intended use, concrete is composed of a mixture of water, sand, fine stone, and a binder such as Portland cement that hardens to a stonelike mass. Early in this century concrete block was promoted as a building material especially suited to the owner-builder who could buy the necessary equipment from a major retailer such as Sears Roebuck and mold blocks with any face he desired in his own back yard. Precast, hollow, or solid block was also used in residential and commercial construction, with brick, stucco, or paint applied to the outside surfaces.

Poured concrete walls for foundations and above-ground walls have also been a vernacular material. But the use of finished and unpainted walls did not blossom until the 1930s. The raw concrete look was never very popular in house design, but warehouses and other industrial buildings often used exposed and finished concrete piers which formed a precise framing system enclosing brick panels. Concrete used in this manner, and in most heavy construction, was strengthened with wire mesh, steel bars or rods, or even steel beams.

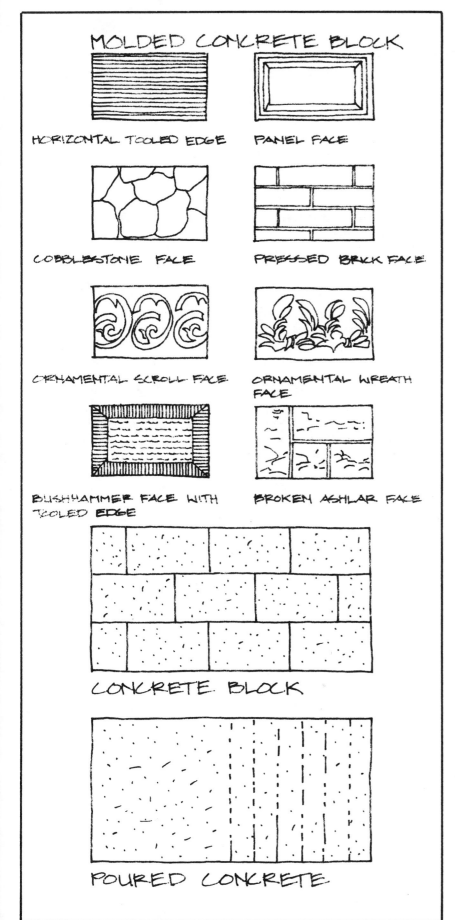

MOLDED CONCRETE BLOCK

HORIZONTAL TOOLED EDGE

PANEL FACE

COBBLESTONE FACE

PRESSED BRICK FACE

ORNAMENTAL SCROLL FACE

ORNAMENTAL WREATH FACE

BUSHHAMMER FACE WITH TOOLED EDGE

BROKEN ASHLAR FACE

CONCRETE BLOCK

POURED CONCRETE

Although concrete has taken a back seat to other design materials, it has served as a less expensive alternative to masonry construction. It did not require the presence of a skilled craftsman on the building site to cut the stone blocks. Early in its history, concrete was looked upon as both utilitarian and decorative. It could be used both ways in the same building—in poured or block foundations, with molded blocks for walls or porch piers—and it was a "democratic" material: the rich and the poor both had access to it.

When molded, concrete blocks were subject to the same design opportunities and limitations as brick and stone. Pattern, especially on the face, was at the heart of each design scheme.

Painted concrete block houses and commercial buildings have been built in most sections of the country, but they seem most popular in warm climates. Poured-in-place buildings seem to have been speculation projects, with some eye toward campaigning for the "modern" design sensibility.

PORCELAIN ENAMELED PANELS THAT ADHERE TO metal by fusion became a commercial cladding in the 1920s. Used originally as a paneling for interiors, they became an exterior material during the 1930s. The glasslike surface was easy to clean, withstood wear well, and created an image of modernity. Companies such as the White Tower restaurant group changed their corporate image forever when they began renovating their interiors and covering their exterior brick walls with white porcelain enamel sheets.

Glass cladding such as Vitrolite was also used during this same period. Vitrolite panels and spandrels were brittle, opaque sheets that were more expensive than porcelain. Although the desire for color was a major factor in using glass, the material was also used in place of stone, especially marble. Vitrolite was the trade name for this product; several other products with the same composition went by other names.

Iron was used only sparingly as a wall covering, but extensively for exposed cast-iron columns, beams, and cornices that together created a frame for commercial buildings. Façades on these buildings were usually clad with masonry. Cast pieces of iron were made by pouring molten iron, high in carbon, into green sand molds. The cornices, surrounds, and panels used to sheath projecting bays were also made of thin plates of iron or steel that were tinned, stamped into architectural forms, and assembled. Tin and cast-iron forms complemented each other and were integrated into a single building system.

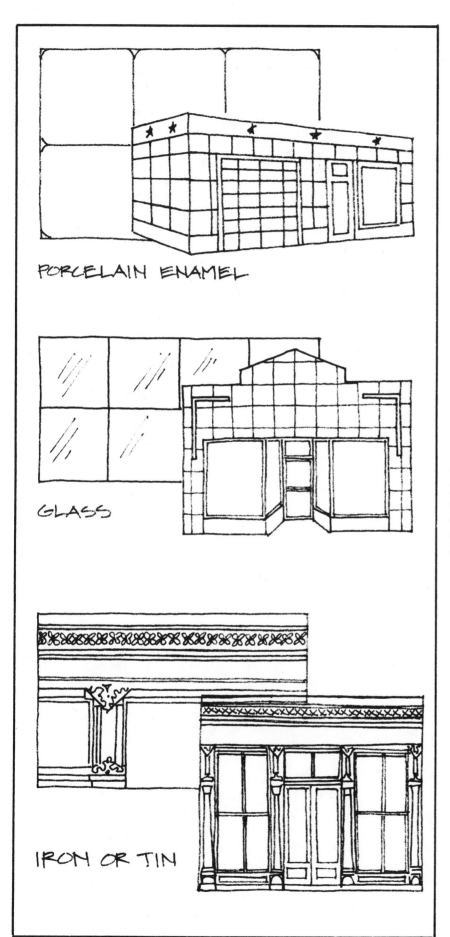

PORCELAIN ENAMEL

GLASS

IRON OR TIN

Panels of porcelain and glass function much like any other modular building unit, with one great exception—the use of light. As reflective surfaces they rely on the play of light on all parts of the surface. They catch light and reveal low-level reflections of the immediate environment. The joinery is most often tight with these materials, but this did not prevent the use of high-contrast mastics or mortars or even metal bands over the joints. The panels were also helpful in defining an overall shape for an entire building, which is one reason why structures using these cladding materials often have only one story.

Iron fronts with tin accents rely on the traditional classical compositions that derive from post-and-beam construction. Strong vertical elements such as columns are linked by strong horizontal elements. Since iron parts were molded, most elements use pattern, particularly continuous pattern, to enhance the surfaces. In terms of organization, iron fronts also rely on proportional relationships among design elements.

THE *GABLE* ROOF TAKES ITS NAME FROM THE TRI-angular portion of the wall, the gable, that carries the pitched roof. The *straight gable* roof has a gable at each end. Gable roofs may be altered to include secondary gables along the side, as in the *center gable* type, or to extend the roof by means of sweeping or *flared* rafters that project the roof beyond the walls. The gable may also be *clipped,* so that the apex of the gable is cut off and laid back (hipped) toward the ridge. In addition, a gable may be *stepped*—that is, graduated in its rake from the eaves to the ridge. In some locales a stepped gable is called a crow gable or crow-stepped gable. The gable end may be tied by a *pent,* a narrow roof attached to and sloping from a wall. A *parapet* gable extends the gable portion so that it passes above the roof. The extension usually includes a top or coping to seal its edge. The *intersecting gable* roof form is composed of two straight gables of similar or different sizes, usually intersecting at a right angle.

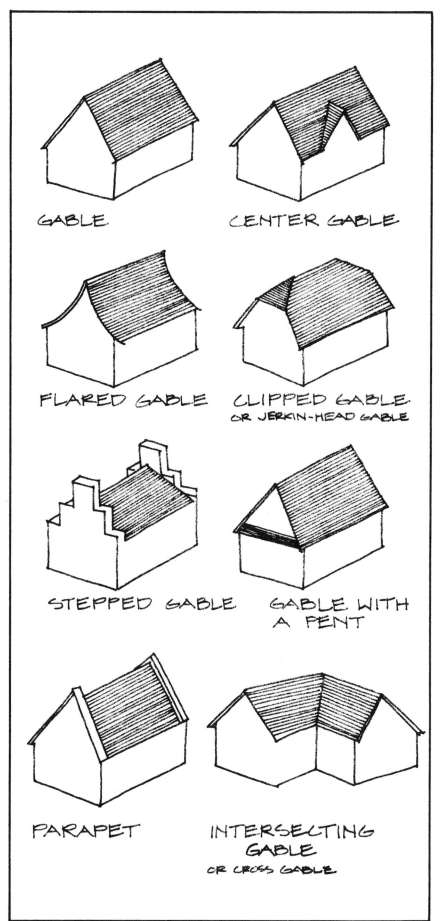

GABLE

CENTER GABLE

FLARED GABLE

CLIPPED GABLE
OR JERKIN-HEAD GABLE

STEPPED GABLE

GABLE WITH
A PENT

PARAPET

INTERSECTING
GABLE
OR CROSS GABLE

A gable roof has such a strong geometric form that it tends to dominate design. Its visual impact derives from the broad expanses of roof, from major accent points along the roof's lines, and from the gable end itself. Variations of the gable roof have been used mostly in house design, occasionally in commercial buildings. The gable may face the street or run its ridge parallel to the street. Each case offers different design opportunities, especially as regards entrance location and any system of ornamentation. The center gable has been used extensively to mark the entrance and to encourage symmetrical design. Flared roofs and clipped gables are used in designs attempting to convey rustic effects. Stepped and parapet gables generate unusual profiles. Their shapes allow the gable to contend more intensely with the broad roof, so that the wall becomes an equal partner with the roof in integrating the upper levels of a building. The pent ties the roof and wall together by extending the roof concept across the wall. The pent diminishes the wall and divides it into two geometric shapes. Straight gables seem to have a point beyond which their length is neither practical nor aesthetically pleasing. Intersecting gables allow for more interior space planning and the massing of large design elements.

A *HIP* ROOF SLOPES UPWARD WITH THE SAME PITCH from all four sides of a building. Some hip roofs have equal sides, but most do not. The shorter sides are roofed with sloping triangles called the hipped ends. The hips themselves are the intersections of the slopes at the corners. Occasionally the ridge of the hip roof may be flattened to form a *deck*. In some treatments the deck may support a wood balustrade or some wrought-iron cresting. Picturesque effects available in designing with hip forms include *flaring the eaves;* adding a second and smaller hipped portion onto the first roof, so that the roof has a *hip on hip; extending a short gable* from the ridge to the hipped ends; and *combining a hip roof with other forms.* All these strategies alter the profile, and some alter the volume of attic space available.

The *mansard* roof resembles a hip roof but is divided into two slopes on all sides. The lower slope is longer and steeper than the upper and may incorporate dormers. Mansard profiles are also susceptible to alteration. Popular shapes include extending the sides into a very steep pitch that is almost straight, and curving the sides into a convex or concave form.

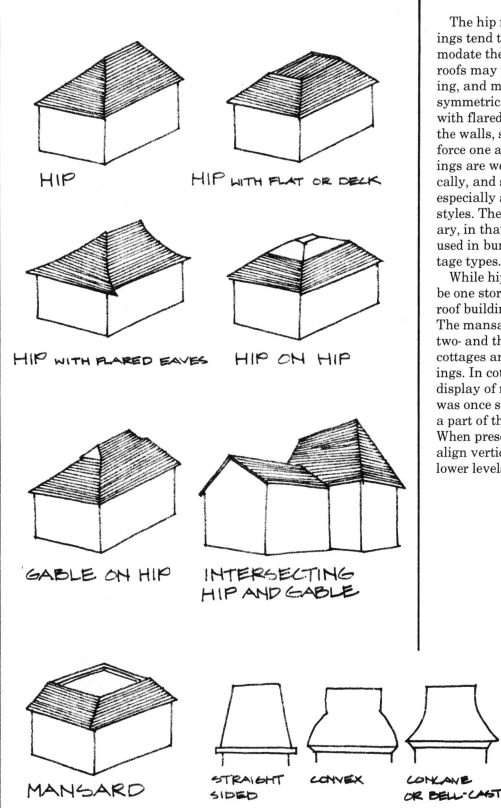

HIP

HIP WITH FLAT OR DECK

HIP WITH FLARED EAVES

HIP ON HIP

GABLE ON HIP

INTERSECTING HIP AND GABLE

MANSARD

STRAIGHT SIDED

CONVEX

CONCAVE OR BELL-CAST

The hip roof is a low roof; buildings tend to spread out to accommodate them. Equal-sided hip roofs may produce a cubical building, and many hip roofs stimulate symmetrical designs. Buildings with flared eaves may also flare the walls, so that the profiles reinforce one another. Hip-roof buildings are well established historically, and some hip forms are especially associated with revival styles. They are also contemporary, in that the hip roof has been used in bungalow and small cottage types.

While hip-roof buildings tend to be one story in height, mansard-roof buildings are rarely that size. The mansard is often found on two- and three-story single-family cottages and multifamily buildings. In cottage design the broad display of roofing material, which was once slate shingles, is as much a part of the design as the profile. When present, mansard dormers align vertically with windows on lower levels.

THE *GAMBREL* ROOF IS ANOTHER VERSION OF THE two-slope roof, but this type utilizes the ridge of the upper portion. The roof slopes on both sides of a gambrel have two different pitches, and specific roof designs depend on the relationship between the upper and lower roofs. In the *New England* type, the upper slopes are steeper than the lower. The *Dutch* version features short upper slopes with flared lower slopes. Gambrel roofs of the same size have also been intersected at a right angle, although this produces an unusually large roof.

Regionally the same roof shape may have different names. In New England the wood-frame *saltbox* house often has a short roof pitch on the side that faces the street and a long roof in the back. In Southern states such a roof is referred to as a *catslide*.

The *barrel* and *rainbow* roofs have very unusual shapes: the former is a half cylinder on section, while the latter is slightly convex.

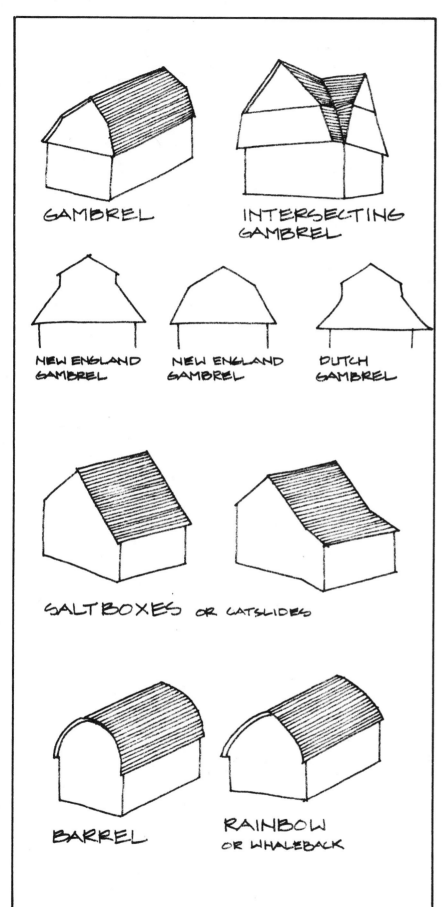

GAMBREL

INTERSECTING GAMBREL

NEW ENGLAND GAMBREL

NEW ENGLAND GAMBREL

DUTCH GAMBREL

SALTBOXES OR CATSLIDES

BARREL

RAINBOW OR WHALEBACK

The gambrel roof is almost exclusively a cottage roof that has been associated with revival styles, particularly several versions of the colonial house. The broad gable formed by the roof shape provides an opportunity for window treatments, including Palladian motifs, and for end-wall chimneys. Dormers have been added to the lower slope to extend the attic space. The gambrel is mostly found on two-story buildings. It is such a weighty roof visually that it often needs a moderately large building to be an effective design element. The saltbox and rounded roof shapes are so strong that they tend to outline the entire building. The rounded shapes and straight saltbox tend to make a house look like a container, with the roof simulating a lid.

THE *FALSE-FRONT* ROOF IS ACTUALLY A COMBINA-tion of an extended wall, which helps to create the illusion that the building is taller than it really is, and a flat or shallow gable roof. In vernacular design a *flat roof* is rarely literally flat; rather, it carries a slight pitch to aid in draining the roof surface.

The *lean-to, shed,* and *half-span roofs* have a single pitch that is carried on a wall that is higher than the roof. A lean-to is usually pitched against and leaning on the adjoining wall of a building. The shed roof is most often incorporated into a section of a building—for instance, as a cover for a back room.

A *monitor* roof is a raised structure that straddles the ridge and provides lights or louvers for the interior. This kind of roof has been used extensively in industrial buildings. The *semimonitor* has only one raised portion that projects at the ridge. A *saw-tooth roof* is formed from a number of trusses and catches north light; when viewed from the end, it has a toothed profile similar to the teeth of a saw.

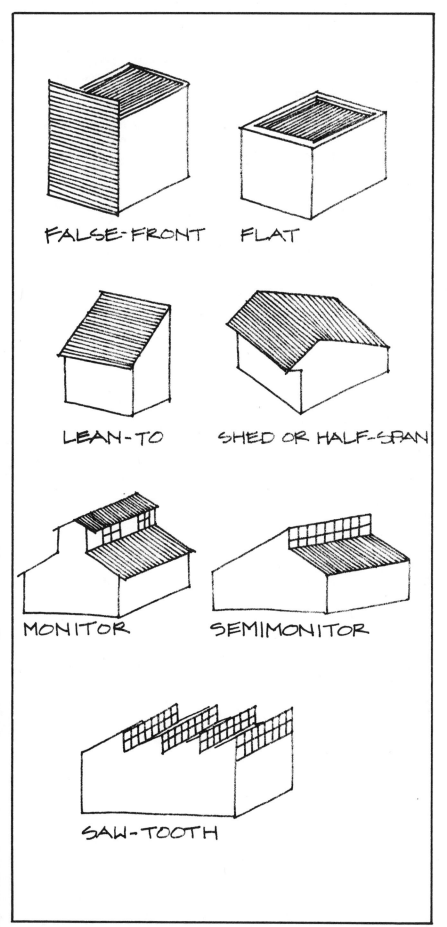

FALSE-FRONT

FLAT

LEAN-TO

SHED OR HALF-SPAN

MONITOR

SEMIMONITOR

SAW-TOOTH

The false-front roof depends on the character of the broad plane of wall for design; the roof proper is a secondary design feature. Most flat roofs are obscured from vision by a parapet. The lean-to has a dramatic angle that needs to be integrated into the geometry of the main building. The shed roof seems easier to accommodate and looks less like a late addition. Many house types employ a shed roof for kitchen, pantry, or storage areas at the back of the building. Monitor roofs have excellent lines; the width of the monitor, its height, and its broad row of lights can add considerably to design. Most monitors have a proportional relationship to the overall volume of the building. The saw-tooth relies on the pattern and rhythm inherent in the structure. Saw-tooth roofs are especially effective designs on long, low buildings.

A *PYRAMIDAL* ROOF IS A HIPPED ROOF WITH EQUAL sides and relatively short ridges that come to a point. This kind of roof shape is also referred to as a pavilion roof. The *conical* roof, which was used in historical styles including Victorian and Queen Anne–type buildings, has an exterior surface shaped like a cone. The *bell-shaped* roof has a cross section shaped like a bell, which means that the roof is concave at the bottom and convex at the top. The *tent* roof, like the pyramid and cone, is used to cap a small tower or turret. A tent roof normally has six sides meeting at a point. Roof forms may be altered to break the regularity of the form, as when a pent is added to a tent roof. Such manneristic gestures were part of the vocabulary of picturesque design.

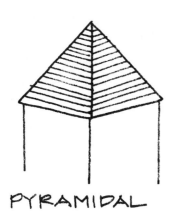

PYRAMIDAL

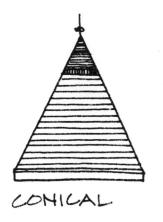

CONICAL

BELL

TENT

TENT WITH PENT

All these specialty roofs rely on their geometry for design effects. They may top off an unusual form and yet look integrated and logical—that is, they may look like they grew out of the tower. At other times they may separate visually and declare their individuality. In either case they are intended as relief against the mass of the main building. In some cases the relief may approach whimsy; in others, such works are orderly asides to a grand gesture.

MATERIALS FOR ROOFING ARE EXTENSIVE; SEVERAL types that may be thought of as generic are presented here. The use of *tile* in American vernacular design is generally associated with historic styles of building such as Italian and Spanish. Two tile forms were especially popular: plain or flat, and sectional. The latter was used more frequently than the former, perhaps because it produces ridges and valleys, usually semicircular in section, so that one unit covers the joints between tiles of another unit. Burnt clay tiles are the oldest and most widely used; red seems to have been the most popular color.

Slate roofs are composed of pieces of slate sawn or split into geometric shapes and nailed to sheathing boards or decking. Slate comes in colors and is laid in rows to make patterns.

Metal roofing in vernacular design refers to tin plate, terne plate, or galvanized sheet metal laid in strips and seamed.

Shingles, whether natural or man-made, cover most vernacular roofs. Most are wedge-shaped and nailed in overlapping courses.

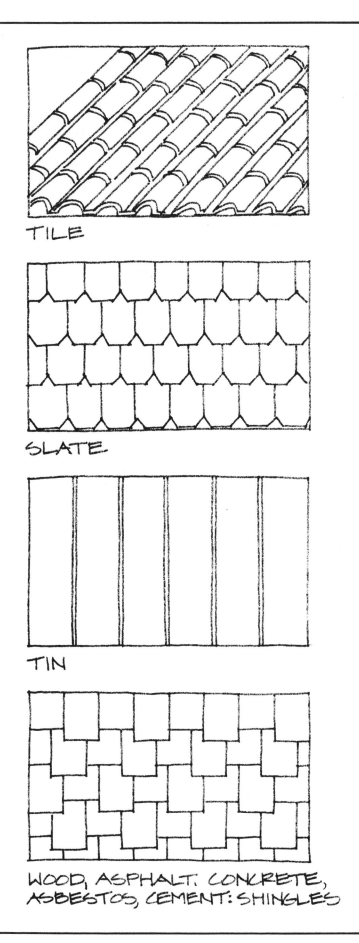

TILE

SLATE

TIN

WOOD, ASPHALT; CONCRETE, ASBESTOS, CEMENT: SHINGLES

Roofing materials play several roles in design. They add color and texture, and they help determine whether the roof itself plays a minor or major role in a design.

The texture of roofing materials acts as visual point or counterpoint to the cladding. Roofing texture also casts an overall impression on a building. Burnt clay tiles, for example, make almost any building look vaguely Mediterranean, even oriental. Historically, clay tiles have been important in Italian and Spanish treatments of masonry buildings.

Color in roofing seems to center on two kinds of design choices: using solid color either to cap the building or to separate the roof shape from the building; and using it as part of a polychromy scheme that is related in value and hue to cladding, trim, and foundation colors.

Most roofing materials add pattern to design and therefore serve as part of the system of ornamentation. Slate and shingle roofs may use several patterns in orderly sequences. A metal roof is particularly monolithic; it binds the roof into a single form with color, reflected light, and seam patterns as ornamental effects.

Most roofing materials are used on almost any kind of building, though tiles are rarely found in rural areas, and metal use varies regionally. Shingles are found everywhere.

ROOFS: DETAILS

ROOF DETAILS VARY ACCORDING TO STYLE AND method of building, but a number of elements are basic to roof treatments. *Rafters,* the boards to which their ends are attached, and the boards that support rafters, are generic elements in a roof. The common rafter extends from the eave to the ridge board. *Purlins* are horizontal pieces of timber laid between the common and the principal rafters; they run parallel to the ridge. The shape of sections or of the entire roof may depend on *trusses*—structural frames with intermediary supports. The slope or inclination of the rafters determines the *pitch,* expressed in degrees, of the roof. If the rafters' ends are covered, the cornice is closed; conversely, open rafters denote an open cornice.

A *fascia* board is used primarily as a cover for the ends of the rafters. Gutters are attached to fascia. *Friezes* may be horizontal boards or bands of brick or stone that appear near the top of a wall but below the cornice. In vernacular building, a frieze may be part of the ornamentation, in that it may have a decorated face or support other decoration.

A *bed molding* is used where the eaves of a building meet the top of the outside walls. A *crown molding* is placed at the top of the cornice and immediately beneath the roof.

Soffits are the underside of any projection such as eaves, arches, or cornices. In a gable roof, a *raking cornice* slopes from the apex of the gable to the eave. It is rather common in house design to have the cornice turn back toward the gable; such a change in direction is called a *return.* If the cornice is closed in and forms a boxlike shape, it is referred to as a *boxed cornice.*

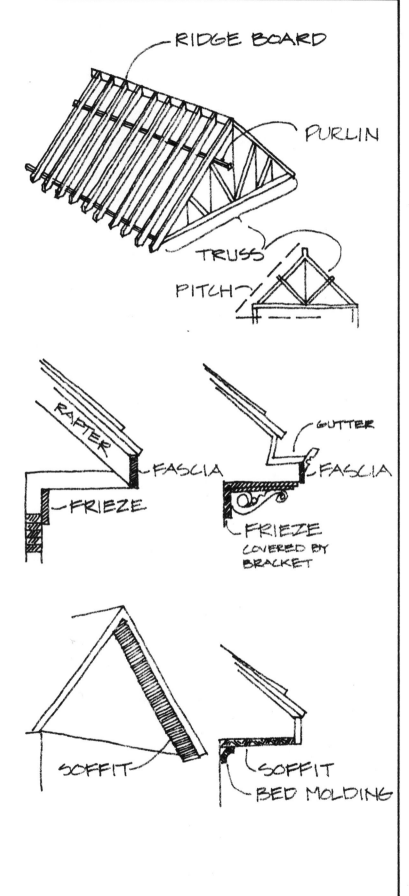

RIDGE BOARD

PURLIN

TRUSS

PITCH

RAFTER

FASCIA

FRIEZE

GUTTER

FASCIA

FRIEZE
COVERED BY
BRACKET

SOFFIT

SOFFIT
BED MOLDING

Roof details play minor roles in design. Roof structure is hidden, but the shapes it creates add character. The edges of roofs provide opportunities to use moldings, such as the crown molding that often runs at the top of the cornice just below the roof. The point where soffits and walls meet may also receive a bed molding. Any flat surface such as a fascia may be decorated, and the proportional relationship among all trim boards can contribute to the sense of order in the design. For example, fascia and corner boards of the same size will help frame the walls and outline the shape of the building. The rafters of an open cornice have often been designed—that is, cut with a scroll saw into an unusual profile. Occasionally, soffits may receive a special treatment, which most often entails the use of a particular material, as for instance narrow tongue-and-groove boards.

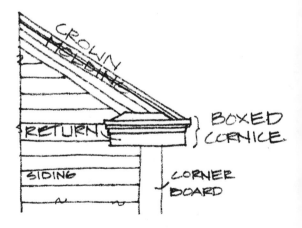

CROWN

RETURN

BOXED
CORNICE

SIDING

CORNER
BOARD

IN MOST VERNACULAR DESIGN, *BRACKETS* ARE composed of stickwork. They do not support other elements, but are used as decorative details for eaves and end walls. In masonry construction, brackets may be built into the wall and carry some kind of projection.

The use of *dentils* derives from historic architecture, especially styles employing classical motifs. Dentils help to articulate the eave as an important juncture of wall and roof. They are usually brick or wood, in rectangular blocks closely set in a row for ornamental effect by alternation of light and shadow. Sometimes a dentil band may serve as a bed molding on a cornice.

Modillions are horizontal brackets that may be designed as plain blocks or be decorated. They are most often shaped in the form of a scroll with an acanthus leaf. Modillions derive from classical architecture; their use is primarily relegated to revival-style buildings. In high-style design, modillions are usually made of stone; in the vernacular they are most often wood but sometimes brick.

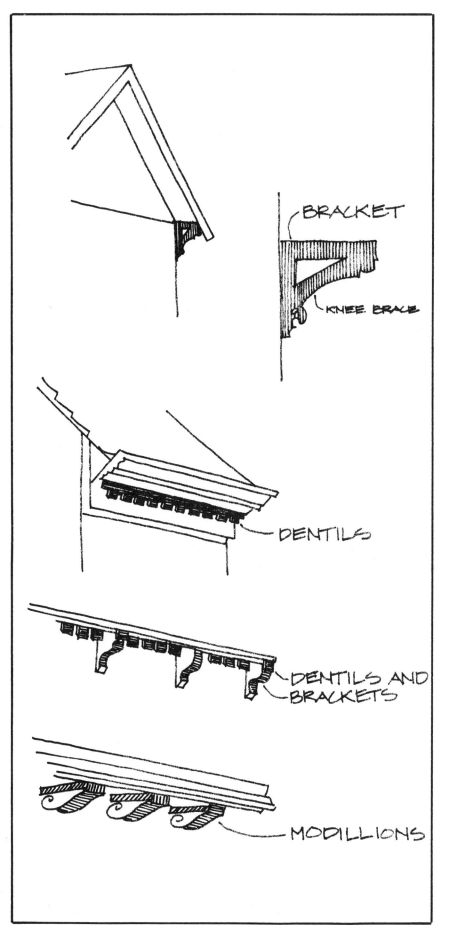

BRACKET

KNEE BRACE

DENTILS

DENTILS AND
BRACKETS

MODILLIONS

Brackets are frequently a three-part configuration: a wall piece, a piece perpendicular to the wall, and a brace. All three pieces may be integrated to look like one unit, or the individual parts may keep their identity. Any and all parts may be decorated—either shaped; sawed through to form patterns, slots, natural forms; or carved. Brackets may detail the corners or, through repeats, delineate the eave line around an entire building.

Dentils may serve as a bed molding covering the joint between the roof boards and the wall. Whether coursed in masonry building or nailed on in wood construction, dentils may be used as individual pieces, known as cogs or teeth. It is not unusual to find combinations of elements at the line of the eave. All these treatments function as transition points where the materials and forms shift from the wall to the roof.

Modillions are unique brackets made of stone, wood, or stamped metal. Like most repeated three-dimensional attachments, modillions rely on the play of light and the use of pattern to enhance design. Originally modillions helped to support the cornice, but in vernacular design, like most brackets, they are ornamental.

A *ROLLED ROOF* IS A STYLIZED ROOF IN WHICH THE roofing material has been bent and laid so that it curves over the roof boards and around the eaves and fascia. The roof simulates a thatch roof and is especially appropriate for one-story cottages in the English country mode.

Polychromy in roofing materials involves the use of multicolored shingles in some kind of composition, laid in courses to emphasize their color differences. Often the coursing and the placement of color outline a pattern.

Ridgerolls are special coverings made of metal, composition roofing, tiling, or wood that cover and finish the ridge. Many have a rounded section over which flashing is secured as a covering for the ridge. The *Boston ridge* consists of shingles saddled over the ridge, intersecting with the courses of shingles from both sides of the roof.

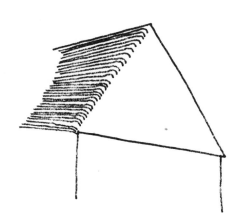

ROLLED ROOF

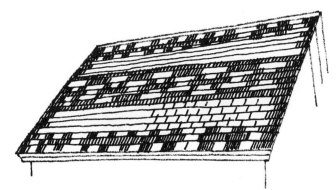

POLYCHROMED ROOF

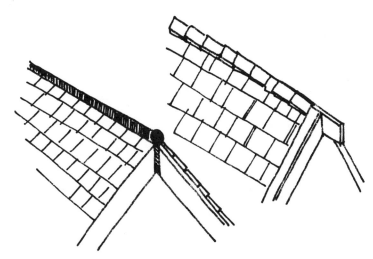

RIDGEROLL   BOSTON RIDGE

The rolled-edge roof relies on its unusual profile and its extra bit of texture and color to offset the roof as a distinctive element in design. These roofs are asymmetrical in that the coursing is irregular. All this adds picturesque effects—the simulation of a rural English thatch roof—to the overall design.

A polychromed roof lightens the impact of the shape and weight of the roof. The addition of color and pattern reduces the role of the roof as cap or lid. Visually it pulls the eye toward the planes of the roof and away from the edges.

Ridge ornamentation, whether cresting or a special ridge cap, outlines the ridge and adds linear qualities to the roof. Some treatments crown the building, while others are part of an extensive system of edge treatments that might be coordinated with stickwork and bracketing along other edges.

VENTILATORS COME IN VARIOUS SHAPES, ALL OF them architectural compositionally, but their functions remain the same: through convection or mechanical means, they ventilate hot air or other used air through the attic. To prevent downdrafts, most are covered with louver boards that overlap slightly.

A *crest* may be used as a decorative device to finish the top of any structure. In vernacular use, most crests are placed along the ridge of a roof. While crestings take almost any profile, most are perforated.

Finials are special terminal ornaments found at the top of a gable, a pinnacle, a spire, or a newel. Finials usually have several component parts and may be made of metal or wood.

Weathervanes, devised to indicate wind direction, are pivoted so as to rotate freely. Most have a platelike form.

Roof flats or decks dramatically terminate the ascending lines of a roof's shape and provide opportunity for ornamental accents such as *balustrades* around the edge. Balustrade styles depend on the style of the building. Most are made of metal (preferably wrought iron) or wood. The corners get a newel post.

A *battlement* is a general term for a particular treatment of a parapet wall. Derived from historic architecture, battlements serve as ornament for masonry buildings. In design a battlement consists of alternate solid and open sections. In many vernacular buildings the battlement may be only symbolic—that is, there are a few solid portions with wide openings between them.

VENTILATOR

LOUVERS

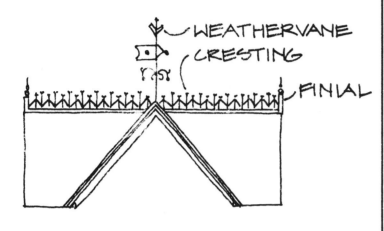

WEATHERVANE

CRESTING

FINIAL

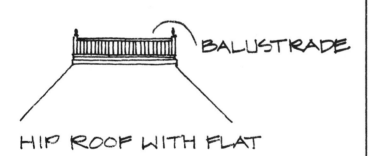

BALUSTRADE

HIP ROOF WITH FLAT

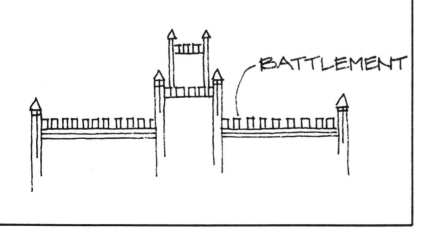

BATTLEMENT

Ventilators, like cupolas, look like terminal design elements. Because of their relatively small size and varied placement, ventilators do not have a dramatic impact on overall design.

Weathervanes do not build up form but rely for effect on a few clean lines and a recognizable shape, sometimes charming or deliberately humorous. Their placement is often tied less to design than to convenience and visual access from the ground level.

Finials usually have architectonic compositions with an ascending profile of forms from the base to the top. These small vertical accents tend to lighten the visual impact of the gable.

Any kind of decking, with or without an enclosing balustrade, visually lightens the roof. Balustrades reinforce the effect of lightness in that they are usually slotted, so that the individual balusters are matched by slots of light; thus the roof's profile terminates in airiness.

Battlements add dramatic profiles, no matter what their arrangement of solids and voids. They may crown a wall or lift a façade; the top of the latter is their primary location. Through rhythm and pattern, they can also add formal order to an otherwise undistinguished wall.

A *TOWER* IS A TALL STRUCTURE, EITHER INDEPEND-ent or part of a building, with lights, internal works such as stairs, and a distinct roof.

A *steeple* is the main vertical feature of a church or public building, comprising both the tower and the spire. The term is also used to describe the whole structure from the ground level up. In either case sections of the steeple—from the tower to the lantern and the spire—usually diminish in size from bottom to top.

A *turret* is a small tower most likely engaged with the wall of a building and topped with a spire or a pyramidal or tent roof. Turrets may be small, with some unusual lights, or large enough to serve as a special interior space on an upper level.

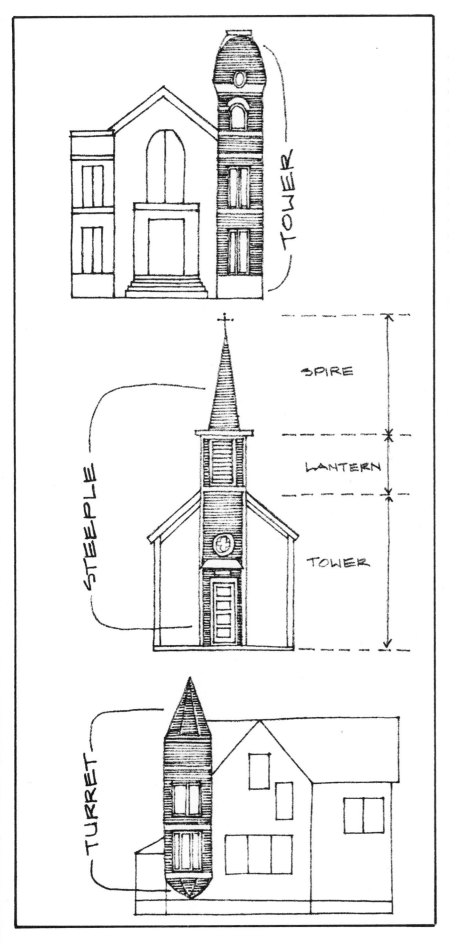

TOWER

SPIRE

LANTERN

STEEPLE

TOWER

TURRET

Towers and steeples both tend to be layered and add or subtract elements at will. First-story sections often align with first-floor ceiling or window heights, thereby creating horizontal continuity. Subsequent divisions may align with upper-level portions of the main building or reflect a proportional relationship to the entire tower: that is, they may be a fraction of the whole, or a multiple of the first section. Towers also tend to have their own fenestration pattern, including the size and shape of windows, and a unique roof.

Turrets, perhaps because of their diminished size, seem designed as a single element with less subdivisions than a tower. Even a unique base or roof seems not to detract from the sense of unity in the turret shape.

TOWERS, STEEPLES, TURRETS, SPECIAL STRUCTURES

MOST VERTICAL ELEMENTS, BECAUSE OF THEIR high-profile qualities, are adaptable to stylistic treatments and special-use construction. Lanterns, belvederes, spires, belfries, cupolas, and domes are typical of these kinds of elements.

A *lantern* is a roof superstructure built to admit either light or air. Often without its own floor, it takes a square, circular, or polygonal shape. A *belvedere* is a special roof structure built for the enjoyment of a view. Large belvederes may be found as independent buildings in gardens or other picturesque locations.

Spires are tall pyramidal, polygonal, or conical structures rising from a tower or a roof and terminating in a point. Spires can be made of masonry or wood and are covered with roofing material. Many take an octagonal shape, especially when rising from a square tower. The *belfry* of a steeple is the upper portion arranged for housing bells. The term can also describe the timber frame to which the bells are attached.

Cupolas are terminal structures, from square to round in plan, rising above a main roof. A cupola's roof is a small, hollow dome with a small base, often set on the ridge of a roof. *Domes* in vernacular design are usually small roof structures that exhibit variety in plan and section. Most span a modest space and may assume the shape of an onion, tulip, bell, or semicircle.

Since all these structures are often the last design element on a building or on the uppermost part of a building, they tend to be lightweight in appearance, graceful, and ornamented. They serve as a special punctuation mark, the last comment on a style—for example, a lantern with small paned windows on a building with colonial motifs. Or they may serve as a final statement in an assortment of stylistic gestures—the last hurrah in an eclectic design. Except for spires, which can be quite large, most of these structures seem to be human in scale: it is not hard to imagine sitting or standing beside one of them. Perhaps the spire, with its thrust toward infinity, asserts human spiritual concerns as well.

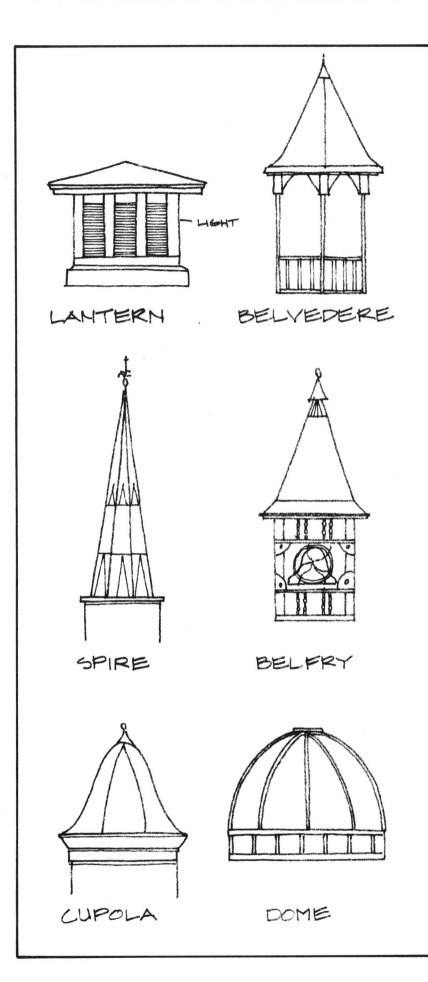

LANTERN

—LIGHT

BELVEDERE

SPIRE

BELFRY

CUPOLA

DOME

CHIMNEYS ARE ESSENTIAL ELEMENTS IN VERNACU-lar design. Most are obvious in terms of their function, containing a flue or flues that conduct the smoke, fumes, and gases of combustion to the outside air. Chimneys in vernacular design most often connect to heating systems. Secondary uses include connections with fireplaces or wood- or coal-burning specialty stoves. Many vernacular buildings have more than one chimney, and multiple chimneys may play an important role in design. Brick is the predominant chimney building material, but stone, metal, and concrete chimneys are common.

Chimney types are defined by their placement on a building: a *gable-end* chimney is located at one or both gables; an *interior* chimney is placed in the interior of a building, often centrally located; and an *end-wall* chimney is usually exposed on a side elevation or the facade.

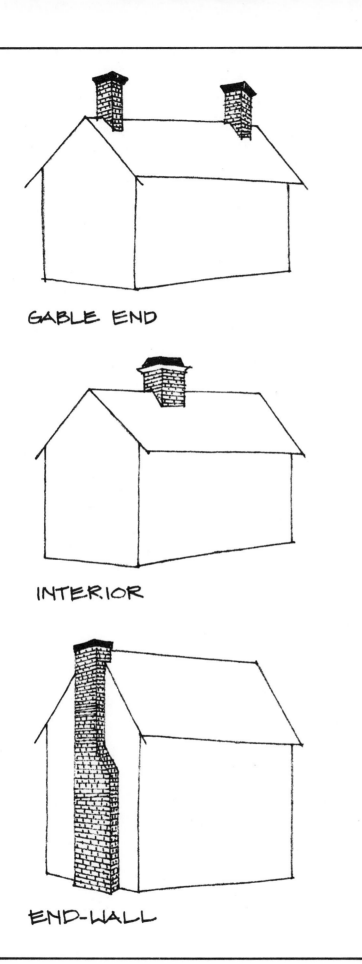

GABLE END

INTERIOR

END-WALL

In gable-end and end-wall placement, a single chimney can pinpoint a special space, such as a living room with a fireplace, and convey a feeling for the homey quality of the design. Double-gable-end or end-wall chimneys help to balance a design and terminate the form: the chimney marks the end of the building.

Interior chimneys may locate the center of a house so that all other elements—especially in buildings with symmetrical fenestration—divide equally along the chimney's axis.

The end-wall chimney appears in colonial treatments. These chimneys are partially or fully exposed. Most often they are built of brick, but combinations of brick and stone are common. When the end-wall chimney is broadened and given a prominent location on the façade, it becomes part of the design vocabulary for the so-called English bungalow or cottage.

CHIMNEYS ARE COMPOSED OF PARTS, WITH MOST attention in design being given to the *stack,* the vertical exposed portion that covers the flue, and to the *cap,* which tops the stack. Chimney caps (sometimes called bonnets or hoods) are often designed to improve draft and ornament the chimney. The most popular vernacular cap is a *corbeled* one in which the cap is built out from the stack by projecting successive courses of bricks beyond those below. If built back again toward the stack, the cap has a stepped profile on top and bottom.

A *chimney brace* ties the stack to the roof, just as a *chimney iron* may tie the stack to the gable. Chimneys that are referred to as stacks are very often large chimneys carrying multiple flues. Many have distinct shapes on plan. Chimney pots are a continuation of the chimney; once made of pottery, they are now made of metal or brick. Older pots may be of any shape, since the material out of which they were made could be molded. Generally, pots are used to improve draft and carry off smoke, but they can add ornament to a roof system.

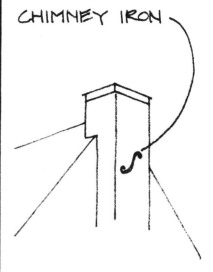

CHIMNEY IRON

CORBELED CHIMNEY CAP

CHIMNEY BRACE

CHIMNEY STACK

PIERCED STACK

T-SHAPE STACK

DIAMOND CHIMNEY POTS

CIRCULAR CHIMNEY POTS

Chimney details provide accent and profile for the roof system. Accents such as unusual caps, chimney hardware, and decorative panels in stacks enliven and relieve massive roof forms. Chimney caps also add profile character to the roof. Corbeled caps, in particular, stand out clearly against the skyline. Shaped stacks are obviously more sculptural than straight stacks: they have multiple surfaces, entertain the play of light and shadow, and offer opportunity for interaction with other design elements. Chimney pots are picturesque effects and reminders of older traditions. They tend to understate the chimney and suggest a rustic quality.

A *DORMER* IS A WINDOW OR OTHER OPENING, SUCH as a louver, projected through a sloping roof and provided with its own roof. The dormer frame is usually placed vertically on the rafters of the main roof. Occasionally one finds an internal dormer that has no roof other than the main.

The term "dormer" (from the French *dormoir,* dormitory) refers to its common use as sleeping quarters. Dormers take more specific names from their placement or their roof shape. A *gable dormer* carries a gable roof, usually with the same pitch as the general roof. Gable dormers are set at 90 degrees to the main roof and may be paired or repeated on the opposite side.

Hipped dormers are commonly found on houses with hipped roofs. *Shed dormers* carry a gently sloping shed roof whose eave line is parallel to the eave line of the main roof.

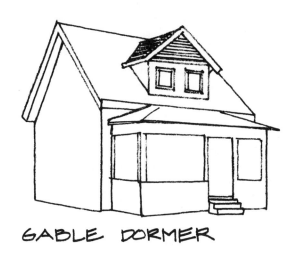

GABLE DORMER

HIPPED DORMER

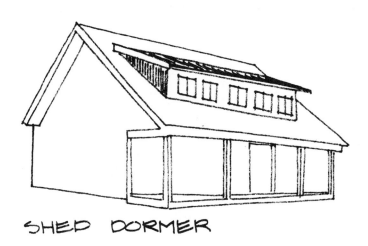

SHED DORMER

Besides their purely functional attribute of providing head room, light, and air to an attic space, dormers can play a role in design. They may align with the center axis of a house, which is usually established by the entrance door on a formal or classical front. If the entrance is offset, the dormer may reestablish the center. Dormers may also be used to balance elevations, with the single dormer usually placed in the center position. The hipped dormer lends itself to repetition easily, thereby adding pattern to the roof. Wide dormers help to accent horizontal lines and break the severity of a broad gable roof.

Dormers also contribute to design through their roof shape, which either repeats the main roof shape in a proportionately smaller size, or uses a new form in an effort to ornament the roof. Glazing patterns are used in the same way, either as echoes of the main pattern or as alternatives to it.

MOST DORMERS ARE REFERRED TO AS *ROOF dormers* because they rise from the slope of a roof. When a dormer is in the same plane as the wall, it is called a *wall dormer*. These dormers, like all dormers, expand the head room of an attic or upper-story room so as to utilize the space better. They can also be used to project a single-story house into a story and a half, especially if they cover most of the width of the roof.

Dormers are integrated into a building's overall design by shape, placement, and relationship to fenestration. Dormers may reinforce design, as when their placement echoes the symmetrical placement of windows, or they may be used for contrast or accent. The latter is true in buildings with picturesque effects. The dormer window itself usually has the same shape and glazing pattern of other windows in the building, but it too may be used for accent.

WALL DORMER

DORMER WITH BALCONY

BALCONY

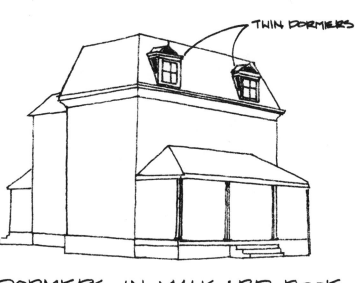

TWIN DORMERS

DORMERS IN MANSARD ROOF

Visually, a wall dormer may be strong enough to give the appearance of a second-story space. To carry through with this effect, the dormer often has a broad gable with a large proportion of wall devoted to glass. Such handling emphasizes the vertical thrust of the dormer, thereby making the house look larger than it is. Dormers with balconies suggest small upper-level porches that were once popular in cottage design and bring more of the outside into the inside. The pairing of most elements is a formal device that often reinforces symmetrical fenestration. Dormers are common on mansard roofs; they provide a pattern to the roof line and an orderly rhythm that may be a repeat of the placement of lower-level windows.

THE SPECIALTY DORMER HAS A UNIQUE PROFILE
that helps to ornament the roof. Dormers with *flared roofs*
and walls are part of the cottage tradition of flaring main
roofs, porch roofs, and walls. *Gambrel roof dormers* seem to
be restricted to gambrel roof houses. In some cases the
dormer appears to be a miniature version of the house
proper.

Clipped gables on main roofs or dormers have been part of
the vocabulary of rustic treatments that some cottages and
bungalows, such as the English styles, have used with great
success.

The *triangular dormer* is a small accent unit that may
employ diamond pattern glazing, if the English mode is
used, or a louver. *Bay dormers* are unusual; on plan, they
are the same as ground-level bays. The *eyebrow dormer* is a
special type that has been applied to cottages and bungalows. It is a low dormer over which the roof is carried in a
wave line similar to the arch over the eye. The eyebrow is
frequently a ventilator.

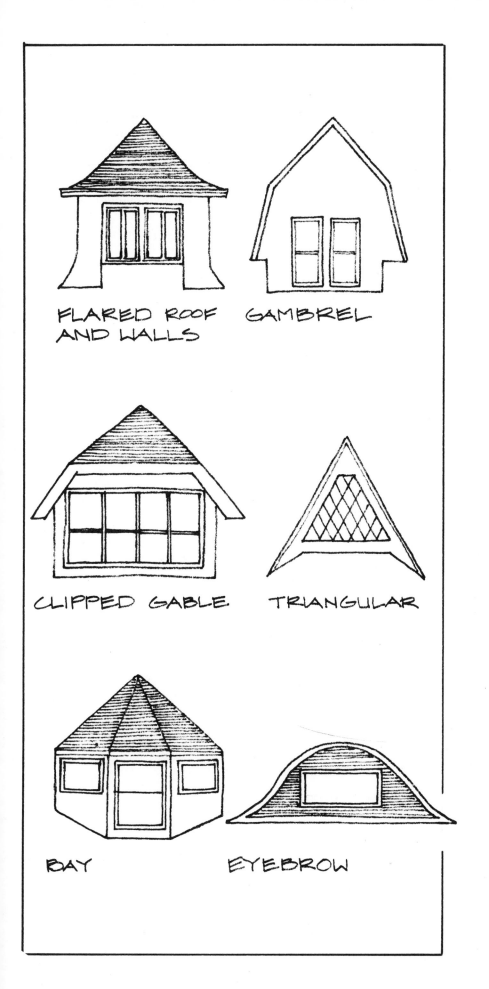

FLARED ROOF
AND WALLS

GAMBREL

CLIPPED GABLE

TRIANGULAR

BAY

EYEBROW

THE SHAPE OF A DORMER WINDOW IS LIMITED ONLY by the size of the dormer and its framing. Almost every kind of window treatment has been used in dormers, including round-, flat-, and triangular-headed units. Dormers borrow pediments from any aspect of historic architecture. Through window shape and pediment, a dormer may contribute to a visual pattern established in the fenestration, or it may function as an independent ornament. The latter use especially prevails in the curvilinear dormer found on buildings with general Mediterranean styling.

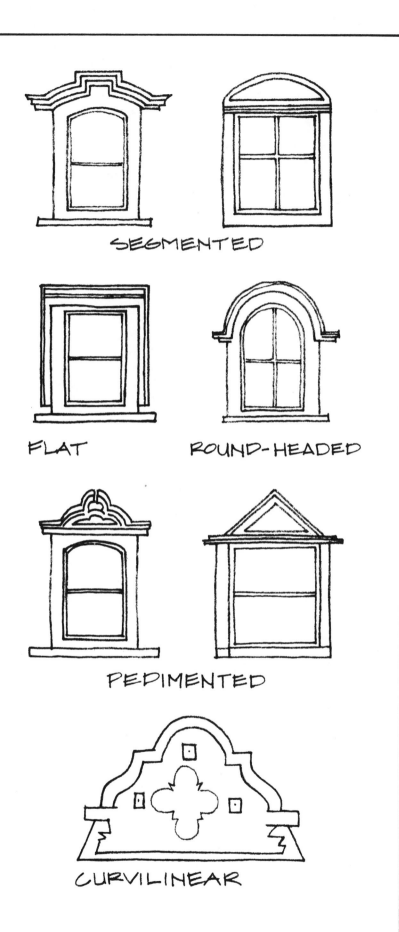

SEGMENTED

FLAT   ROUND-HEADED

PEDIMENTED

CURVILINEAR

THE *GABLE END* OF A BUILDING IS THE TRIANGU-lar portion of a building's end wall with a sloping roof. Gables may be either of the same material as the rest of the wall or of a contrasting material, texture, or appearance. Typical of a change in texture and materials is a clapboard house that has shingled gables.

Bargeboards cover the edge of the projecting portion of a gable roof and are set back under the roof's edge. "Bargeboard" and "vergeboard" have become synonymous terms, although historically the first derives from the second. Bargeboards have been ornamented through carving or sawing and may be integrated into a large gable ornamentation scheme. A *collar beam* is a tie beam that spans the gable opening and connects the two end rafters. A popular motif, it appears in both curved and straight form.

Gable finish refers to various kinds of bargeboards, blocks of wood, and specially cut pieces that have been used to ornament the gable. Most pieces of finish are of three classes: those that trim the edges of the roof, those that span the gable, and those that are attached to the gable wall.

A *pent roof* is part of the gable system; it is attached to and slopes from the wall. A pent is usually placed above the first-floor windows; if carried around the house, it is called a skirt roof.

An *open gable* has no connecting elements that span the gable opening, while a *closed gable* spans the opening with a pent, moldings, or ornamental pieces.

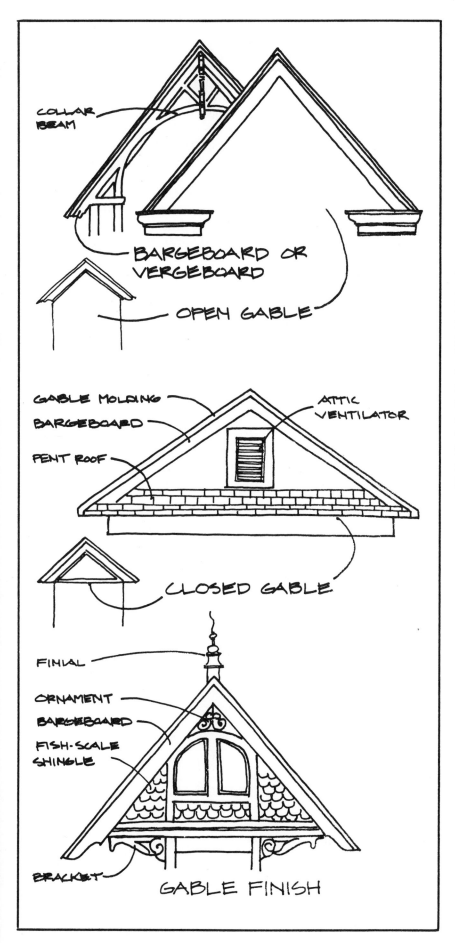

COLLAR BEAM

BARGEBOARD OR VERGEBOARD

OPEN GABLE

GABLE MOLDING

BARGEBOARD

ATTIC VENTILATOR

PENT ROOF

CLOSED GABLE

FINIAL

ORNAMENT

BARGEBOARD

FISH-SCALE SHINGLE

BRACKET

GABLE FINISH

In design the gable end of a building may play many roles. Each treatment has a different effect on overall composition. The plain gable emphasizes the wall; the roof plays a minor part. The introduction of gable finish, or of specific gable motifs such as stickwork, beam and truss forms, and decorated bargeboards, gives the gable its own identity. A hipped gable breaks the formality of the triangular shape and introduces rustic qualities. A pent can turn the gable into a pediment that can be dressed up with windows or left plain; as a pediment, the gable may be an integral part of a formal—even classical—scheme. The most complex condition includes the application of ornament on the walls and at the edges (bargeboards and ridge). In this case the gable separates itself from the wall and must be integrated into the total house design. Such integration is often done by repeating the pattern in other gables.

AS A RULE, THE SHAPE OF A GABLE FOLLOWS THAT of a roof form, so that the *gambrel gable* results from the break in the angle of pitch between the ridge and the eaves.

Curvilinear gables project above the roof edge and outline geometric curves in convex-concave configurations.

The *stepped gable* has a number of common names, including crow gable and crow-stepped gable; but whatever the name, the gable wall is finished in steps instead of a continuous slope.

The *pedimented gable* has a clearly defined triangular face. In its classical form, its base rests on an entablature and includes an order of architecture or the visual equivalent of an order, pilasters or cornerboards.

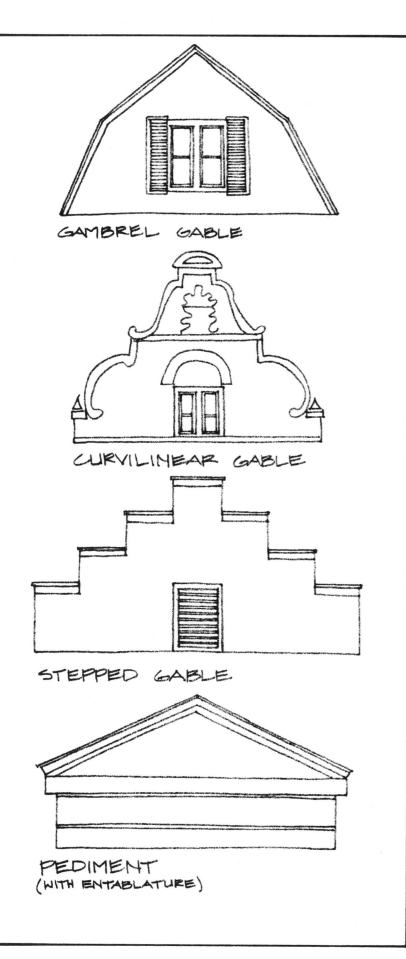

GAMBREL GABLE

CURVILINEAR GABLE

STEPPED GABLE

PEDIMENT
(WITH ENTABLATURE)

Gable ends rely on geometry to express design. Most gable types have a strong outline that may be reinforced by bargeboards, as in the gambrel or pediment, or by caps as in the curvilinear and stepped forms.

A second characteristic centers on the relationship between the overall shape and the implied center axis that runs from the apex of the gable to the base. Most gable ends will center an element on this axis. Windows or ventilators are the most common element used in this way.

The broad face of a gable is susceptible to ornamentation, including shingle treatments, stucco and stickwork, moldings along the edges, and window treatments.

STICKWORK IS ORNAMENTAL WORK DERIVED FROM the precise placement of individual pieces or groups of pieces of millwork. Stickwork has been made in various widths and lengths with planed and molded faces. The gable ends of buildings have been used extensively as grounds for stickwork figures.

Half-timbering is really a misnomer in vernacular architecture, because very few walls are built of whole timbers with the timber faces exposed on the inside and outside of the walls. Instead, sticks applied to stuccoed walls simulate the timbers. Such wall treatments are found in what are referred to as Tudor or English styles.

Sunrise or sunburst motifs derive from the overlapping of wedge-shaped sticks to create a radiating pattern. Just as the sticks imitate the rays of the rising sun, the *herringbone pattern* imitates the spine of a herring. Herringbone patterns are also found on brick walls or walkways and on ornamental interior wood or brick floors.

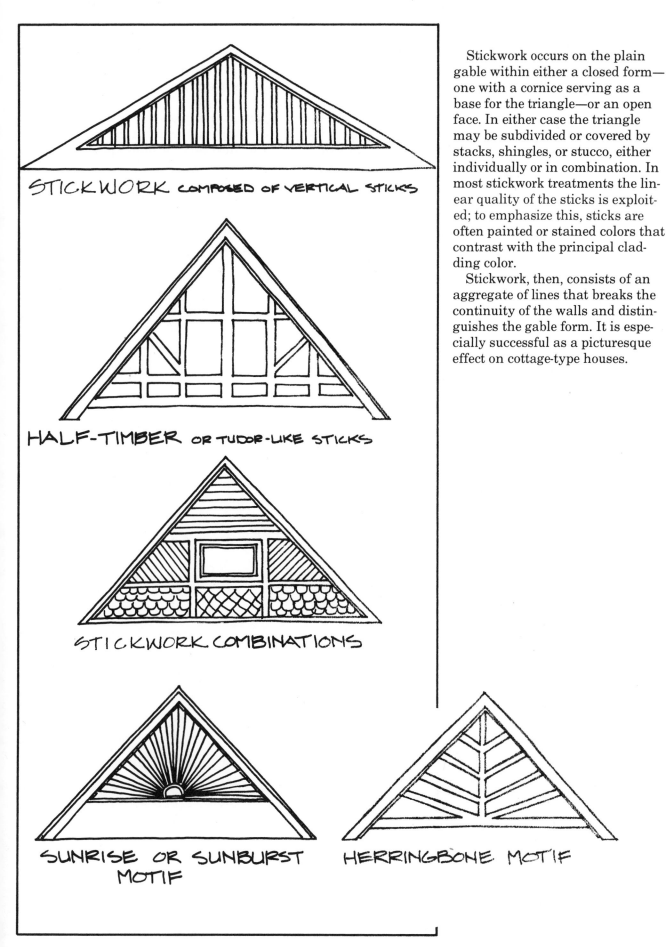

STICKWORK COMPOSED OF VERTICAL STICKS

HALF-TIMBER OR TUDOR-LIKE STICKS

STICKWORK COMBINATIONS

SUNRISE OR SUNBURST MOTIF

HERRINGBONE MOTIF

Stickwork occurs on the plain gable within either a closed form—one with a cornice serving as a base for the triangle—or an open face. In either case the triangle may be subdivided or covered by stacks, shingles, or stucco, either individually or in combination. In most stickwork treatments the linear quality of the sticks is exploited; to emphasize this, sticks are often painted or stained colors that contrast with the principal cladding color.

Stickwork, then, consists of an aggregate of lines that breaks the continuity of the walls and distinguishes the gable form. It is especially successful as a picturesque effect on cottage-type houses.

SOME GABLE TREATMENTS REQUIRE SPECIALLY cut boards. This is particularly true with the so-called *canoe motif* found in the gable of the porch roof on bungalow houses.

Scrollwork—openwork cut with a scroll saw or a jigsaw—has been a popular gable treatment because of the multiplicity of shapes the saw can produce and the unusual designs that the assembled pieces make.

The *kingpost,* like bargeboards, alludes to the truss that supports a gable roof. But while bargeboards may imitate or serve as rafters, the kingpost echoes the central upright piece of the triangular truss against which the rafters abut.

Tumbled brick is a special pattern of coursing that gives the brickwork a tumbled, tossed, or cascading appearance.

CANOE MOTIF

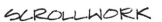

SCROLLWORK

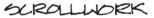

SCROLLWORK

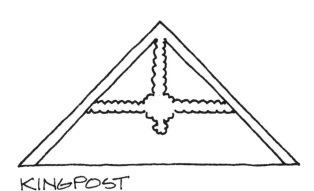

KINGPOST

TUMBLED BRICK

Openwork is a distinct category of ornamental motif; it projects from the surface of the wall, aligned in the same plane as the edge of the roof. The profile of the design elements against the openings is the most important design feature for flatwork such as the canoe motif. Scrollwork tends to lie close to the wall; therefore it often appears to project toward the viewer. Scrollwork and truss patterns work well on cottages. The kingpost is a sculptural form relying on light and shade and the visual texture for its numerous parts. In its plain form, the kingpost can be a bungalow motif.

Tumbled brickwork has an unusual pattern. Like all the motifs on this page, it is a picturesque treatment.

HISTORICALLY, THE FRAME THAT HOLDS THE WINdow glass in position has been called the *sash*. Such windows have been movable or fixed; they may slide up or down, pivot from one side only as in the casement, or not move at all. In the course of time, sash has most commonly referred to those windows that slide up or down by means of pulleys or metal tracks. The most common form of sash is the *double-hung,* in which both sashes slide. From 1870 to 1930, the most popular double-hung sash was that which was balanced by sash cords attached to weights passing over a sash pulley.

Panes of glass cover the openings between rails and muntins, or between stiles and muntins, and are referred to as *lights.* A light may be an entire glass or a section. Dividing the glass into sections, *muntins* or *glazing bars* separate the lights and hold the glass in place. In the past, all glazing bars were called "muntins" and the top, bottom, and side frames were called "rails." The *meeting rail* overlaps where the upper and lower window meet; it is where the window lock is mounted on a double-hung sash window.

The *casement* is an old window form. It contains one or more lights and opens on hinges much in the manner of a door. *Fixed windows* are lights or parts of a large window that do not open. Both *awning* and *hopper* windows open on the horizontal, with the awning hinged at the top of the frame and the hopper hinged at the bottom and opening inward.

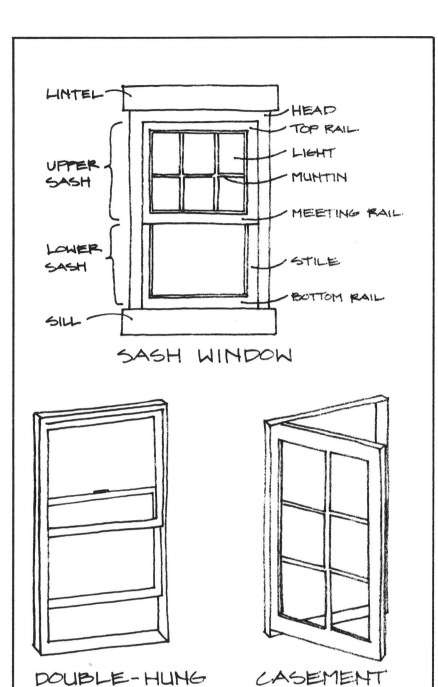

LINTEL

HEAD
TOP RAIL
LIGHT
MUNTIN

UPPER
SASH

MEETING RAIL

LOWER
SASH

STILE

BOTTOM RAIL

SILL

SASH WINDOW

DOUBLE-HUNG
SASH

CASEMENT

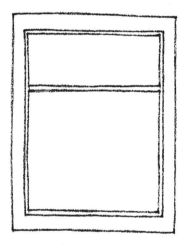

FIXED

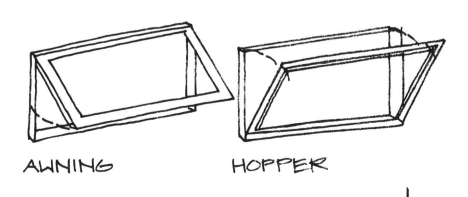

AWNING

HOPPER

Window construction and design involve the systematic organization of window parts. In the typical sash window, the horizontal elements—rails, lintel, and sill—have to be integrated with verticals—stiles and muntins—which really go in both directions. Integration involves the kinds of material used, dimensions, and profiles.

No matter what the window type, the design process is the same. Fixed windows may have fewer parts to integrate than operable windows, but their design and overall impact on a building starts with the assembly of parts. The assembly creates a pattern that, when repeated, becomes a rhythm, perhaps a module.

WINDOW PLACEMENT—THE DISTRIBUTION OF WIN-
dows on walls and their relationship to interior spaces—has
changed with time. Some placements are tied to styles of
building, but a few, such as the single-paned, double-hung
sash, are ubiquitous. Windows are also combined into
pairs, triples, or *bands.* When they are combined, individual
window sizes may be adjusted so as to keep a sound proportion of windows to wall area. The unique *corner window* is a
modern concept: visually, it eliminates part of the bearing
wall and wraps light around the corner.

   Stepped placements are used on large walls to light stair-
cases or large rooms.

   The *skylight* is usually a fixed window, although some
have movable sections that serve as ventilators. Skylights
have been used to light interior hallways or rooms. Most are
not visible from ground level because they are hidden by
parapet walls or other roof forms. The most extensive use of
skylights has been in industrial buildings.

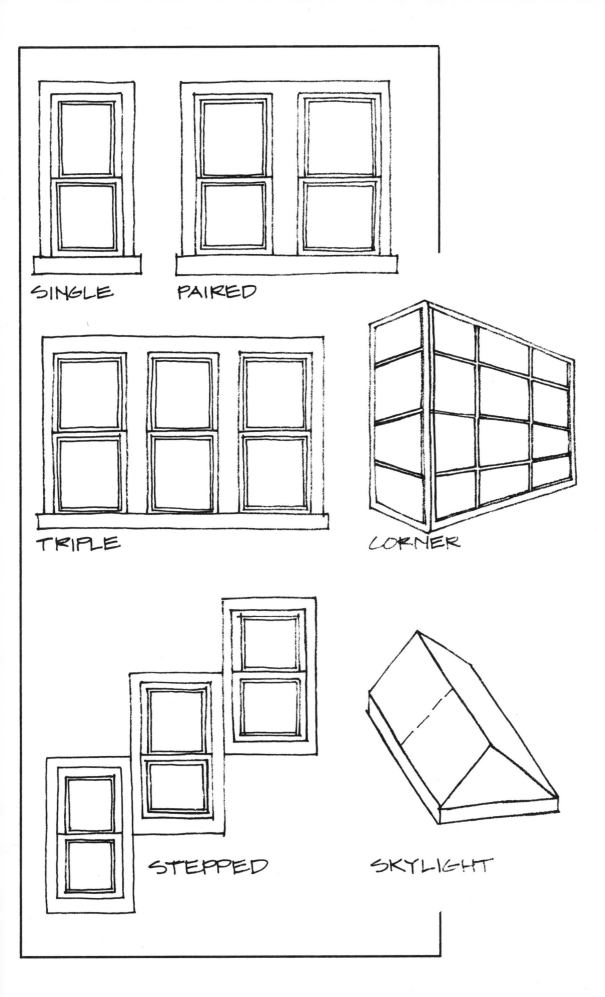

SINGLE   PAIRED

TRIPLE

CORNER

STEPPED   SKYLIGHT

IN BUILDING DESIGN, FENESTRATION REFERS TO the arrangement of windows and other openings, especially the patterns that such an arrangement defines. Generally fenestration has come to refer to windows only. Window size and design may play a role in determining pattern, but more often than not, pattern gets divided into two gross categories—*asymmetrical* and *symmetrical* placement. In the asymmetrical pattern, windows are placed so as not to be arithmetically balanced, or so that one-half of an elevation is not a mirror image of the other half. Balance among elements in an asymmetrical pattern is achieved by adding and subtracting shapes, sizes, and the relative visual "weights" of each window. Symmetrical fenestration emphasizes a steady, replicatable rhythm, even mirror image—the kind of alignment where the spectator may anticipate and predict placement.

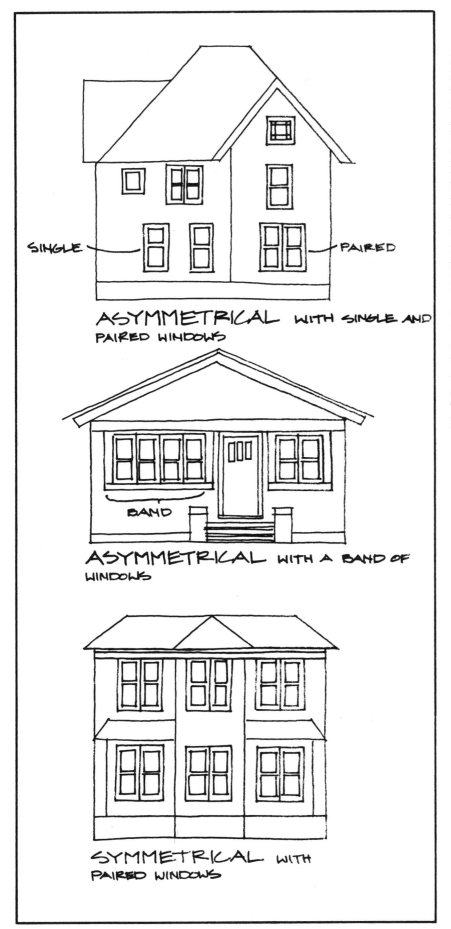

ASYMMETRICAL WITH SINGLE AND PAIRED WINDOWS

SINGLE — PAIRED

ASYMMETRICAL WITH A BAND OF WINDOWS

BAND

SYMMETRICAL WITH PAIRED WINDOWS

The kind of asymmetrical placement illustrated has been especially associated with the design of the cottage, where asymmetry is associated with picturesque effects. A related device could be used in a bungalow, where the center line (from the apex of the gable to the foundation) is violated by placing the entrance off-center. The grouping of windows may be used in either fenestration, but the use of windows in bands has been particularly successful in the early twentieth-century cottage and bungalow.

Symmetrical placements effect design on the horizontal whereby windows help delineate floor levels and spread the building out from the center. They also effect design on the vertical whereby stacking creates bays or columns of light. The tension between the two forces helps unify the design.

A *CLEARSTORY* (OR CLERESTORY) IS A SPECIAL group of windows that admits more air and light to a building. In recent vernacular usage, the term has come to designate the row of transom lights above the display windows on a storefront, as well as the row of windows that rises above a lower roof and is set back through the next roof's slope, as in the monitor roof of an industrial building.

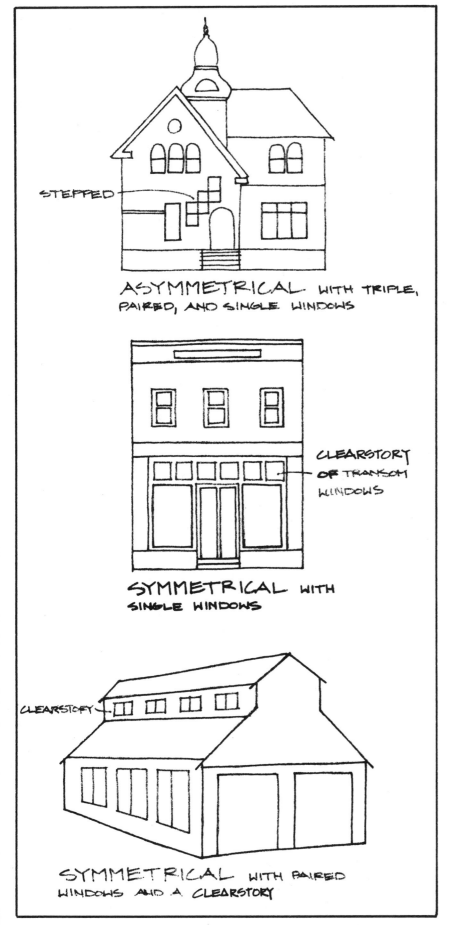

ASYMMETRICAL WITH TRIPLE, PAIRED, AND SINGLE WINDOWS

STEPPED

CLEARSTORY OF TRANSOM WINDOWS

SYMMETRICAL WITH SINGLE WINDOWS

CLEARSTORY

SYMMETRICAL WITH PAIRED WINDOWS AND A CLEARSTORY

In a moderately large building, fenestration may affect the massing of design elements. For example, windows may help to create a lighter or heavier appearance for an element or relate to the building's materials in a special way or be integrated into other elements as when a stepped window lights a stair.

In storefront design, transom lights often cap the display windows. They may also tie the façade together horizontally into a band or clearstory. In vernacular buildings the clearstory was usually a row of windows that, though practical, was well integrated into design through regular and orderly placement and proportional integration of the windows.

ORIEL WINDOWS HAVE BEEN USED LESS EXTEN-sively than other kinds of bay windows. Nevertheless, they are found on several house types and commercial buildings. A part of the vernacular vocabulary, the oriel projects out from the wall of an upper story. On plan it may be two-sided or three-sided, as in half a hexagon or in segmental or semi-circular design. It has its own tent or half-dome roof, and its base may be carried on corbels.

The *bay window,* strictly speaking, is the window portion of a projecting bay, but the term has come to stand for the entire structure. Unlike the oriel, the bay is carried on foundations outside the wall line. Bays may be single, or stacked to cover two or more stories. On plan the three-sided bay, with two canted walls and one parallel to the main wall, is the most popular. Some three-sided bays have their projecting walls perpendicular to the main wall. Occasionally one finds a curved bay with a bow window.

Oriels and bays have a special effect on design. They are more successful on second- or third-floor side elevations where their three-dimensional qualities may be enjoyed. The oriel is somewhat restricted in size, no doubt because of its method of support, but bays, either canted or perpendicular to the wall, have a wide range of sizes. Both window types have been associated with picturesque design and certain historical styles, and both have been used in residential and commercial design to gain variety in wall treatment.

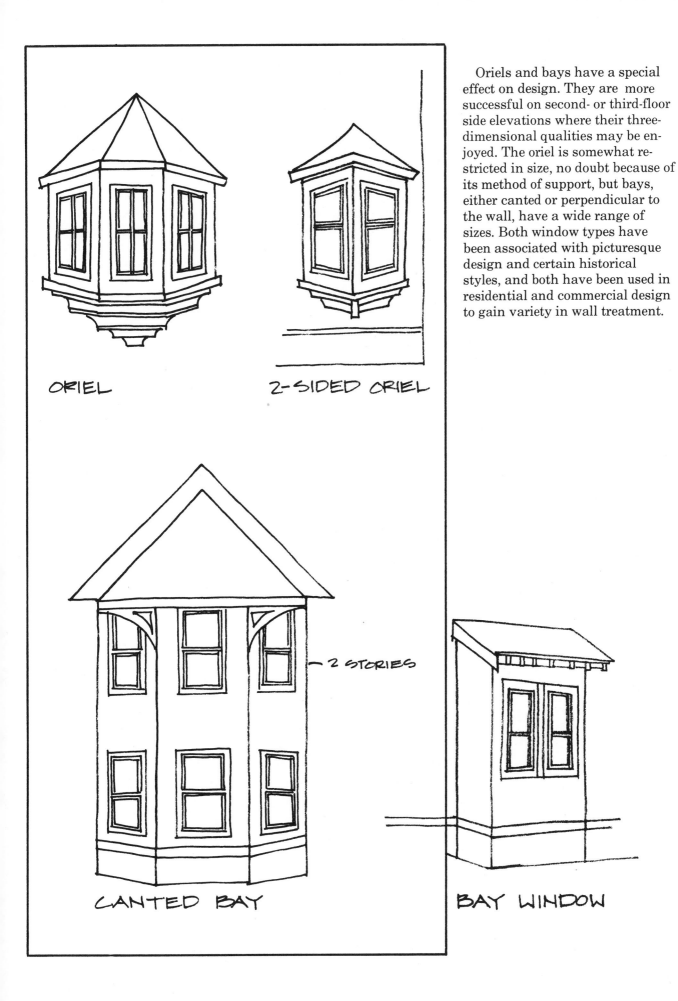

ORIEL

2-SIDED ORIEL

— 2 STORIES

CANTED BAY

BAY WINDOW

THE *BOWED* OR *BENT* WINDOW, FOUND IN TOWERS and curved walls, projects directly from the wall. Such a window is a segment of a circle on plan.

Art glass has been the vernacular equivalent of contemporary hand-crafted stained glass. Square pieces of art glass were utilized on the borders of cottage windows, and smaller pieces were assembled to create naturalistic or geometric designs in fixed windows or as the head portion of a large window. *Leaded glass* is an arrangement in which the lights are held together with lead or zinc bars. *Beveled glass* is composed of pieces that have been cut on a slant along their edges; the cut is a bevel.

The *lunette* window is small in size and serves as an accent window. It has a semicircular shape and may feature a single light, art glass, or unusual glazing. In some buildings the glass has been replaced by louvers that help ventilate an attic space.

The *Palladian* or *Venetian* window is the most elaborate of vernacular windows. In many applications the original structure of colonnettes or pilasters, rectangular windows with rounded tops, and a large, round-headed center window has been reduced to a three-part arrangement without columns or an entablature. Only the primary shape remains. Some Palladian forms have been so reduced as to remove the rounded heads of the windows.

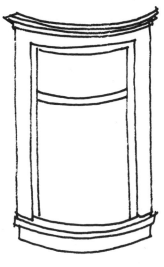

**BOWED OR
BENT WINDOW**

SASH WINDOW
WITH LEADED GLASS
AND ART GLASS

LUNETTE.

LUNETTE
QUARTER CIRCLE

PALLADIAN WINDOW

PALLADIAN TYPE

The windows on this page could be used to accent a wall, as in the case of the bowed window and the lunette; to emphasize a shape, as when a bowed window is placed in a tower; to emphasize a portion of a wall, as with a Palladian; or to provide special light for an interior space with special glass or a grand design. Windows with leaded, beveled, or art glass were usually placed so as to take advantage of sunlight. Lunettes were most often placed in gables or opposite stair landings. The Palladian could light a stair, a hallway, and an upper-level social space. Drastically reduced in size and design, it could also serve as a gable-end light for an attic.

THROUGHOUT THE LAST QUARTER OF THE NINE-teenth century, sash windows were given a variety of head portions in order to expand their usage. Some designs tried to relate to specific styles, while others were created for use as accent windows. *Pointed* or *Gothic* shapes were especially designed for use in vernacular churches, while circle-top and segmented windows were used in commercial buildings and houses.

The *transom* in an entrance system is specifically the wood bar that separates the light from the door, but as in so many other cases, the term has been expanded and now stands for the light as a whole. Transom windows are either fixed for light or operable for light and air.

A *fanlight* is another overdoor or transom window, semi-elliptical or semicircular in shape, with radiating wood muntins or strips of lead between the panes. Such windows may be either fixed or operable.

CIRCLETOP
(ROUND-HEADED)

SEGMENTED

GOTHIC HEAD

PEAK HEAD

TRANSOM

TRANSOM

FANLIGHT

In vernacular design the shape of the upper portion of a window may be reinforced by similar shapes above the window. For example, a circle top or segmented top may have a circle-top or segmental lintel above the window, or a peak head may have a triangular lintel and a wide peaked casing to reinforce its shape. The repeated form also strengthens the rhythm that the windows may establish on the walls.

Although transom lights are low-key design elements, a storefront may have an elegant transom to enhance its entrance.

Generally, fanlights have been associated with colonial design motifs, and may be accompanied by side lights beside the entrance door. Fanlights, however, are not limited to colonial styles; they are also found in cottage types.

SASH BOARDS, LIKE OTHER KINDS OF STICKWORK, were cut and shaped in any way machines allowed. Thus it was possible to develop a series of small windows for use in gables and on elevations. Designs were limited only to what the door and sash companies were willing to offer as stock for sales catalogs, or to what the carpenter was willing to make on the job.

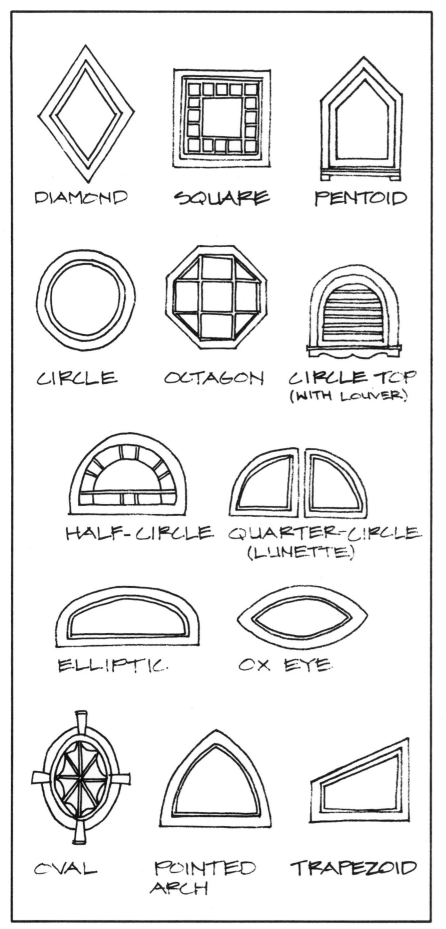

DIAMOND SQUARE PENTOID

CIRCLE OCTAGON CIRCLE TOP
(WITH LOUVER)

HALF-CIRCLE QUARTER-CIRCLE
(LUNETTE)

ELLIPTIC OX EYE

OVAL POINTED
ARCH TRAPEZOID

This page displays a general assortment of the specialty windows most often found in the gable ends of houses. They may be integrated into a stickwork design or stand alone. Secondary uses include ornamental lights for walls or towers (the latter in churches) and accent lighting for stairs. These windows are small in size and usually fixed.

Occasionally one finds a different window in each of the gables of the same house. Stylistically, the half-circle, quarter-circle, elliptic, and oval have been used extensively in colonial treatments, but all these shapes have been used on most house types.

THE MOST EXTENSIVE USE OF *LINTELS* IS IN MA-sonry construction. Structurally, a lintel is a horizontal beam that bridges an opening and supports the weight above it. In window treatments a lintel spans the opening above the head of the window. Lintels have been carved from stone, planed from timbers, and cast from cement. They have basic geometric shapes such as rectangles or pentoids and various segments of a circle. A *surround* is a special element that combines a lintel into a whole piece enclosing a doorway, a window, or a fireplace opening.

Where lintels head a window or a door, sills underline the same openings. Both elements have similar functions, in that they can throw off water. Lintels built to throw off water are called *dripstones, hoodmolds,* or *weather molds.* Special sills include the *slip sill,* which lines up evenly with the window casing, has no projections or lugs, and is not built into the masonry; and the *lug sill,* which projects beyond the window casing and has its ends built into the masonry. A *continuous sill* connects each window on an elevation and ties the windows into an overall pattern. Visually, such a sill can work like a belt course: it projects from the wall plane, and its finish, size, and material may be different from the wall material. It can also bind all four walls together into horizontal planes and neatly delineate story levels.

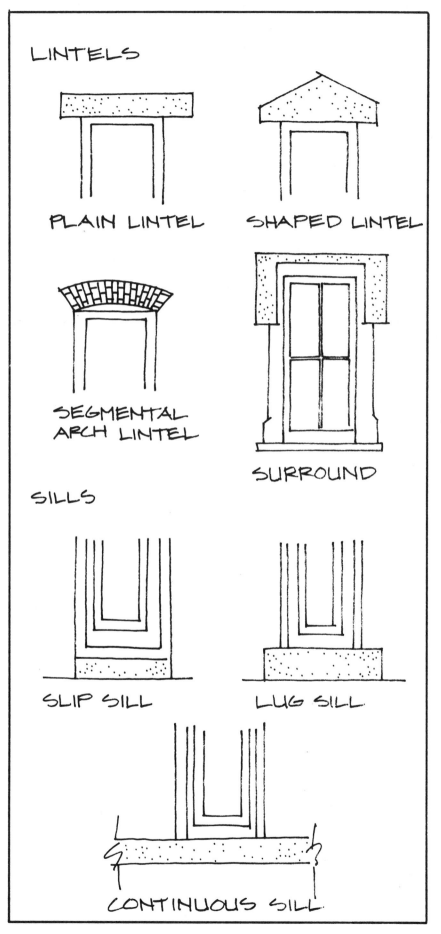

LINTELS

PLAIN LINTEL

SHAPED LINTEL

SEGMENTAL ARCH LINTEL

SURROUND

SILLS

SLIP SILL

LUG SILL

CONTINUOUS SILL

Lintels and sills accent window treatments and punctuate fenestration. The shape of a lintel may contrast with or reinforce the shape of a window, whereas sills have less range in shape. The material used in either may complement the wall material or contrast highly with it.

Another design consideration for lintels and sills occurs in the connections that can be made among them. Lintels and sills may both be continuous, so as to band windows into a grand pattern. Lintels of different types—say, plain and segmental—have been used to create an integrated system of ornament. To describe this kind of arrangement, one might assign a label—*a* for the plain and *b* for the segmental. If an elevation has five windows beginning and ending with a plain lintel, the rhythm for that elevation would read *a b a b a*.

SASH WINDOWS WERE IMPORTED INTO ENGLAND from Holland in the late seventeenth century; soon after, they made their way to America. This window rose to preeminence when window production—with rails, stiles, muntins, and sheets of glass easily produced in large quantities—developed into a major component of architectural materials manufacturing. Sash, door, and blind companies used a wide variety of cutting machines, most with the revolutionary rotary cutting blades, to create the stickwork needed for windows, doors, and interior shutters.

Queen Anne was the trade catalog name for the double-hung sash that contained small panels of colored glass or unusual glazing in the upper sash. The term *cottage window* was also a trade name for prominently placed windows that were wider than other types and carried a header. Cottage windows also often contained art glass and beveled or leaded glass, and they had disproportional sections of sash.

SOMETIMES COLORED GLASS PANELS

QUEEN ANNE WINDOWS

QUEEN ANNE WINDOWS

Many design qualities associated with cottage types derive from the style known as Queen Anne. Picturesque and otherwise rustic effects were common to the style, including unusual glazing patterns. Such patterns gave the windows a contrived rural look and reinforced the active and agitated surfaces that Queen Anne design promoted. In a sense the kind of stickwork that prevailed on walls, porches, and in gables was displayed in windows.

The extra-wide cottage window that served the parlor or dining room helped integrate inside and outside space. In the ever expanding sense of space that characterized modern design, these windows were a window on the world from the inside out and from the outside in. Proportionally the cottage window had unequal parts, with the top or head usually smaller than the lower portion.

COTTAGE WINDOW 2 FIXED LIGHTS

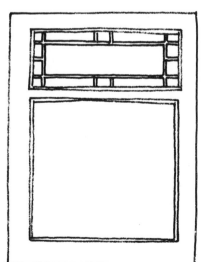

COTTAGE WINDOW DECORATIVE HEADER

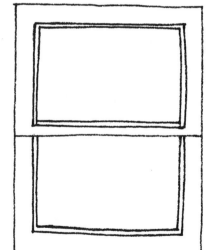

COTTAGE WINDOW SASH

BOTH PRAIRIE AND BUNGALOW HOUSES HAD LONG horizontal forms. The placement and design of windows could break up the wall planes and add vertical accents. Glazing design was especially effective, in that the muntins or glazing bars took on a very linear quality. Muntins divided glass into vertical elements, and sash division occurred not only at the usual locking rail but also at the upper quarter or third of the window. The effect of this change in composition was to lengthen the window and focus on the vertical. When these windows were grouped, they formed a finely wrought panel of glass tightly bound by the vertical thrust of the stiles and the horizontal thrust of the rails.

Sash windows predominate in prairie- and bungalow-type houses, but the distribution of glass and the arrangement of muntins is different from cottage design. Here the emphasis is on linear qualities, especially the vertical. Glass is divided into strips and panels of glass. Right angles dominate and a grid is implied in the overall design.

Both prairie- and bungalow-style buildings extend the horizontal planes of the design. Both open interior space until individual spaces flow easily into one another. The new open plan relied on light to activate the space and cross-ventilation so as to modify the environment. The few vertical accents in these kinds of houses were often left to the windows, particularly in bungalows.

WINDOWS: PRAIRIE AND BUNGALOW

SEVERAL KINDS OF SASH WINDOWS WERE USED IN buildings with colonial motifs. Essentially, colonial patterns called for many ridges on the sticking, and a division of the lights—particulary on the upper sash—into multiple panes.

Design for colonial styles centered on a rational, well-ordered appearance. The division of glass into neat, proportional elements reflected the general belief in a rational and balanced world. These windows were often wide and tall in order to shed great light on the orderly and proportional interior spaces. The light in this case was emblematic of general attitudes about the value of colonial design, many of which derive from nineteenth and twentieth-century revivals of the colonial, rather than from the historic Georgian or federal styles of building. Arithmetic proportions favored over time include 1:1, 2:1, and 4:1, and multiples of the numbers 3 and 4, with an occasional 5.

GLASS BLOCK IS A HOLLOW GLASS BUILDING BLOCK that admits light but provides privacy (because of the patterns molded on both faces); it also insulates against noise. It is not used in load-bearing walls. While found mostly in commercial and industrial buildings, it has been used in various modern (often masonry) house types.

Steel-framed windows have been popular for commercial and industrial use because of their strength and low maintenance costs. Such lights have few divisions, so that large panes may admit as much light as possible. Other commercial types include wood sash and fixed windows. Sometimes these windows have wire mesh in the lights; intended for safety and security, the mesh also adds visual texture to the walls.

One of the most successful turn-of-the-century windows was the so-called *Chicago window.* The size, shape, and practicality of this window suited both high-style and vernacular design. The Chicago window is oblong, with a wide, fixed, central light flanked on each side by narrow, movable sash windows. This kind of window expanded greatly the area devoted to windows on an elevation and increased the amount of light admitted to the interior. It also encouraged thinner exterior walls, which increased floor space.

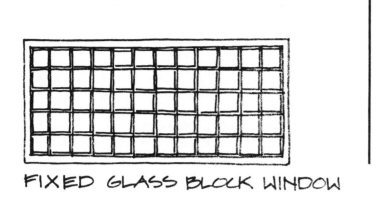

FIXED GLASS BLOCK WINDOW

STEEL
CASEMENT

WOOD
SASH

FIXED COTTAGE
WITH FAN-LIGHT

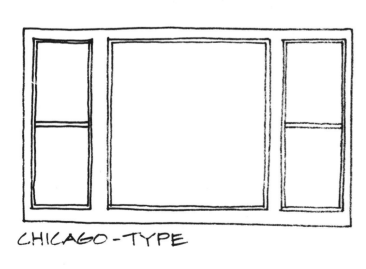

CHICAGO-TYPE

WAREHOUSE
CASEMENT AND
TRANSOM

GENERALLY, A *PORCH* IS A COVERED ENTRANCE TO a building. While traditional porches have their own roof, and the porch proper projects from the main wall, other kinds of entrance designs have become known as porches. The *porch that covers an entire facade* and utilizes the main roof of the building for cover is one of these. The porch's relationship to the building depends on the architectural style being used, but its basic components include entrance steps that are open or are closed with wing walls; porch piers bearing that portion of the roof; and a porch wall or rail to enclose the porch space.

The *entrance porch* with a separate roof is common to most styles in vernacular design. As part of the entrance, this porch may vary a great deal in size, roof shape, roof support (piers or posts), and placement. The *cutaway porch* results when a portion (usually a corner) of a building is cut out, so that the porch is recessed under the main roof.

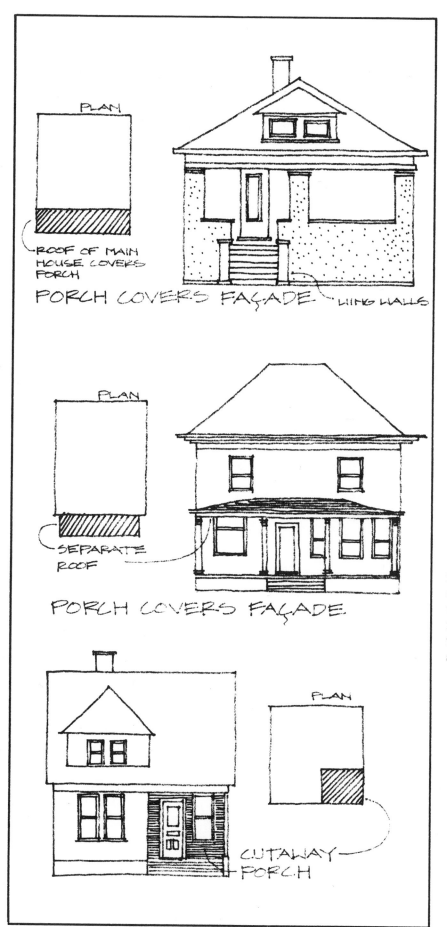

PLAN

ROOF OF MAIN
HOUSE COVERS
PORCH

PORCH COVERS FAÇADE — LIING WALLS

PLAN

SEPARATE
ROOF

PORCH COVERS FAÇADE

PLAN

CUTAWAY
PORCH

Entrance porches are major design elements in vernacular houses, and minor elements in other building types. An entrance porch that covers an entire façade can determine a good deal of the effect of the design. In the design illustrated, the porch helps to frame the building visually; it organizes the façade into two bays, establishes strong corners through the design of the piers, and in this case, despite the offset door, adds a bit of formality.

The projecting porch seems to derive from the portico, which may account for the formality—even the classical nature—of these porches. Porch fronts are usually divided into bays organized by columns or posts that carry a full or partial entablature. The projecting porch ceiling height aligns with the ceiling height of the interior, and the depth of the porch is influenced by the flow of interior space. Designs that emphasize continuous space tend toward deeper porches with windows and porch open space aligned.

The cutaway porch is frequently a proportion—in the illustration, about half—of the width of the façade. Steps are often under the cutaway, so that the porch is contained within the plane of the façade. The depth too is proportional, averaging less than half the square footage of the front room.

A *VESTIBULE* IS A SMALL HALL OR PASSAGE THAT serves as intermediary space between the exterior and the interior. Most nineteenth-century vernacular houses with vestibules included them within the volume of the house. In a number of twentieth-century designs—especially English cottage types and the colonial revival houses referred to as Cape Cod—the vestibule projects from the facade. In these types a shallow vestibule with its own roof serves as a porch and an air lock for the interior.

The entrance porch of some churches and other public buildings has a vestibule form without walls. It is a shallow porch with its own roof, a small porch floor, and railings.

A *porch with a hood over the door* is the most understated entrance porch. The hood projects over a portion of the porch area and is most frequently furnished with brackets. Hoods are found on a variety of house types and are used as canopies for secondary entrances to other kinds of buildings. Hoods may be flat or half-round in section and may carry an ornamental balcony and decorative moldings.

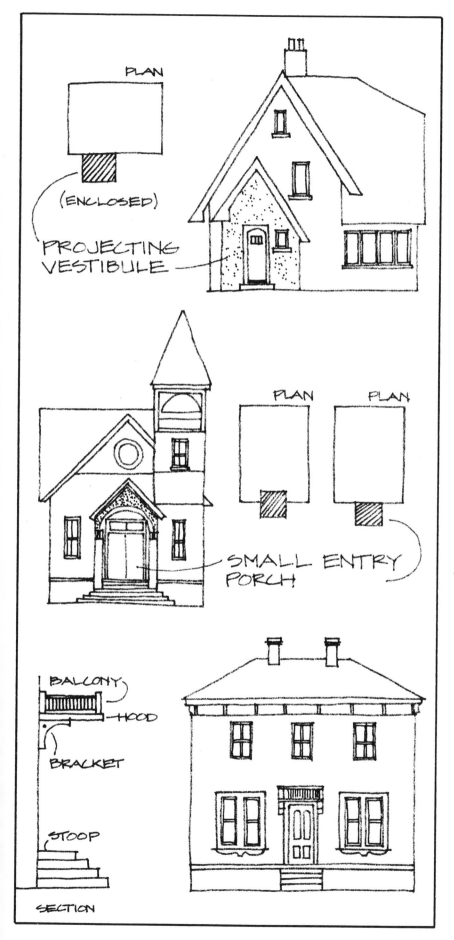

PLAN

(ENCLOSED)

PROJECTING VESTIBULE

PLAN   PLAN

SMALL ENTRY PORCH

BALCONY

HOOD

BRACKET

STOOP

SECTION

A projecting vestibule is not a large design element, but it can reinforce other elements. In the illustration, the gable roof line has been repeated in the vestibule roof, so that the entire vestibule looks like a miniature of the gable façade. Vestibules are used in wood-frame and masonry houses, and the cladding material is usually the same as the main section of the building. Placement depends upon overall style: center placement is used in colonial and classical fronts, whereas off-center placement is tied to picturesque and rural effects.

The small entry porch on churches or other public buildings is so shallow as to really be part of the facade. In some designs the void of the porch area is used to counter the mass of a tower or a corner. Since many of these entrances have double doors, the opening in the wall is larger than any other opening.

Because of their size and somewhat unobtrusive placement, porch hoods can be thought of as ornamental as well as practical. The depth of a hood is about the same as the depth of the steps, so that their relationship is integrated.

PORCHES: PORTICOES

A *PORTICO* IS A FREESTANDING STRUCTURE WITH a roof supported by columns. In the course of time the portico has been integrated into vernacular design as a porch. Most vernacular versions of the portico are either one or two stories in height and one or two bays wide. Both single and multistory porticoes may carry a balcony or pediment, the latter being traditional. Columns are most often classical—an order of architecture with an entablature. In vernacular design, porticoes are wood and are built with millwork elements.

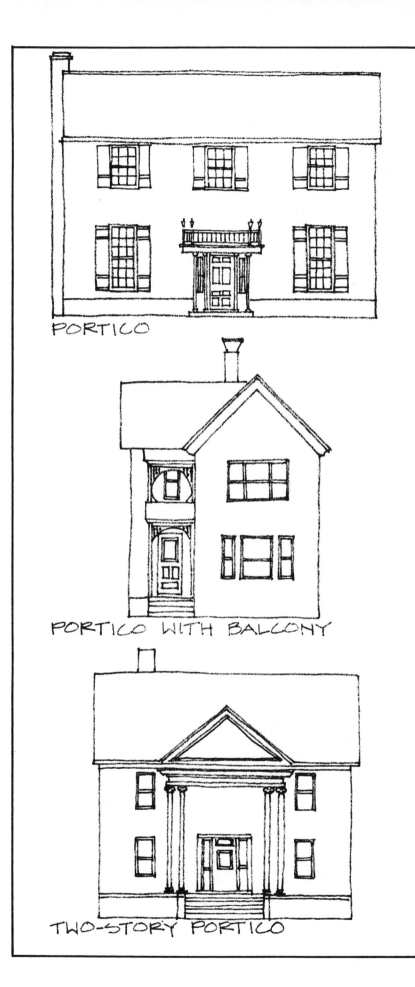

PORTICO

PORTICO WITH BALCONY

TWO-STORY PORTICO

Porticoes are most prominent as center axis structures, a kind of placement most often related to symmetrical design. In trying to analyze the portico's relationship to the entire design, one needs to consider the extent to which formal, classical vocabulary has been used, and the proportional relationship of the portico structure to the rest of the façade.

Porticoes are used in a wide range of scales, from the delicate unit that characterizes the entrance to a building to the two-story, full-façade type, with a balcony at the second-story floor line and a full pediment above that. The grandeur of the portico sets a tone that strongly influences the remainder of the design elements, including the interior millwork and arrangement of spaces. Thus a large-scale full-portico treatment encourages use of a central hall or large receiving hall, as well as the repeat of pediment or column forms in door casings, lintels, and fireplace surrounds. A less stylized piece may contribute only moldings to the ornamentation.

NINETEENTH-CENTURY LITERATURE DOES NOT provide clear distinctions between verandas, porches, and piazzas. Indeed, designers and writers of the period and compilers of architectural dictionaries seem to use the terms interchangeably. In this book a *veranda* is a special porch characterized by openness, lighter posts and rails, and continuous space that links at least two sides of a building. The space created by this porch is a key to its definition: gallery-like, it is intended for walking, socializing, or sitting. A veranda carries its own roof and may have more than one access from inside and outside.

An *end-wall porch* may be a primary or secondary entrance, depending upon siting and building form. In the illustration, the end-wall porch is the secondary entrance; it covers most of the end wall and is clearly an extension of the main house.

A *porte-cochere* is a porch arranged as a side porch and side entrance with a roof that once protected passengers getting into and out of carriages; as automobiles became wider, it disappeared as a porch type. In its time, the porte-cochere also served as an access road to a carriage house or garage area.

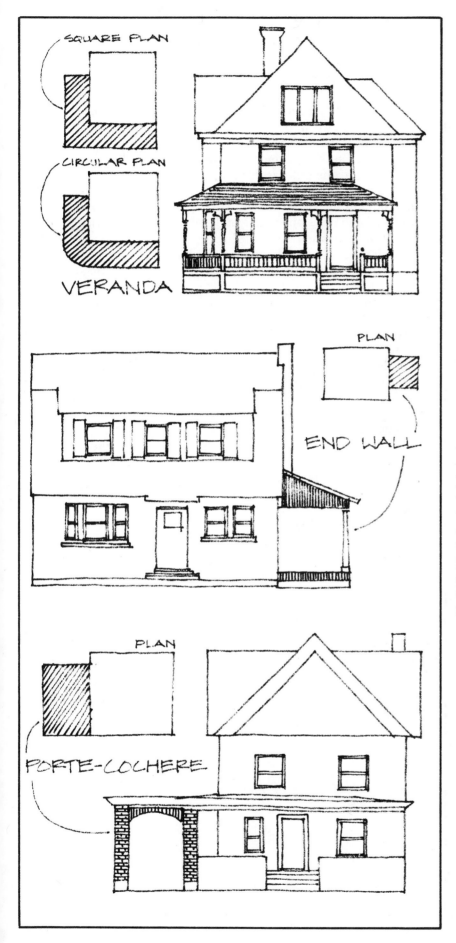

SQUARE PLAN

CIRCULAR PLAN

VERANDA

PLAN

END WALL

PLAN

PORTE-COCHERE

Verandas are strong design elements, being large enough to affect elevations and light enough visually and structurally to help ornament a building. As porches they tend to engage the house rather than the grounds: they are so well integrated that they seem to serve the inhabitants as secondary living space, yet offer easy and direct access to the outdoors.

Success in integrating an end-wall porch depends on the style of the building and the scale of the porch. As illustrated, single-story porches—no matter what the character of their elements—appear to be dependencies. But two-story porches—or single-story ones that carry horizontal lines from the façade, including the foundation window lines—look like sections of the main house. When an end-wall porch is the primary entrance, it often has a formal composition that clearly marks it as such.

The porte-cochere usually carries lines from the main building—whether a porch roof, as illustrated, or other lines. Most porches of this kind have strong architectonic qualities, in that columns or piers with broad arches or an order of architecture are common. Porte-cocheres are built of masonry or frame construction.

PORCH COMPOSITIONAL DETAILS DIVIDE INTO
two integrated types: roof support, and enclosure elements
such as piers, posts, walls, rails, balusters, and lattices. *Piers*
usually have at least two parts: a base such as a pedestal,
and a shaft with a capital or bracket that serves as an intermediary between the shaft and the first member of the
roof. Porches are also organized with columns and entablatures in which the treatment is formal, usually identifying
the main entrance. Regardless of their placement, ornamentally styled porches have relied on turned posts, balusters,
and spindles for visual effects. Turned work was mass-
produced on lathes; the pieces had extraordinarily varied profiles of historic and free-form shapes.

Porch enclosures could be suggested directly by *open rails,*
that is, organized by slotted balustrades, or *closed* rails, the
intervals between posts being filled by a wall. Open rails—
more frequently used than closed ones—were composed of
two rails terminated by newel posts, with a row of vertical
balusters between the rails. The closed type relied on horizontal organization, especially employing clapboards or
shingles to cover the wall.

A *pergola* is a freestanding structure open to the sky. Its
vertical supports are columns or posts, and its roof is composed of girders and cross-rafters whose ends are usually
tail-cut. Pergolas are popular bungalow elements but are
also found as entrance porches with a full roof on other
buildings. They are often enclosed on one or more sides by
lattices—openwork made of interlaced strips of wood that is
frequently covered with vines or other climbing plants.

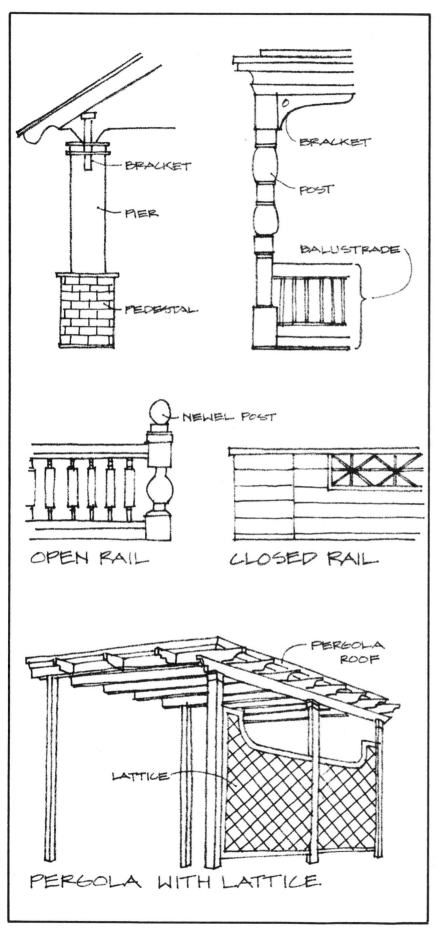

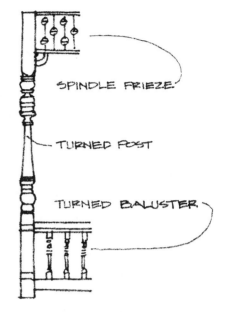

SPINDLE FRIEZE

TURNED POST

TURNED BALUSTER

BRACKET

PIER

PEDESTAL

BRACKET

POST

BALUSTRADE

NEWEL POST

OPEN RAIL

CLOSED RAIL

PERGOLA ROOF

LATTICE

PERGOLA WITH LATTICE.

Porch details have a wide range of design uses. Buildings with little ornamentation may use porch elements as the sole decorative portion of the design. Highly decorated buildings may integrate the porch elements into an overall scheme. Piers and posts mark edges of buildings, and as edges their profiles are taken into account. Rails or balustrades of any kind function as walls, as elements of enclosure. Combined with their supports, walls and rails indicate the boundary between inside and outside space. Accordingly, they may suggest continuity of space or make a clear delination between inside and outside domains. The pergola is a special element: it may augment design as a freestanding structure or be an end-wall element, or portions of it may be used as ornamental divides. In the latter case, a small pergola roof may cover an entrance porch.

THE ORDERS OF ARCHITECTURE HAVE A DISTIN-
guished history as load-bearing support systems, as design
systems, and as systems of ornamentation. In vernacular
building and design, the use of the orders has been primarily decorative; in most cases, they appear as scaled-down
versions of their original selves. Basic properties and qualities may remain part of the order, but features have been
stripped away.

The *Doric* is the oldest order. It is characterized by a thick,
tapering shaft that has no base and a plain capital. Columns in the Doric order have fluted edges. In the Roman
version of the order, the *Tuscan,* the flutes have been removed, the shaft has a base, and the ornamental details
(moldings) have been removed. The Tuscan is probably the
most popular order in the vernacular tradition. The Doric
entablature may have some ornament on the frieze, but the
Tuscan is most often plain.

The *Ionic* order is taller and more slender than the Doric
and is characterized by the scroll-like ornaments of the capital. The Ionic capital has four volutes or scrolls, and while
most were made of wood, molded clay capitals are not uncommon. The entablature is plain and the architrave may
be divided into two or more fascia boards. The *Corinthian,*
the most ornamental of the orders, is characterized by a bell-
shaped capital adorned with an acanthus-leaf design. Ionic
and Corinthian shafts were usually fluted.

In vernacular use of the orders of architecture, builders
took some license with the forms. In general, moldings were
applied less frequently, and if applied, they have plain faces;
entablatures are also plain. Most vernacular orders are
made of wood, but masonry orders are found on public and
commercial buildings.

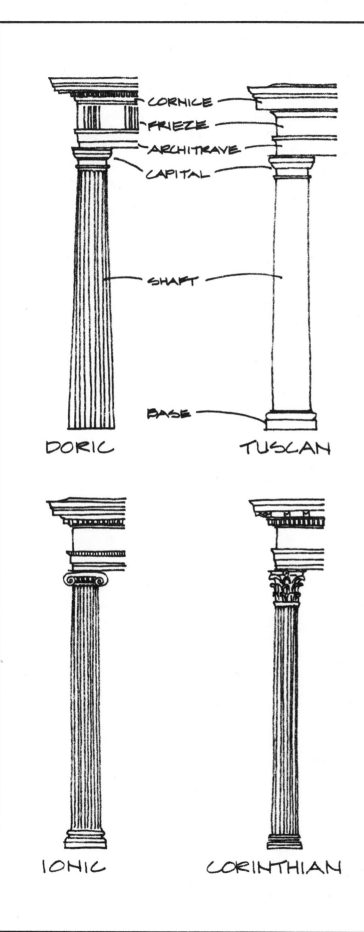

CORNICE

FRIEZE

ARCHITRAVE

CAPITAL

SHAFT

BASE

DORIC

TUSCAN

IONIC

CORINTHIAN

Original uses of the orders included a design system, in that the orders could be modular. As yet, there is little evidence to suggest that the orders were used in this way in vernacular design. As part of the organization of elevations or as part of a system of ornamentation in vernacular, the orders play an important role. As part of an organizing system, they help to divide walls into bays or to proportion vertical elements on a facade. When columns carry an entablature or a pediment, they tend to give overall shape to a building or to that section with which they are most involved.

As ornament, the orders help organize porches, articulate entrances, and establish rhythm; their use causes architraves or friezes to become significant elements in horizontal organization. As ornament, the orders are likely to be used eclectically, with the addition of bases to Doric columns, the removal of cornices from entablatures, and a general borrowing of moldings among the orders. Sometimes the orders are enlarged to a giant scale; at other times they are reduced to miniatures.

IN VERNACULAR ARCHITECTURE, COLUMNS, POSTS, and piers have limited structural use but play a large role in ornamentation. The *column* is traditionally circular in section and usually consists of a base, a shaft, and a capital. When columns are used for support in vernacular design, they most often carry the roof of a porch, a veranda, a portico, or other entrance element.

Piers are usually rectangular in section and either hollow or solid; many support walls or carry horizontal elements or arches. Piers may be stacked one upon another to concentrate the load of the roof and to support internal floors.

In vernacular architecture, columns and piers are often set on a *base* or a pedestal. The bases are integrated into the overall design and usually reflect the style of the building. *Pedestals* are usually rectangular in section; many are battered so that the top is smaller than the bottom. Pedestals in wood may be ornamented with moldings and inset panels. Most often made of wood and built in sections, columns have been shaped to round or flat patterns and are almost always hollow. Piers may be hollow, too, to save on weight; they are primarily of brick.

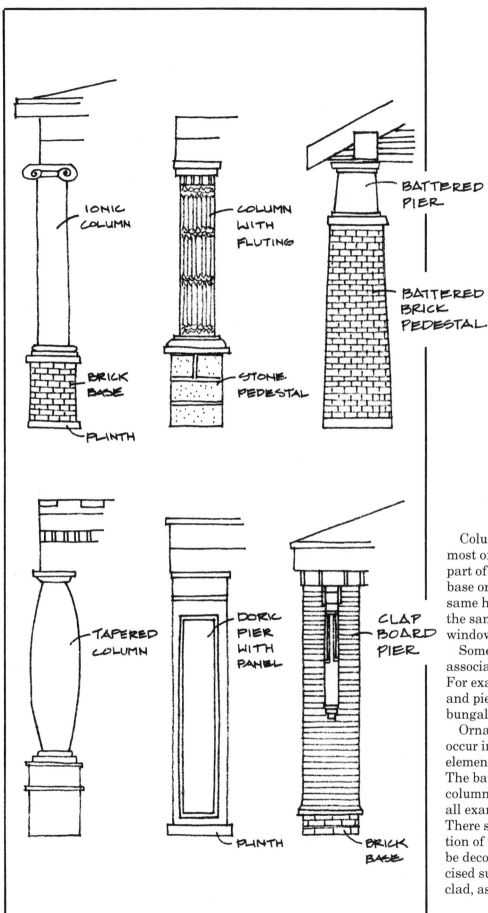

IONIC
COLUMN

COLUMN
WITH
FLUTING

BATTERED
PIER

BATTERED
BRICK
PEDESTAL

BRICK
BASE

PLINTH

STONE
PEDESTAL

TAPERED
COLUMN

DORIC
PIER
WITH
PANEL

CLAP
BOARD
PIER

PLINTH

BRICK
BASE

Columns or piers on pedestals most often support porch roofs. As part of an entrance system, the base or pedestal may stand at the same height as the porch rail or at the same height as the first-floor window sill.

Some pedestal and pier forms are associated with particular styles. For example, the battered pedestal and pier were used effectively in bungalow- and prairie-style houses.

Ornamentation of an order can occur in any of the compositional elements—base, shaft, or capital. The battered pedestal, the tapered column, and the paneled pier are all examples of this kind of design. There seems to be little manipulation of materials, but columns may be decorated with moldings or incised surfaces, and piers may be clad, as in the clapboard pier.

COLUMNS HAVE BEEN USED IN STYLES THAT RE-
call classical or revival motifs, especially when some degree
of formality is desired. A good deal of *Victorian* design is
visually "busy," in that the surfaces have many parts that
produce elaborate profiles. The Victorian column is no less
busy than any other Victorian design element.

Rustication also derives from historic vocabularies. In this
treatment—primarily tied to masonry building—blocks of
stone or bricks alternate larger with smaller or plainer with
richer or protruding with nonprotruding units. Often the
edges of the blocks have been beveled to create deep shadow
lines. Rustication on vernacular piers is usually quite simple
and direct, with little attention to the texture of the blocks'
surface.

Cast-iron columns or piers appear in numerous shapes,
with a range of ornamental treatments. Classical shapes are
common but so are generally abstracted and flattened forms
as in the capital of the illustration.

Paired columns have been used to add variety to a façade
design and to develop an alternative rhythm and an alternative light and dark pattern. The same is true for *colonnettes*, which, though miniature columns, vary a good
deal in size. The *pilaster* is a flattened column or pier, attached to walls, that helps organize and frame portions of a
design. An *engaged column* is built into the wall, rather
than laid on it like most pilasters. In vernacular design,
however, the distinction between engaged and attached
elements blurs.

In the Victorian column, the overall shape comes from the cumulative parts, and each major section of the order has multiple shapes. Thus, the play of light is enhanced by this design.

Rustication is infrequently done in isolation, but it is possible to find the treatment on one portion only of a design. Rustication may be carried out in wood as well as masonry.

Paired columns rarely appear as engaged elements. Their primary use in design is as freestanding supports for porch roofs. The colonnette is more adaptable: it can be made small enough to ornament a window or large enough to support a small roof.

Pilasters and engaged columns seem relegated to ground levels in vernacular design. they are, however, also present in vernacular interiors.

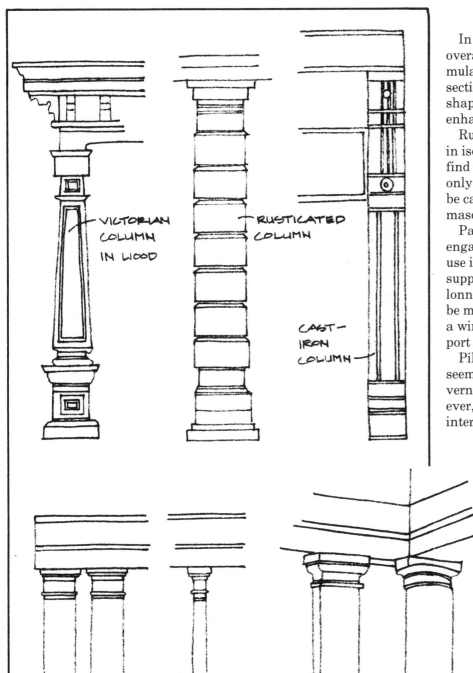

VICTORIAN COLUMN IN WOOD

RUSTICATED COLUMN

CAST-IRON COLUMN

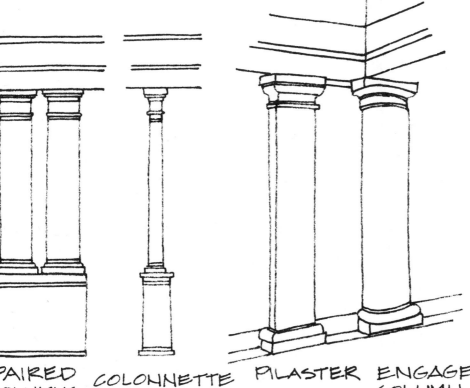

PAIRED COLUMNS   COLONNETTE   PILASTER   ENGAGED COLUMN

TAKEN AS A WHOLE, THE ENTRANCE SYSTEM FO-cuses the design of the elevation on which it is located. The entrance sets a tone for the entire stylistic treatment. In cottage types, the entrance received a great deal of attention. To be understood completely, it must be seen in concert with the porch and the approach to the house.

In the area immediately around the entrance door, the design vocabulary consists of an ornamented door: multiple panels, often with glass; numerous moldings, transoms, and rectilinear and curvilinear forms; and coloration through paint, stain, or glass—all conceived to enhance the play of light on the surfaces and to delight the eye.

Cottages with Victorian schemes tend toward tall, narrow double doors. The windows in these buildings have the same narrow shape. Ultimately the Victorian door gave way to the general cottage door of the 1880s and 1890s—a single door of panel and glass construction.

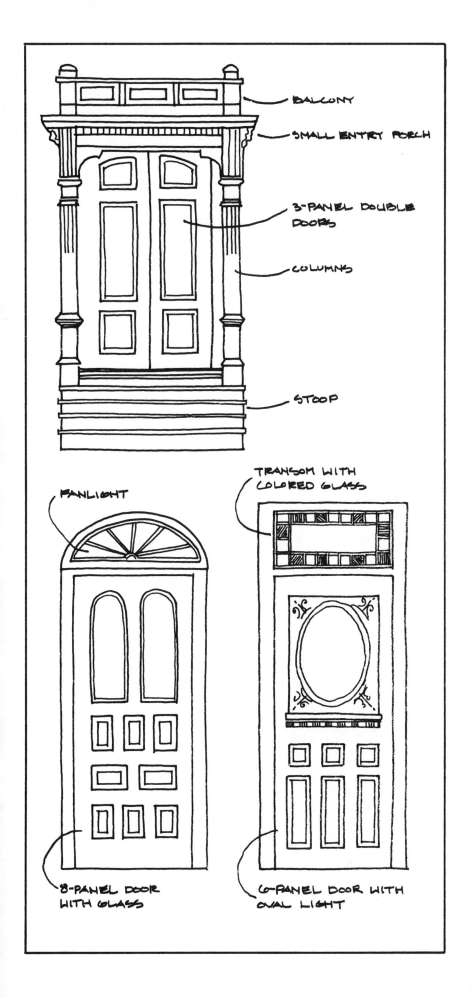

BALCONY

SMALL ENTRY PORCH

3-PANEL DOUBLE DOORS

COLUMNS

STOOP

FANLIGHT

TRANSOM WITH COLORED GLASS

8-PANEL DOOR WITH GLASS

6-PANEL DOOR WITH OVAL LIGHT

PRAIRIE AND BUNGALOW TYPES EMPLOYED EITHER wide, open porches with thick pedestals and piers for the porch roof (in which case the entrance was diminished by the depth of the porch or the broad gable of the porch roof), or a small stoop with a hood supported by brackets. In either case the door and its peripheral elements were severely and precisely geometrical.

Sidelights have been part of entrance systems throughout most of the 1870–1940 period. They are generally associated with colonial treatments and most often light an entrance vestibule. In the modern style, sidelights have sometimes been included in entrance design, but their organization is restrained and integrated into a unified door and sidelight composition. The number of panes is reduced drastically and the accent is on verticality, the linear quality of the muntins, and the use of geometric design as ornament.

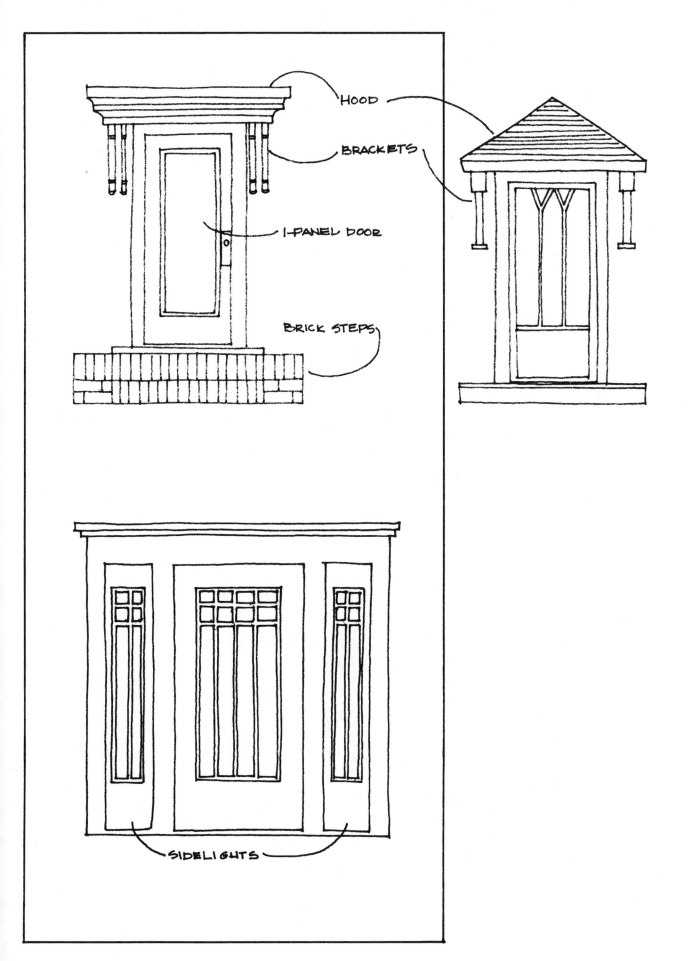

HOOD

BRACKETS

I-PANEL DOOR

BRICK STEPS

SIDELIGHTS

COLONIAL SYSTEMS MAY VARY IN THE DETAILS OF their treatment but most rely on engaging a classical front. The simplest system employs an order of architecture in either literal or abstracted form, with some reference to a pediment. Pilasters seem to be more common than engaged or freestanding columns. Among the details in the system illustrated, the round-headed panes, varying from three to five in number, are common elements in colonial doors. Ornaments on broken pediments include urn forms and the old emblem of hospitality, the pineapple.

Another prevalent system includes a small portico in which the Tuscan order is the most widely used. The porch is shallow, and the door is very often surrounded by sidelights and a fan-shaped transom. Door and sash companies sold entrances as systems, but the whole package need not be bought, in which case the door and its accompanying lights might not have a portico at all.

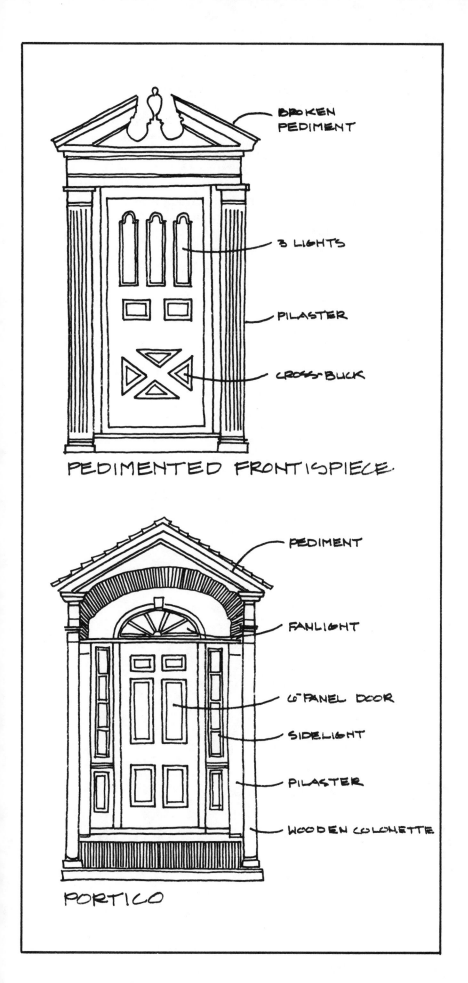

BROKEN
PEDIMENT

3 LIGHTS

PILASTER

CROSS-BUCK

PEDIMENTED FRONTISPIECE.

PEDIMENT

FANLIGHT

6-PANEL DOOR

SIDELIGHT

PILASTER

WOODEN COLONETTE

PORTICO

NINETEENTH-CENTURY COMMERCIAL ENTRANCES employ many of the same devices used in residential design, achieving formality characterized by strong vertical and horizontal organization. With display windows increasing the size of the entrance opening, the vertical elements dominate. Both cottage types and iron fronts rely on detailing, including moldings and changes in texture through the fluting or smoothing of columns. Later designs remove surface details and emphasize the clean, finished surface. Most of these systems use metal doors and metal mullions to divide window glass into large panes.

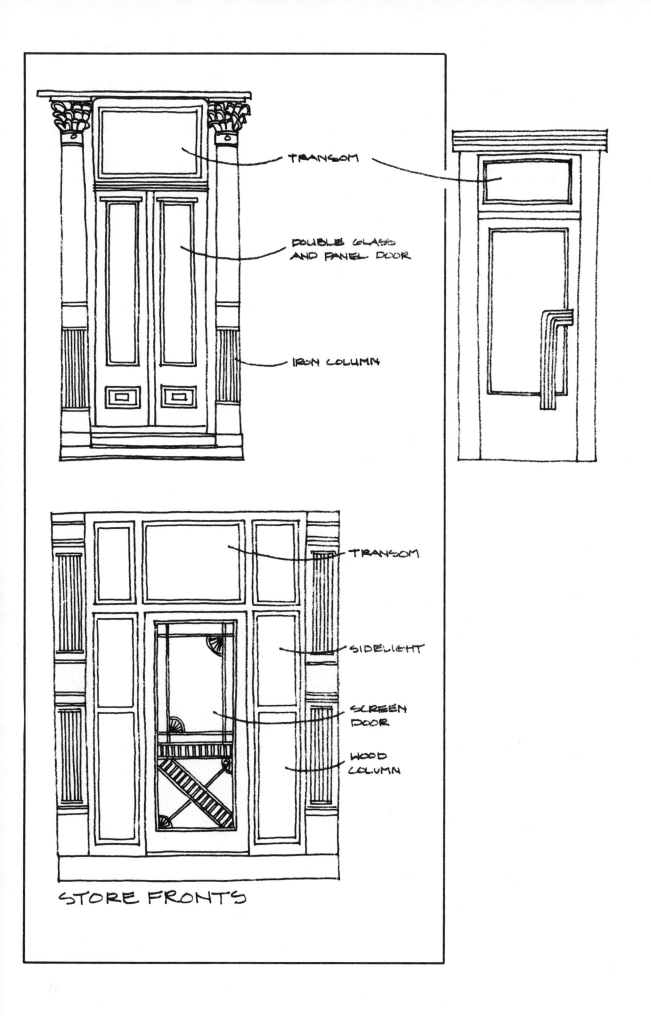

TRANSOM

DOUBLE GLASS AND PANEL DOOR

IRON COLUMN

TRANSOM

SIDELIGHT

SCREEN DOOR

WOOD COLUMN

STORE FRONTS

ENTRANCES TO VERNACULAR PUBLIC BUILDINGS are larger than entrances to houses but are usually more restrained. Paired doors are common, as they allow for easy access. Sidelights and transoms that light vestibules or corridors are also popular. Church or school entrances may employ an order of architecture; Tuscan and Corinthian seem to prevail. Most entrances are close to ground level, and many are recessed into the wall with shallow porches.

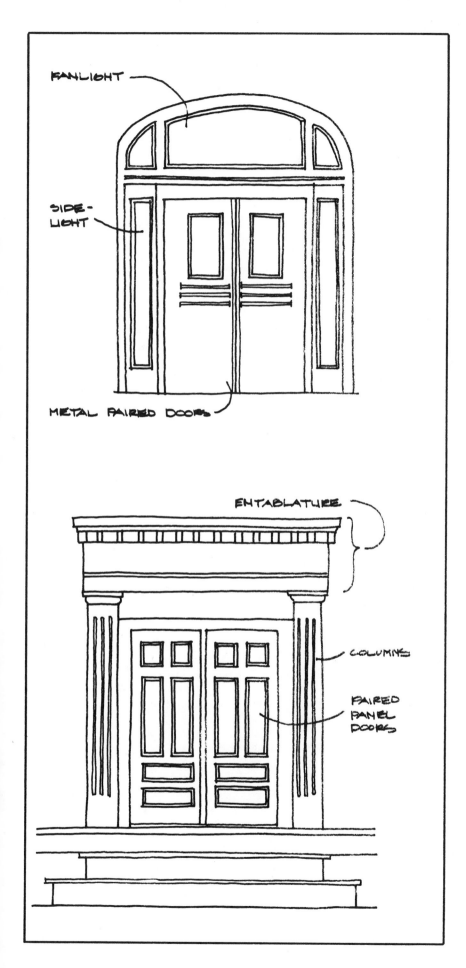

FANLIGHT

SIDE-
LIGHT

METAL PAIRED DOORS

ENTABLATURE

COLUMNS

PAIRED
PANEL
DOORS

PAIRED PANEL
CHURCH DOORS

THE ENTRANCE DOOR PLAYS A MAJOR ROLE IN THE development of an entrance system. A panel door includes stiles and rails that run vertically and horizontally respectively and form the frame of the door, panels, pieces of glass, muntins, and moldings. *Panels* are flat surfaces recessed below the plane of the framing and set off by one or more moldings. Panels may be embossed or be stained or painted a different color from other door elements. Some doors have different-size panels; thus in a series of cross or horizontal panels, the lowest panel may be much wider than the uppermost. Panels may also be placed in vertical positions.

A *slab door* is a modern door with a clean, planar, flush surface. The slab may be painted, stained, or varnished. Although it owes much of its use to its association with modern design, the slab has also been preferred because it admits less moisture through the door than paneled models.

Combinations of panel and glass or of slab and glass are common, and a few combinations have become part of specific stylistic treatments. Whether inset panels are of wood or glass, door elements are designed to be proportional. In the two-panel door, the lower panel is half the size of the upper. In the five-cross-panel door, the panel becomes a modular unit upon which the door is organized.

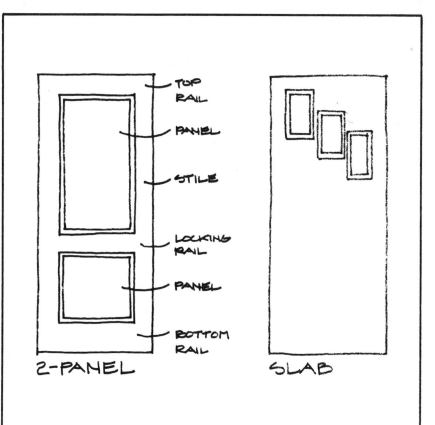

TOP RAIL

PANEL

STILE

LOCKING RAIL

PANEL

BOTTOM RAIL

2-PANEL

SLAB

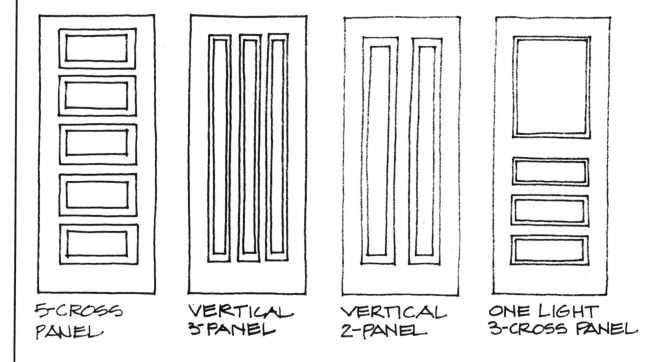

5-CROSS PANEL

VERTICAL 3-PANEL

VERTICAL 2-PANEL

ONE LIGHT 3-CROSS PANEL

The *all-glass door* is a modern design that consists of a large glass panel or plate, two stiles, and two rails of wood or metal. The so-called *French door* is the most popular glass-panel door. It usually has a top and bottom rail, two stiles, and small panes of glass arranged in pairs over its entire length. French doors are hung in pairs hinged at the jambs. These doors serve as both windows and doors and may be found opening onto special porches and outside spaces, or serving as entrances to special rooms such as dens, libraries, and dining rooms.

Double doors are used in residential and commercial vernacular design. Double doors are most often paneled doors with meeting stiles, hung in a frame with no mullion.

Panel size, placement, shape, and organization are taken into account in all door design so as to produce a balanced effect. Even the depth of cut on the moldings that trim the panels is controlled, so as to be proportional to the depth of the panel surface. With this kind of organization, entrance doors look precise regardless of size, shape, or location.

4 PANEL   5 PANEL   GLASS DOOR
(METAL OR WOOD)

FRENCH DOORS

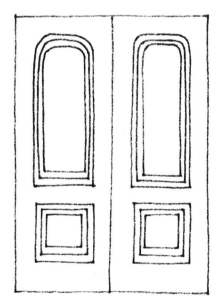

PAIRED OR DOUBLE
DOORS
DECORATIVE PANELS

PEDIMENTS ARE ONE OF THE PERIPHERAL ELE-ments of an entrance system. They derive from classical architecture, and their vernacular use centers on ornamentation over doors and windows. Pediments may be curved or triangular and may be made of stone, wood, metal, or cement. They are used over entrance doors to emphasize the importance of this special opening. An entrance pediment may be repeated to establish a rhythm on the façade or another important elevation.

The *triangular* pediment is one of the most traditional pediments used over doors and windows; it is composed of one or more moldings or cornices in each leg of the triangle, and the height of the pediment is low compared with the width of its base. *Segmental* or curved pediments have an arc of less than 180 degrees. *Broken* pediments have interrupted cornices at the top, leaving a space that is sometimes filled by an ornament. A *scroll* pediment may be complete or broken; it has a free-flowing profile. The *entablature* type is a scaled-down classical entablature with an architrave, frieze, and cornice.

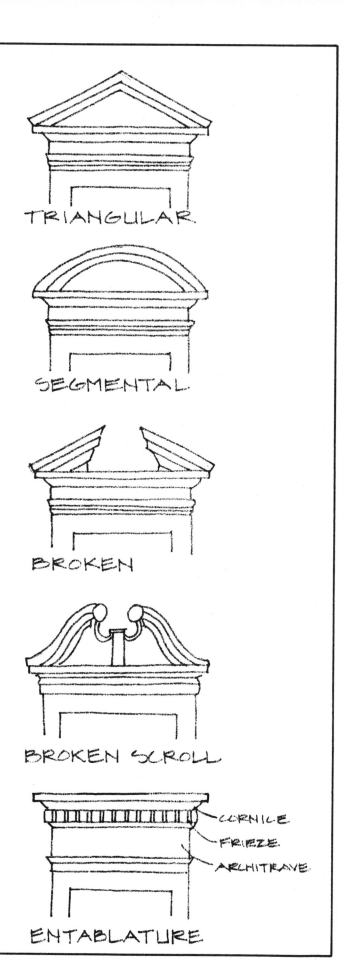

TRIANGULAR

SEGMENTAL

BROKEN

BROKEN SCROLL

CORNICE

FRIEZE

ARCHITRAVE

ENTABLATURE

COTTAGE DOORS—BOTH ENTRANCE AND INTERIOR doors—exhibit a great deal of ornamental detail. Stiles and rails are often cut with a number of inside edges or finished with moldings to ease the frame into the panel. Much of this work is delicate and greatly influences the overall appearance of the door.

Panel and glass combinations are most popular in cottage types. The glass may be colored, etched, or beveled. Panels themselves may also receive special treatment: they may have additional moldings or be beveled or be raised in successive planes. Even the screen door or storm door can carry picturesque motifs, echoing the stickwork of the porches.

PANEL AND
GLASS

6 PANEL WITH
QUEEN ANNE
LIGHTS

COLORED
LIGHTS

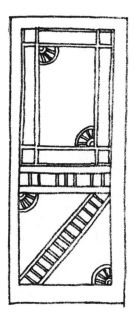

2 PANEL
WITH CIRCLE-
TOP LIGHTS

DECORATIVE
PANEL

SCREEN
DOOR

SPATIAL CONTINUITY BETWEEN INSIDE AND OUT-side spaces—a design characteristic of most prairie and bungalow types—is enhanced by large glass panels in doors. Window and door patterns in both these styles tend toward rectilinear geometric forms. Because of its lack of ornament, the slab door is also a "modern" door. The Craftsman style, pioneered by Gustav Stickley, also employs rectilinear yet bold motifs.

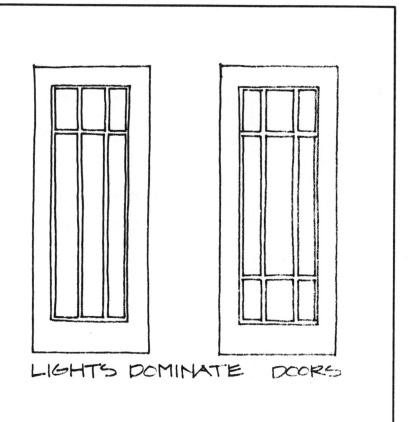

LIGHTS DOMINATE DOORS

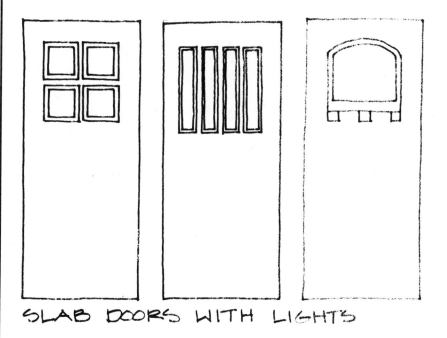

SLAB DOORS WITH LIGHTS

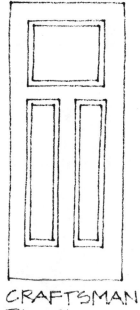

CRAFTSMAN
PANEL

DOORS USED IN COLONIAL TREATMENTS MAINTAIN a remarkable continuity of design throughout numerous revivals of the style. The six-panel door, for example, seems to show up in each revival. Although the panel and glass and the cross-buck and glass were most often used as back doors, they may be found at the front entrance too.

Colonial styles were ornamental, and the colonial door had an active surface. Since some colonial motifs were integrated with others, it is not uncommon to find colonial doors on the bungalow or other house types. Similarly, entrance doors were sometimes thickened to give them a heavier, more rustic appearance. When glass was part of the design, the muntins were scaled up to match the stiles and rails.

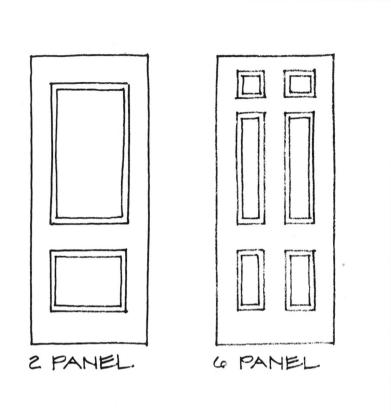

2 PANEL.   6 PANEL

CROSS-BUCK   4 PANEL   12 LIGHTS
WITH LIGHTS   WITH LIGHTS

PICTURESQUE STYLES—ESPECIALLY THOSE ASSO-
ciated with rustic treatments or flavored with a particular
culture, such as the general Mediterranean—used specially
shaped or specially ornamented doors. Some companies actually produced plank doors with or without battens, but
many created the same effect with slab doors grooved with a
V-joint and strap iron hardware; the latter shows up in
colonial design as well.

Rounded, pointed-head, or Tudor-headed doors—perhaps
combined with a V-joint slab—were used with Mediterranean, medieval, or renaissance styles. Small glass panels in
these kinds of doors were often leaded.

SLAB
V-JOINT

HALF-CIRCLE

SEGMENTAL
HEAD

GOTHIC-HEAD
V-JOINT

A *FAÇADE* IS, STRICTLY SPEAKING, THE ENTIRE exterior of a building, especially the front. Some prefer to think of it as the face of a structure or as the front elevation.

An *elevation* is a particular kind of geometrical drawing on a vertical plane, showing the external upright parts of a building. With time, the term came to refer to the sides and back portions of a structure.

A *bay* is the space or division of a wall within a building between two rows of columns, piers, or other architectural members. A bay may also be a space between a row of columns and a bearing wall. This kind of bay can be ascertained not only through visual inspection, but by examining the plan of a building. In vernacular design a bay may also result from vertical alignment, as for instance from the way windows or other openings on each floor relate.

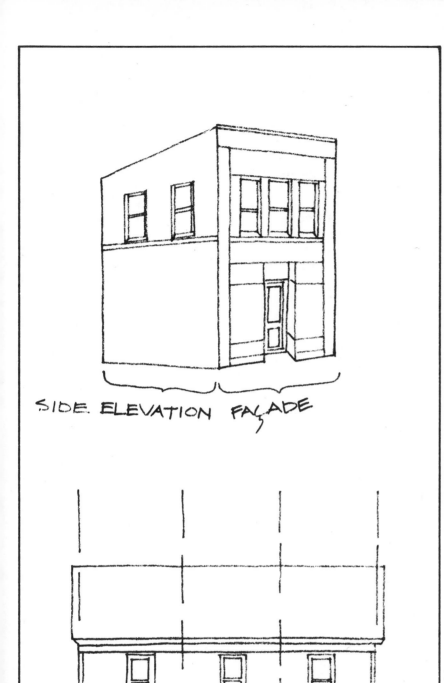

SIDE ELEVATION   FAÇADE

BAYS

1   2   3

This section describes design elements that contribute to the organization of walls. Walls are most often analyzed one wall at a time, with the wall that faces the street or the wall that functions as the principal wall getting most of the design attention. Elevations are also referred to by their placement—side, front, rear—or by their directional names: north, south, east, or west. But façades and elevations should be seen both as whole units, each systematically designed with vertical, horizontal, projecting, receding, and ornamental aspects, and as units that relate to one another.

One method of vertical organization is the division of the wall into bays. Bays may alternate different types of window, ornament, or even building material.

BASIC *STOREFRONT* ORGANIZATION IS RATHER direct, in that façades employ large-scale elements in both vertical and horizontal organization. The vertical bay—that portion between adjacent piers or columns on a large building, or that portion of vertical organization characterized by first- and second-story alignment—is one such major element. Depending upon the time of construction and the general notion of style then prevailing, display windows, entryways, and informational signage may serve as vertical or horizontal organization. Low-rise stores often use a mullion in the windows or a strong corner to create some vertical feeling. A two- or three-story building may try to band the windows by placing them close together on the façade or another elevation or may use a transom over each façade window so that the units appear linked on the horizontal. On a building built on a narrow lot, this can help reduce the impression of narrowness. In most storefront designs, such things were done systematically to create a unified design that admitted light to interior spaces and at the same time displayed wares or services. Most façades were basically plain rectangles; therefore variations in window size and window placement, decorative panels placed at the sidewalk level or as friezes near the top of a wall, as well as cornices, pilasters, and the like, constituted a fundamental vocabulary to be married to an overall shape and to the use of materials to make one store distinctive from another.

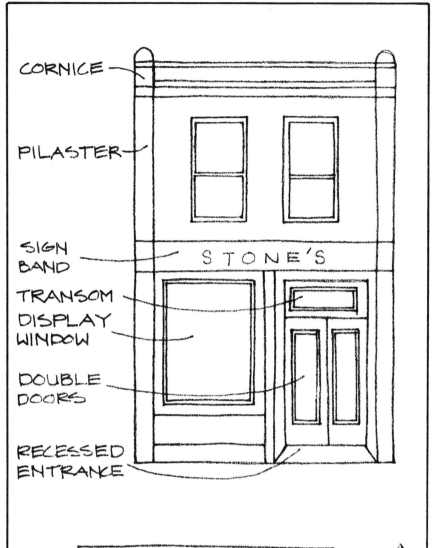

CORNICE

PILASTER

SIGN BAND

TRANSOM

DISPLAY WINDOW

DOUBLE DOORS

RECESSED ENTRANCE

STONE'S

PARAPET

FRIEZE

CLEARSTORY OR TRANSOM

DISPLAY WINDOW

KICK PLATE

THE USE OF *QUOINS*, WHICH DELINEATE CORNERS or dress and integrate walls, stems from historical masonry construction. Quoining in vernacular building may be executed in stone, brick, or wood. Quoins are laid or nailed in patterns and may differ substantially from the pattern of the principal cladding in size, cut, joinery, or texture.

Cornerboards are trim boards used to finish the corner and may vary greatly as to their width and their visual likeness to pilasters.

Flared walls break the plane of the original framing on elevations and porches, with the lower portion of each wall flaring beyond the foundation. The flaring of walls, by building a curved, concave firring under the cladding, was popular in several vernacular house types. The flare adds character to the building's profile and belongs to the picturesque tradition. Houses carrying flared walls sometimes had flared eaves as well.

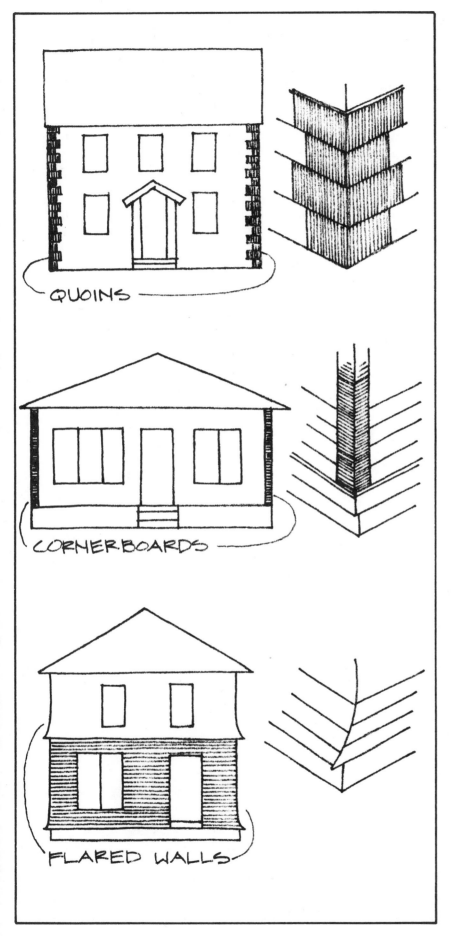

QUOINS

CORNERBOARDS

FLARED WALLS

From a design point of view, quoins provide strong edges for buildings and relieve the pattern of the cladding material. Cornerboards not only strengthen the appearance of the edges of walls, but also help to divide walls into panels or frame (enclose) an entire elevation. In some cases cornerboards may be designed to look like pilasters and may carry an entablature at the eaves.

The manipulation of wall surfaces, whether flared out above the foundation or curved in toward windows, is characteristic of picturesque design. The abrupt change in the flow of the plane of the wall works against the geometry of the overall shape of the building, rendering a rectilinear and geometrical shape more organic, more sculptural.

A *FOUNDATION* IS THE LOWEST STRUCTURAL DIVI-sion of a wall elevation. The building is erected on this part of the wall. Many vernacular buildings do not have full foundations that enclose a cellar, but instead have short stem walls or intermittent piers upon which the building sits.

A *water table,* which may be wood or masonry, is fixed to the foot of a wall or projected on the outside of the founda-tion to protect it from rain by throwing water away from the wall.

Plinths are used primarily to establish a base for a column or a pedestal, but occasionally the base courses of a building may be laid so as to give the appearance that the building rests on a platform.

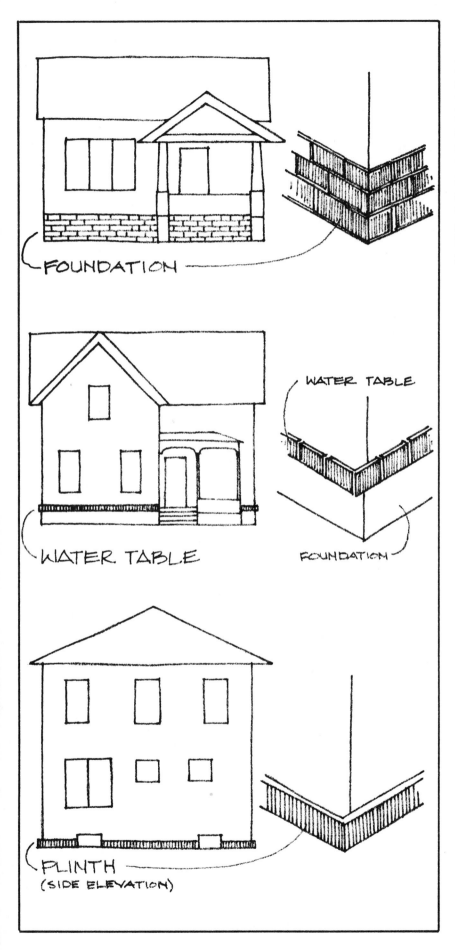

FOUNDATION

WATER TABLE

WATER TABLE

FOUNDATION

PLINTH
(SIDE ELEVATION)

The bases of walls help to establish horizontal design elements, including proportion (the height of the foundation in relation to other heights on the elevation), color, and texture. Foundations may be of a different material than the walls (stone is common in the vernacular tradition) and function as a continuous element that helps to tie a design together. Water tables and plinths alter the profiles of buildings and provide opportunity for ornamentation.

THE *CURVING OF WALLS* IS AN OLD TRADITION IN architecture and building. In vernacular work, only portions of walls receive curved treatments, although there are a few styles such as art deco, art moderne, or what some call drugstore modern, in which extensive curving is encouraged. In most cases an understructure is built up to which the cladding material may be attached. In masonry construction, tiles, bricks, and blocks were molded into curved forms, while in wood construction, boards could be steamed and clamped to create a curved form. Metal panels were pressed or bent to assume the desired shape.

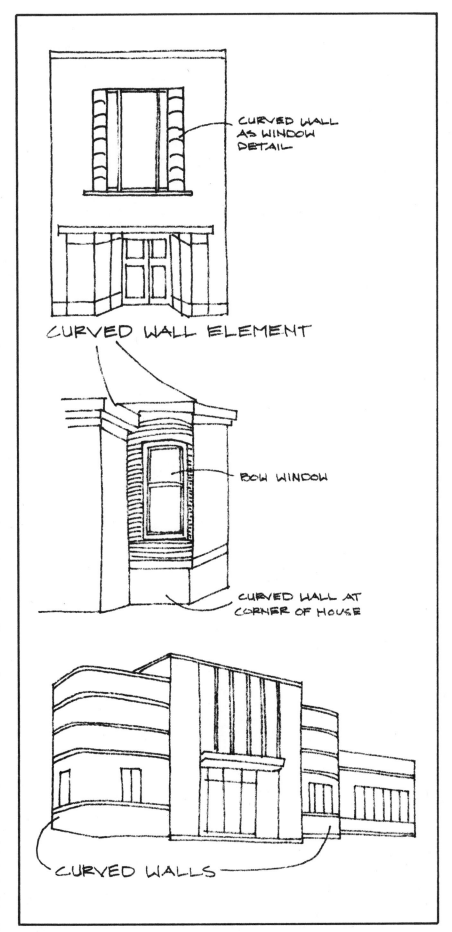

CURVED WALL AS WINDOW DETAIL

CURVED WALL ELEMENT

BOW WINDOW

CURVED WALL AT CORNER OF HOUSE

CURVED WALLS

In commercial design, curved walls produce a streamlined or sculptural form. These highly reflective, hard surfaces suggest modernity and urbanity and represent one of the instances in which technology is flaunted in vernacular architecture.

Curved surfaces are novelties in house design, with the exception of the curved porch or extended veranda. The curved window complete with curved glass can punctuate the wall of a cottage, but most curved walls form towers or turrets.

A FALSE-FRONT WALL EXTENDS ABOVE THE ROOF of a building to create the illusion that the building is larger and taller than it really is. Such fronts were popular in developing towns throughout the midwest and west.

Canting a wall means building it to incline at an angle, especially an obtuse angle. An entire corner of a building may be canted. Similarly, a bay window often has two canted walls that project from the main wall. Occasionally a whole element in a design, such as a two-story portion of a house, may be set at a cant to the mass of the main portion of the building.

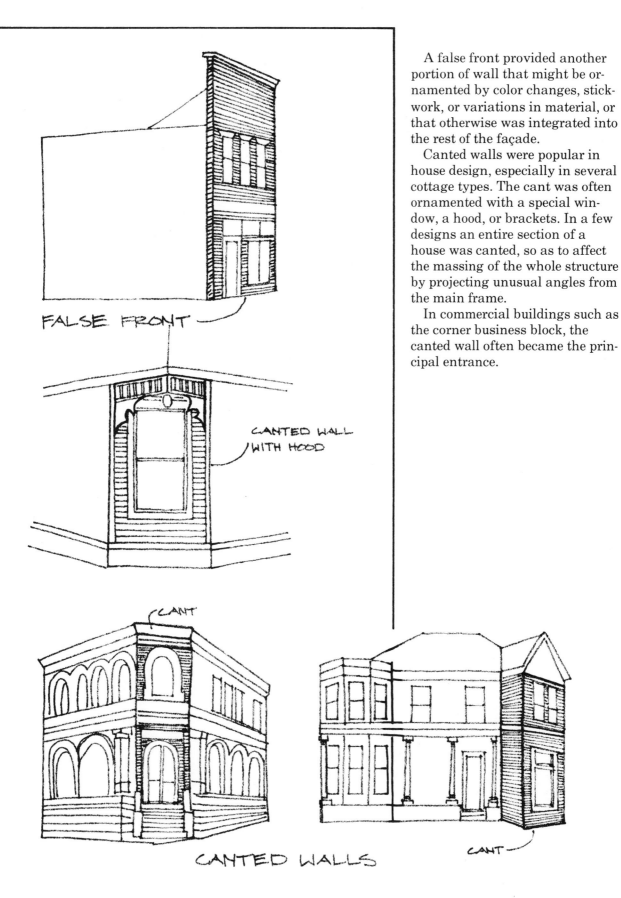

FALSE FRONT

CANTED WALL
WITH HOOD

CANT

CANTED WALLS

CANT

A false front provided another portion of wall that might be ornamented by color changes, stickwork, or variations in material, or that otherwise was integrated into the rest of the façade.

Canted walls were popular in house design, especially in several cottage types. The cant was often ornamented with a special window, a hood, or brackets. In a few designs an entire section of a house was canted, so as to affect the massing of the whole structure by projecting unusual angles from the main frame.

In commercial buildings such as the corner business block, the canted wall often became the principal entrance.

PILASTERS ARE ATTACHED RECTANGULAR PIERS of shallow depth. Most pilasters have the same height and width as columns with similar bases and capitals.

An *arcade* is a series of arches supported by piers or pillars either attached to or detached from a wall. It may be used for a passageway and can support a roof.

Buttresses strengthen a wall. Structural buttresses help a building resist lateral forces in general or specific thrusts from interior structures, though the latter use is infrequent in vernacular design.

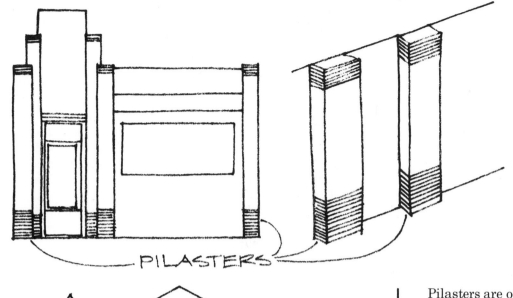

PILASTERS

ARCADE (OPEN)

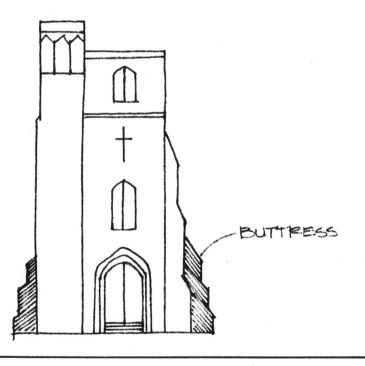

BUTTRESS

Pilasters are ornamental in most vernacular design. They are used with an order of architecture or as generic upright elements. In some twentieth-century styles, terra cotta pilasters are laid on walls in strips, each of which is narrower and perhaps shorter than the one below it.

As design elements, arcades succeed because of their rhythm and the play of light and dark. They also lighten visually the massing of a building. The open space seems to relieve the walls of their load-bearing responsibility and to defy gravity.

While buttresses have practical uses, they also help organize a wall and give an elevation an orderly rhythm.

AN *ARCH* IS A SELF-SUPPORTING ELEMENT THAT IS usually built of masonry. It consists of a number of units spanning an opening in which the downward thrust of each unit is carried to the next unit, until the last unit meets the vertical supports. Arches are described in terms of their interior outline: flat, segmental, semielliptical, and so forth. In vernacular architecture, arches are usually made of brick or wood; in both cases they are more often ornamental than structural.

Flat arch construction has a horizontal profile, while a *segmental* arch has a degree of arc that is less than a semicircle. The *round* arch is half a circle, while the *semielliptical* arch is half an ellipse. The *lancet* is a sharply pointed arch produced by the meeting of two curves. *Tudor* arches have been used for entrances in vernacular designs; they are elliptical in shape.

A *horseshoe* arch is an ornamental arch whose curve is more than a semicircle; in vernacular design these were often executed in wood. An *ogee* arch—rarely seen in vernacular buildings—has a profile consisting of linked concave and convex portions. *Triangular* arches result when members are laid diagonally to support one another.

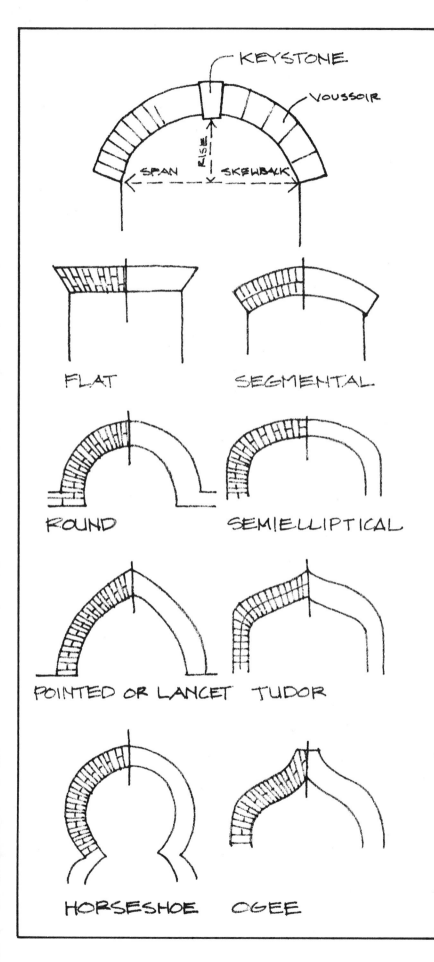

KEYSTONE.

VOUSSOIR

RISE

SPAN   SKEWBACK

FLAT   SEGMENTAL

ROUND   SEMIELLIPTICAL

POINTED OR LANCET   TUDOR

HORSESHOE   OGEE

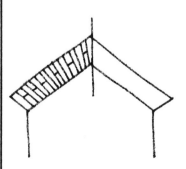

TRIANGULAR

As a design element, the arch is used structurally and ornamentally, with the latter use predominating. Structurally the arch appears in groupings, although a single arch may span an entrance. As ornament, the arch decorates any opening in the wall. It has also been applied as a blind arcade to the wall and may also ornament a portion of a wall, complementing the primary forms or materials.

RUSTICATION IN MASONRY BUILDING INVOLVES the use of squared or hewn stone blocks with roughened surfaces or with roughened or cleanly beveled edges. Such work creates conspicuous joints, textural surfaces, and shadow lines. The principal face of each stone may be *rough* (looking more rocklike), *chiseled* (with teeth marks showing), or *vermiculated* (treated to appear worm-eaten). Blocks are *beveled* on their edges or margins to expose the joint and cast a shadow, but large portions of block face may also be beveled or canted.

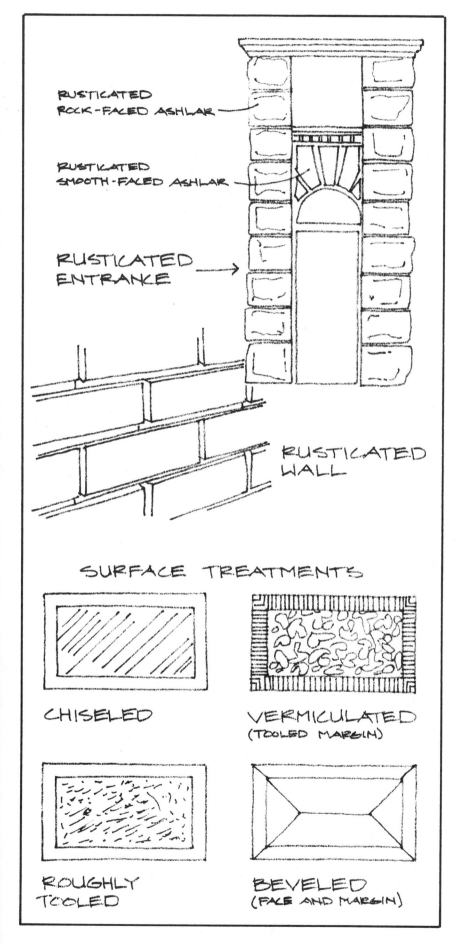

RUSTICATED
ROCK-FACED ASHLAR

RUSTICATED
SMOOTH-FACED ASHLAR

RUSTICATED
ENTRANCE

RUSTICATED
WALL

SURFACE TREATMENTS

CHISELED

VERMICULATED
(TOOLED MARGIN)

ROUGHLY
TOOLED

BEVELED
(FACE AND MARGIN)

Rustication gives pattern and texture to walls. When applied to several courses, rusticated sections provide strong horizontal organization; heavily rusticated walls appear monolithic. Rustication is often reserved for special locations, such as entrances or corners. On corners, rustication is usually part of a quoining pattern. In terms of texture, each block may have a pattern on the margin and on the face.

While rustication has a long history of application in stone masonry, it has also been part of the vernacular tradition of building in brick, which includes rusticated sections of walls and quoins.

PENDANTS ARE ORNAMENTAL PIECES SUSPENDED from above, as for instance from the overhanging second story in the illustration. On section they have a short stem and terminate in a rounded or conic form.

Gutters or eave troughs catch rain water and melting snow and convey them via *downspouts* to the ground, where water is discharged away from the building at ground level or into drainpipes connected to storm sewers. Gutters are hung in the eaves and are normally made of wood or metal.

Tie rods give stability to one part of a structure by securing it to another part. Such rods prevent bulging or separation of elements. Tie rods terminate on the outside of the wall with cast-iron anchors, which are ornamental washers or nuts.

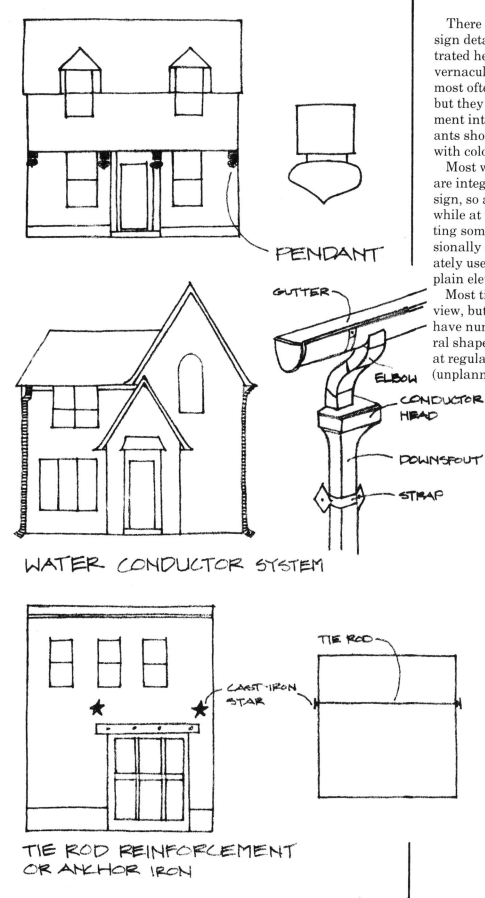

PENDANT

GUTTER

ELBOW

CONDUCTOR HEAD

DOWNSPOUT

STRAP

WATER CONDUCTOR SYSTEM

TIE ROD

CAST·IRON STAR

TIE ROD REINFORCEMENT OR ANCHOR IRON

There are a number of lesser design details on walls. Those illustrated here are common to many vernacular buildings. Pendants are most often found on the exterior, but they have been used to ornament interiors as well. The pendants shown here are associated with colonial revival designs.

Most water conductor systems are integrated into the overall design, so as to function as intended while at the same time contributing something to design. Occasionally downspouts are deliberately used as vertical accents on plain elevations.

Most tie rods are hidden from view, but their cast-iron anchors have numerous geometric or natural shapes that punctuate the walls at regular (planned) or irregular (unplanned) intervals.

COMMERCIAL BUILDING FAÇADES HAVE VERTICAL and horizontal elements that combine into what can be thought of as an implied grid. For example, corner piers or façade bays may be crossed by cornices, friezes, or special courses. Spaces on the grid are filled with windows, panels, ornament, entrances, and the like. Some of these spaces may be filled with identifying information such as a *name plate* (name of the building) or a *date plate* (date of construction).

Manufactured stamped elements in tin, like the cornice in the illustration, give a dramatic finish to a commercial façade. Attached to a wooden substructure, these elements project off the wall plane and terminate the façade's design.

Corbels are a form of bracketing produced by extending successive courses of masonry or wood beyond the wall surface. Rows of corbels, especially in brick, constitute a major wall treatment in vernacular design.

Belt courses have a slight projection from the wall— perhaps the width of a brick—and often mark a major division in the wall plane. Belts are usually carried around an entire building, while *string courses,* which may project farther and appear only on a single elevation, help break the plain effect of a large wall.

Ornamentation on glass or metal panel walls consists of sections of etched glass or bands of colored glass. Glazed surfaces often employ pilasters or other raised elements to break the continuity of the surface. Strips of metal, especially chromed metal, are also used on paneled walls to organize the elevations into rectangular units and to add contrasting color to the hard mirror finish.

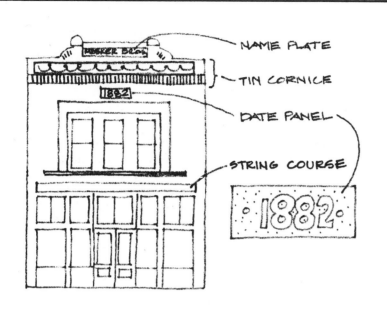

NAME PLATE

TIN CORNICE

DATE PANEL

STRING COURSE

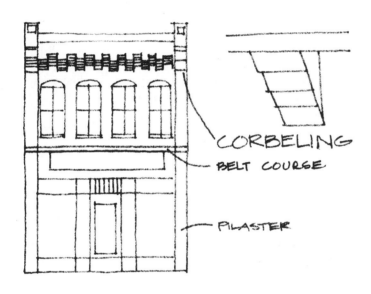

CORBELING

BELT COURSE

PILASTER

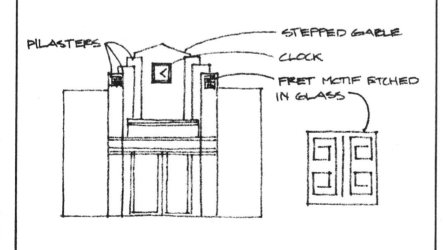

PILASTERS

STEPPED GABLE

CLOCK

FRET MOTIF ETCHED IN GLASS

Ornamental details on commercial fronts are limited to what can be applied to large design elements such as windows, or to what can be used to accent major axes or major grid lines. Name and date plates invariably align with the center axis of the façade. Corbels have enough visual impact to serve as the vertical terminus of a wall and therefore the last horizontal element in the grid. They also integrate into other kinds of cornice designs and are often the only ornament present on a commercial or industrial building.

Wall ornament is most subtle on glass-panel and metal-panel walls. Most designs seek to relieve the surface only. Ceramic treatments, which offer more latitude, may be bold enough to help organize the walls into discrete units.

BRICK PANELS, OFTEN ARRANGED JUST BELOW THE cornice, are a major decorative device for commercial design. Most of these panels are recessed into the wall and exhibit a pattern that is distinct from the pattern of the bonding of the main wall. Diamond shapes, diaper patterns, and contrasting color bricks were all typical treatments.

Wall surfaces have been animated by a variety of ornaments, most of them intended to enliven the wall through changes in color or texture. *Skintled brickwork* is a special scheme that depends upon the irregular arrangement of bricks with respect to the normal face of the wall. The bricks, which usually have a different color from the facing brick, are set in and out so as to produce an uneven effect on the surface. The term "skintled" also refers to a rough effect caused by the squeezing of mortar out of the joints. In either case the wall takes on a rustic appearance.

Shutters are protective coverings for windows. They appear more frequently as interior rather than exterior coverings on vernacular buildings built between 1870 and 1940. Shutters are a type of door used to shut out light or protect from weather. They are solid or louvered and originally were movable.

Latticework is an openwork produced by interlacing thin strips of wood or metal. Its primary use in vernacular design is as a porch apron or skirt. It has also been applied to cottages and bungalows as part of the general vocabulary of rustic effects.

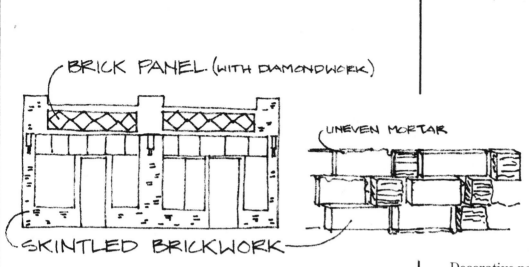

BRICK PANEL (WITH DIAMONDWORK)

UNEVEN MORTAR

SKINTLED BRICKWORK

SHUTTERS

LATTICEWORK

Decorative panels extend a commercial wall to its edges and to the cornice or parapet cap. They may also divide a two-story front into sections.

Skintled bricks have no overall pattern; their placement differs in terms of how far they project from the surface. Color too plays a role, in that many skintled bricks are darker than the face brick, so that their impact is more dramatic.

Design with exterior shutters centers on pattern and color as ornament. But as ornament, shutters become part of the window system and must be integrated with the size and shape of the windows. Most modern house types shun shutters, but colonial revival styles employ them.

Latticework has its own built-in pattern, diamond and square being the most popular. As wall ornament a lattice usually carries a planting—a vine or some other climbing species.

STICKWORK IS GENERALLY ANY KIND OF GROUPING of narrow boards arranged in patterns or applied as ornament to large or small surfaces. The pieces themselves—particularly moldings—are produced by a sticker machine or a saw. As exterior ornament, stickwork may be either of molding or of straight, flat boards arranged in distinctive patterns.

Half-timber treatments are a special pattern associated with what is called the Tudor style. Historic half-timber framing exposed large timbers on the inside and outside of the building; panels of masonry or other material filled in the spaces between frame members. Stickwork imitates the pattern of the original framing. Sticks are usually an inch thick and from two to six inches wide; most are painted a dark color and nailed over a stucco surface.

Polychromy refers to the uses of several colors, either applied to the surfaces or more frequently found inherently in the cladding materials, as a decorative scheme. Polychromy may be of low or high contrast in terms of the intensity of the colors, but the hues are generally closely related. For example, two different kinds of brick color might be used on the same building, both of them basically red, while a third color—a brown or an ocher—may be used on the same building by employing sandstone blocks for the foundation or sandstone sills or lintels. Such an effect reads as a polychromed design.

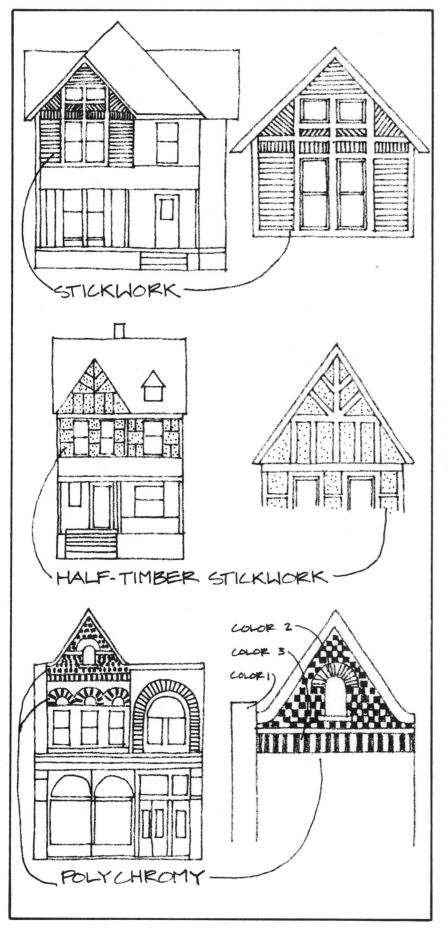

STICKWORK

HALF-TIMBER STICKWORK

POLYCHROMY

COLOR 2
COLOR 3
COLOR 1

Stickwork is arranged in patterns that tend to divide a wall into panels. Half-timber stickwork is always nailed in pattern; herringbone and a general rectangular pattern occur a great deal. While gable ends are most susceptible to this kind of treatment, half-timber motifs have been applied to entire elevations. The stucco work under the boards is also part of the design; the stucco may have a special color, and the finish of the top coat—rough or smooth, with or without trowel marks—also contributes to the design.

In polychromy the entire building must be analyzed to understand the effect of the colors. Pattern is usually involved, and it is often tied to the manner in which panels of color, and the linear elements such as arches or lintels, link sections of the building. Finally, there needs to be some resonance among the colors; in vernacular design, polychromy tends to rely on warm colors.

HERRINGBONE IS A PATTERN IN WHICH BRICK, IN alternate courses, is laid obliquely in opposite directions, forming a design similar to the spine of a herring. *Checkerwork* is any pattern arranged like a checkerboard, alternating light and dark squares. A *zigzag* molding is a series of chevrons that extend in a continuous pattern. *Diamondwork* is another zigzag pattern that establishes continuous diamonds, either plain or with contrasting light and dark values.

The *dovetail* pattern combines trapezoidal repeats in a series of interlocking units. The *fret* is an ancient form characterized by interlocked angular lines. *Guilloche* is a bandlike form made up of interlacing curved lines arranged so as to form wavy or woven motifs with open space. *Running ornament*—a molding—has continuous wavelike forms used in a frieze or a band.

The *rinceau* pattern is set in low relief and consists of a strip of vine, leaf, fruit, or flowers. The *garland* too employs low relief; its swags drape from point to point. *Egg-and-dart* is a molding pattern alternating ovoid forms (eggs) with arrowhead forms (darts). *Scallops* are a shell form that is laid on a continuous band. *Rope molding* simulates twisted strands of rope in low relief. *Floral and plant forms* are sculptural and may be naturalistic or stylized forms of leaves or flowers.

HERRINGBONE

CHECKERWORK

ZIGZAG

DIAMONDWORK

DOVETAIL

FRET

GUILLOCHE

RUNNING ORNAMENT

RINCEAU

GARLAND

EGG-AND-DART

SCALLOPS

ROPE MOLDING

FLORAL AND PLANT FORMS

In using ornamental motifs in design, much depends upon the material and the placement. Flat and low-relief forms with geometric or naturalistic designs lend themselves to continuous patterns, bandlike placements, or relatively isolated relief forms. Especially suitable for continuous pattern are the zigzag, diamondwork, dovetail, egg and-dart, scallop, and rope motifs.

Guilloche and running ornament, and sometimes rope, are usually arranged in bands. Relief forms—some of which may function well as isolated as well as continuous forms—include rinceau, garland, and floriated types.

A *CARTOUCHE* IS AN ORNAMENTAL PANEL, OFTEN in the form of a scroll or tablet, with elaborate borders, and a plane or convex surface that may bear an inscription of date. A *trefoil* is a three-lobed figure that usually looks leaflike. The *fleur-de-lis* is also a flower form, the lily or iris, used in bands or as a finial. *Sunrise* motifs consist of radiating rays from half the sun appearing above the horizon. Sunrise patterns are found in glazing, in the gables of houses, and as isolated molded or carved figures.

The *quatrefoil,* like the trefoil, is a leaflike, four-lobed piece. Ornamentally, lobed works may accent the shapes of the lobes themselves and the terminations of the lobe ends, the cusps. A *palmette* is also a multilobed work. Its thin lobes radiate from a calyxlike base and imitate the leaves of a palm tree.

Rosettes and patera are low-relief sculptural ornaments. The former are conventionalized circular floral motifs, while the latter are disklike ornaments that may carry floriated designs on center. *Animal motifs* and *allegorical figures* are infrequently used in vernacular architecture. They are symbolic forms conveying traditional or special meanings pertaining to the building to which they are attached.

CARTOUCHE

TREFOIL

FLEUR-DE-LIS

SUNRISE

PALMETTE

QUATREFOIL

ROSETTES

PATERA

ANIMAL

ALLEGORICAL

All the figures on this page may be thought of as ornamental accents, in that most have been used as one-of-a-kind ornament. Placement varies and several of these figures may be repeated, especially smaller forms like the fleur-de-lis, rosette, and patera. Banding of these figures is also not uncommon. In vernacular work such banding consists of narrow bands, usually of light hues, across the elevation, with molded pieces evenly spaced in the center of the band.

Elements like the cartouche, the lobed forms, and symbolic flora or fauna are given a prominent location such as the façade, and are close enough to the ground level to be read by passersby. The trefoil and quatrefoil have also been used as accent windows, piercing towers or churches, or as accents on arcades or any other element with a general Gothic flavor.

 **TYPES**

DORMER DOMINATES ROOF

CORNICE RETURN

ENTRANCE DOOR ON-CENTER

2½ STORY   TYPICAL FAÇADE
CENTER-GABLE COTTAGE

CHARACTERISTICS
2½ OR 1½ STORIES
3-5 BAYS
CLADDING:
   CLAPBOARD
ROOF:
   GABLE,
   RIDGELINE
   PARALLEL TO
   STREET,
   DORMER
   DOMINATES ROOF
   OFTEN RETURNS
   OR PENT
CHIMNEY:
   INTERIOR BRICK
DORMER:
   1 LARGE
   CENTER GABLE
   DORMER,
   WINDOW
   TREATMENT
   IN DORMER

THE *CENTER-GABLE COTTAGE* HAS A LONG HISTORY of development that seems to emerge from the application of gables to Gothic revival houses. During the period 1870–1940, the gable itself, while always aligned over the entrance door, lost its narrow, steeply pitched gable roof and widened to function more properly as a dormer. This house, built during the period 1870–90, was rectangular in shape, with the wide side toward the street, and has a central hall plan with four rooms to each floor. The center gable was a frame house with clapboard siding, although shingles were later used in gable ends. The fenestration was symmetrically arranged in three bays. The house had a porch that was shallow in the older models and shallow but wide in the later ones. The porch carried its own roof supported by square posts.

As these houses continued to be built into the cottage era of the 1880s, the porch began to attract brackets and other more delicate stickwork. From 1880 to 1910 the center-gable turned toward colonial revival styles, and the gable began to look like a pediment. The porch became a portico with a full order of architecture. The gable itself underwent transformation in that it received a new window motif—a three-part window that echoed the Palladian—and was given returns and boxed cornices. The window below the gable, whether on the full second story or a half story, became a three-part

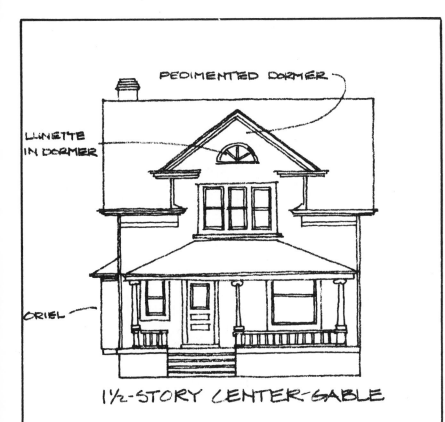

PEDIMENTED DORMER

LUNETTE IN DORMER

ORIEL

1½-STORY CENTER-GABLE

WINDOWS:
SYMMETRICAL FENESTRATION, DOUBLE-HUNG SASH, VARIABLE PATTERN, SOMETIMES ORIEL

PORCH:
WIDE ENTRANCE PORCH

WALLS:
CORNERBOARDS, FAÇADE HAS A TEMPLE FRONT

window or a bay. A few cottages had a second-story door that accessed a balcony on the porch roof. The gable was now wide enough to embrace the space between the second-floor windows or, in story-and-a-half models, to fill half the wall of the upper portion. The gable, however, remained in the same plane as the main house wall.

Like other house forms that entered and endured the grand cottage age, the center-gable cottage displayed cottage detailing. The entrance door began to appear off-center, and the fenestration patterns on the side elevations adopted cottage arrangements, including the grouping of windows into pairs and triples.

The center-gable, then, represents a short history of the development of the cottage. It bridged historical revival styles and at the same time reminded Americans of the design strength of their heritage buildings. The center-gable could be adapted to suit changing family needs, yet still look like an appropriate product of its time.

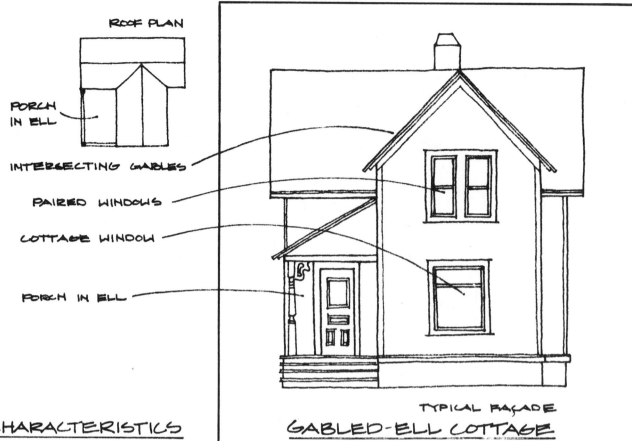

ROOF PLAN

PORCH IN ELL

INTERSECTING GABLES

PAIRED WINDOWS

COTTAGE WINDOW

PORCH IN ELL

TYPICAL FAÇADE

GABLED-ELL COTTAGE

CHARACTERISTICS

2 STORIES

ELL-SHAPED

CLADDING:
   CLAPBOARD

ROOF:
   INTERSECTING GABLES, SOMETIMES 1 CLIPPED GABLE

CHIMNEY:
   INTERIOR BRICK

DORMERS:
   NOT COMMON

GABLE:
   SHINGLES AND STICKWORK

THE *GABLED-ELL COTTAGE* HAS A LONG HISTORY of use in rural, small-town, and small-city development throughout the United States. One of the most ubiquitous house forms ever produced, it prevailed between 1870 and 1920. It was built in successive territories and states as the country developed from east to west.

This house has always been a cottage type susceptible to applications of style on its elevations. The 1870s type was either a simple ell with only a single corner, which was utilized as the entrance, or a simple T shape with the projecting stem toward the street and the cross-piece behind. The T shape often provided an extra porch. The section that projected toward the street—usually a parlor room—was not centered on the crossing portion of the building. The gables of these houses and the gable end wall received systematic applications of stickwork ornament. The May 1879 issue of *Carpentry and Building* has "a study in cheap houses" in which the same gabled-ell gets an "English," "Swiss," "English" with a tower, and "French" treatment. Most of the differences in these styles center on the use of stickwork and other trim boards to create effects. Fenestration in all the examples remains the same—symmetrical.

In the next decade, cottage fever introduced more picturesque elements, including turned posts on expanded porches, shingled gables, bay windows, and canted walls with brackets at the corners. Between 1890 and 1920, how-

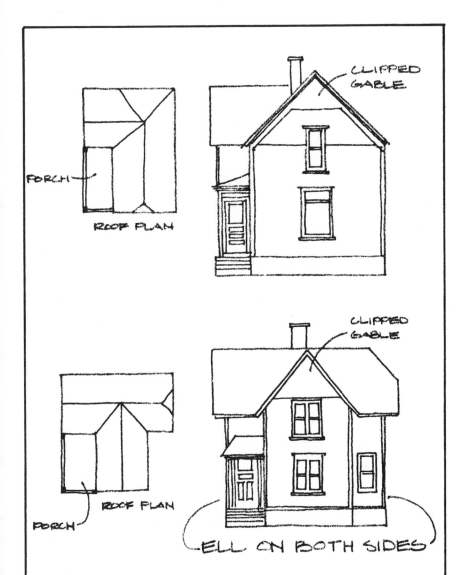

ROOF PLAN

PORCH

CLIPPED GABLE

CLIPPED GABLE

ROOF PLAN

PORCH

ELL ON BOTH SIDES

WINDOWS:

COTTAGE OR PAIRED ON 1ST FLOOR FAÇADE, SOMETIMES A BAY WINDOW ON SIDE, OFTEN PAIRED WINDOWS ON 2ND-STORY FAÇADE, 1/1 MAJOR PATTERN

PORCH:

IN SPACES PROVIDED BY ELL

COLUMNS:

TURNED POSTS WITH ACCOMPANYING STICKWORK

ENTRANCE:

PANEL AND GLASS DOOR

WALLS:

CORNERBOARDS TIED TO A FASCIA

ever, the gabled-ell lost some of its ornamentation. The plan changed slightly, in that the stem of the T became centered on the crossing section. The edges of the houses emerged, as trim boards got wider and were painted a contrasting color. The foundation wall became more prominent so that horizontal division—foundation, wall panels, gable, and roof edge—underwrote the design scheme. Fenestration remained symmetrical. The gabled-ell, then, proved to be one of the hardiest of all vernacular types; it could be modified for most sites (though it was not an inner-city type for very long) and could be embellished to respond to consumer demand.

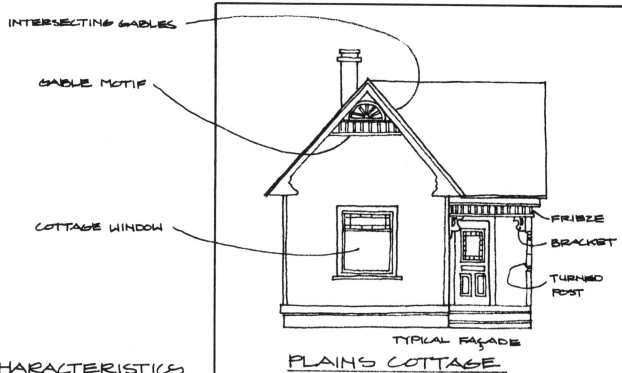

INTERSECTING GABLES

GABLE MOTIF

COTTAGE WINDOW

FRIEZE

BRACKET

TURNED POST

TYPICAL FAÇADE

PLAINS COTTAGE

CHARACTERISTICS
1 STORY,
SMALL DELICATE
HOUSE
CLADDING:
CLAPBOARD,
SOMETIMES
BRICK
ROOF:
COMBINATIONS
OF STRAIGHT
GABLE,
INTERSECTING
GABLES,
CLIPPED GABLE,
OR GABLE-HIP
CHIMNEY:
BRICK, INTERIOR
DORMERS:
RARE

SOME VERNACULAR HOUSE TYPES HAVE NOT BEEN formally identified as having a particular style. One of these is the *plains cottage,* the development period of which coincides with the growth of Queen Anne, Eastlake, and shingle-style cottages. The plains cottage is an extant house type that sits on railroad lots in towns between the Mississippi River and the west slope of the Rocky Mountains. It was also built in the south; in Biloxi, Mississippi, it is referred to as a "bayed cottage."

The plains cottage assumed its overall shape from the intersection of its roof forms, which were usually gables, one of which might be clipped or hipped; from what was usually an ell plan; and from the entrance system nestled into the ell. The cottage was trimmed with machine-made stickwork and had windows with an art-glass header or borders. All the cottage's elevations celebrated the play of light on the surfaces, whether the light picked up the shingle pattern in the gable, pierced the art glass, or cast shadows from the brackets or spindle friezes on the porch or on the gable. Part of the charm of these houses resulted from the freedom with which the builder could manipulate the limited design vocabulary. Besides using ornamentation, the designer could cant the walls or project bays to distinguish one plains cottage from another on the same block. In this flexibility of design, the plains cottage seems to have been the precursor of another small house, the bungalow, in the next century.

These structures were built from railroad-shipped mill materials. Socially they sheltered every class of plains dweller. The plains cottage was in many cases the initial design statement in truly transforming the prairie settlement into a town.

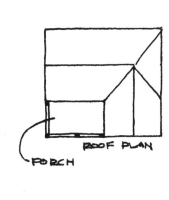

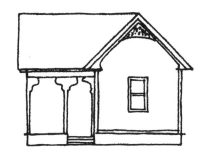

ROOF PLAN

PORCH

HIPPED ROOF

ROOF PLAN

PORCH

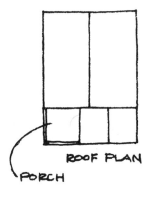

ROOF PLAN

PORCH

CANTED BAY WINDOW

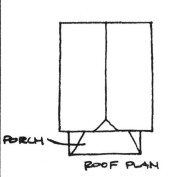

CLIPPED GABLE

PORCH

ROOF PLAN

GABLES:
  TEXTURED AND DECORATIVE, SHINGLES, BARGEBOARD, GABLE ORNAMENTATION, PENT ROOF

WINDOWS:
  1 DECORATIVE WINDOW ON FAÇADE - COTTAGE, QUEEN ANNE, OR BAY

PORCH:
  DELICATE, TURNED POSTS, SPINDLE FRIEZE, BRACKETS, STICKWORK BALUSTRADE

DOOR:
  PANEL AND GLASS, SOMETIMES TRANSOM

WALLS:
  NARROW CORNERBOARDS

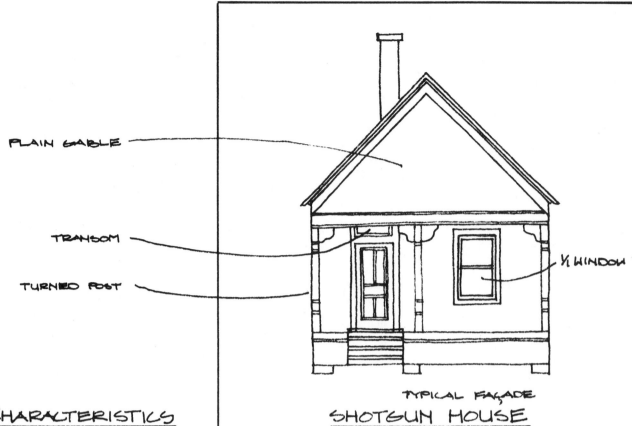

PLAIN GABLE

TRANSOM

TURNED POST

½ WINDOW

TYPICAL FAÇADE
SHOTGUN HOUSE

CHARACTERISTICS
1 STORY,
RECTANGULAR,
2-3-BAY
ORGANIZATION,
1 ROOM WIDE,
3 OR 4 ROOMS
DEEP, ONE
BEHIND THE
OTHER
CLADDING:
   CLAPBOARD,
   BOARD AND
   BATTEN,
   SOMETIMES
   BRICK
ROOF:
   GABLE OR
   HIP
CHIMNEY:
   INTERIOR

THE *SHOTGUN* HOUSE HAS HAD AN INTERESTING social as well as design history. The term "shotgun" refers to the unusual shape and plan of the structure. The folk tale about the house suggested that one could fire a shotgun into the house through the front door and have the shot come out through the back door without hitting any walls. Built as inexpensive worker housing in several sections of the country—but mostly in the near and deep south and the west—the shotgun has emerged as an object of rehabilitation in a number of cities, including New Orleans and Louisville. The house was always simple in concept—three or four rooms attached on a single axis. Frequently built on railroad lots, the houses were narrow and moderately deep. Original shotguns had no running water inside; toilets were outdoors, as were kitchens in warm climates. Later the toilet and kitchen were moved into the house. A few shotguns added an extra bedroom over the back room only, and these became known as "camelbacks."

The shotgun was often built in rows, and at first glance their design schemes seem limited to façade improvisations. While this is true, it does not represent all that was available to the builder. Façades, whether in brick, board and batten, or clapboard, were distinguished from one another in subtle ways, in that lintels, a modest frieze, turned posts, or a corner bracket could be employed to stylize the front. Other possibilities included the variety in floor plan that shotguns offered, such as partial or full-length side porches; window-

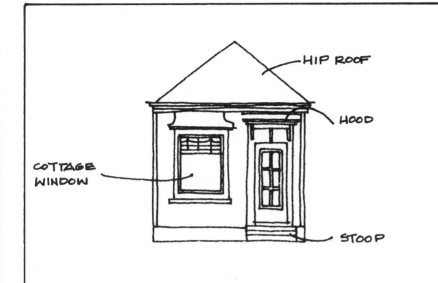

HIP ROOF

HOOD

COTTAGE WINDOW

STOOP

SHOTGUN WITH WING

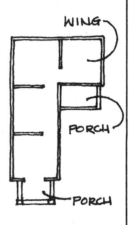

WING

PORCH

PORCH

GABLE:
USUALLY UNDECORATED, SOMETIMES DECORATIVE SHINGLES

WINDOWS:
1/1 DOUBLE-HUNG SASH, 1 OR 2 FRONT WINDOWS, SOMETIMES A COTTAGE WINDOW ON FAÇADE

PORCH:
SHALLOW, TURNED POSTS, SHED OR HIP ROOF, SOMETIMES STOOP AND HOOD

DOOR:
OFF-CENTER, PANEL AND GLASS, SOMETIMES TRANSOM

WALLS:
CORNERBOARDS

less walls on one side, so that windows did not align between houses, which fostered privacy; side entrances that did not abut between houses; art glass; cornice details; full-façade porches with or without rails; some gable detail; and a hipped roof instead of the straight gable. By the early 1920s, the shotgun could be upgraded to include on plan a specified living room, dining space, two bedrooms, kitchen, and bath. All these spaces were small, but they could fit into a 16-by-30-foot building. Many shotgun houses were built by companies for employees and as such were industrial housing. A great number were cheaply made and did not survive more than one generation. Others—especially in large cities—continue to be recycled.

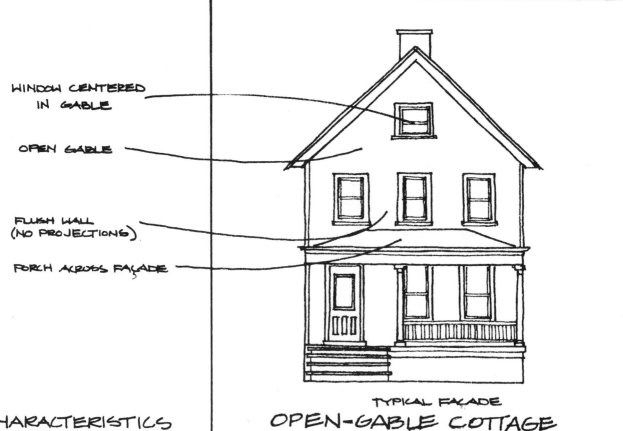

WINDOW CENTERED IN GABLE

OPEN GABLE

FLUSH WALL (NO PROJECTIONS)

PORCH ACROSS FAÇADE

TYPICAL FAÇADE
OPEN-GABLE COTTAGE

CHARACTERISTICS
2 STORIES,
PLAIN, SIMPLE
LINES,
2-OR 3-BAY
ORGANIZATION
CLADDING:
   CLAPBOARD
ROOF:
   GABLE,
   PERPENDICULAR
   TO STREET
CHIMNEY:
   BRICK, INTERIOR
DORMERS:
   SOMETIMES ON
   SIDE ELEVATION
GABLE:
   OPEN

MOST OF THE COTTAGE HOUSES TAKE THEIR basic form from a single feature or a few key design elements. In referring to this cottage as an *open-gable*, we refer to its wide gable and its plain form. It could just as well be called the flush-wall, center-axis cottage, because these features characterize its design, but that would be an awkward label. The open-gable was built for almost 50 years throughout most of the country. It has been a two-story house, though there were one-and-a-half-story versions clad in brick, shingle, and clapboard, the last being the most prevalent.

The *open-gable* cottage has clean lines, simple form, and no projections off the façade; it carries the façade wall up into the gable, with no distinction between façade and gable until the early 1890s. This house has a classical orientation, in that the façade is a linear temple front in which thin corner boards or pilasters carry a low, wide pediment. The introduction of cornice returns reinforces this impression. The façade is organized around a center axis running from the apex of the gable to the ground level. Gable windows are placed on or along the side axis, and porches with three posts have the middle post placed on the same line. What detailing appears is often derived from bungalow or Craftsman design.

The open-gable served as middle-class and working-class housing and as rural, even farmstead, housing.

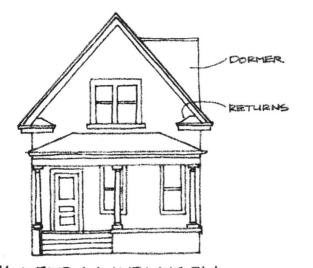

DORMER

RETURNS

1½ STORY VARIATION

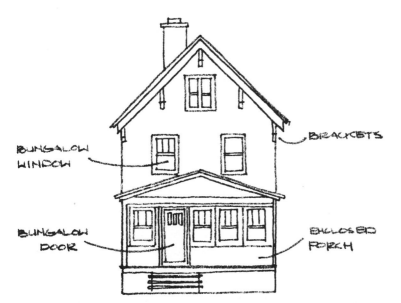

BUNGALOW WINDOW

BUNGALOW DOOR

BRACKETS

ENCLOSED PORCH

VARIATION: CRAFTSMAN DETAILS

WINDOWS:
  1 OR 2 CENTERED IN GABLE, SYMMETRICAL FENESTRATION, 1/1 MAJOR PATTERN

PORCH:
  EXTENDS ACROSS FACADE WITH STEPS TO SIDE, OFTEN SHED ROOF ON PORCH, OFTEN ENCLOSED PORCH

COLUMNS:
  SQUARE POSTS COMMON

ENTRANCE:
  PANEL AND GLASS DOOR

WALLS:
  CORNERBOARDS, FACADE AND ELEVATIONS USUALLY FLAT

It had a rectangular plan with a side hall until the 1890s, when square plans became more popular. The same period used Queen Anne ornamentation on many cottage types, and the town and country absorbed this through porch design and gable motifs.

The *Old House Journal* refers to this house as "the Basic Homestead House"—a designation that certainly captures the spirit of this cottage. It was a straightforward, well-composed dwelling. Suggesting security and clearness of purpose, it stood for the basic requirements of American shelter.

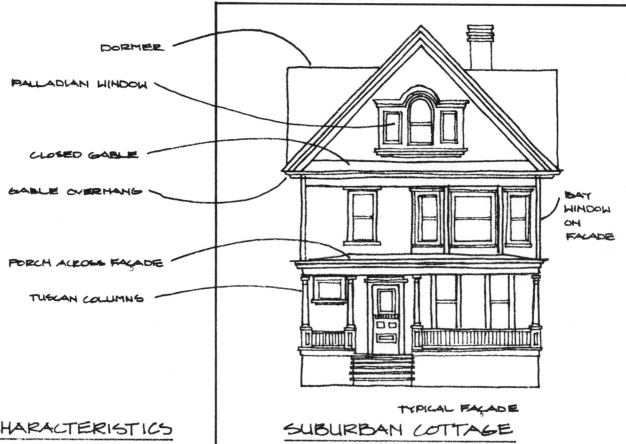

DORMER

PALLADIAN WINDOW

CLOSED GABLE

GABLE OVERHANG

PORCH ACROSS FAÇADE

TUSCAN COLUMNS

BAY WINDOW ON FAÇADE

TYPICAL FAÇADE
SUBURBAN COTTAGE

CHARACTERISTICS
2 STORIES,
3-BAY ORGANIZATION

CLADDING:
CLAPBOARD,
GABLE CLADDING
DIFFERENT
FROM HOUSE

ROOF:
STRAIGHT GABLE,
LARGE OVERHANG

CHIMNEY:
BRICK, INTERIOR

DORMERS:
OFTEN LARGE
DORMERS ON
SIDE

GABLE:
CLOSED,
WIDE,
PROJECTS
BEYOND HOUSE,
A PEDIMENT

THE *SUBURBAN COTTAGE* TAKES ITS NAME FROM its design and location. Throughout a forty-year period, this cottage evolved from a narrow city cottage into a wide-bodied colonial cottage with a large lot or prominent siting. The house remained rectangular on plan and in shape and carried its full two-and-a-half-story height throughout its development. In the 1880s the structure presented its straight gable roof to the street with moldings that spanned the gable and turned it into a pediment. The façade carried a bay window on one or both stories, as well as on a side elevation. The entrance porch was small, with a modest but ornamented hood over the entrance. Queen Anne detailing was present on the porch in the form of turned posts and brackets, and in the gable. Often there were two kinds of cladding, or changes in cladding pattern.

During the 1890s some changes were made in overall design. The straight gable remained, as well as the bay window on the façade, but a distinctive Palladian window was placed in the closed gable, and the entire gable now overhung the main body of the house. The entrance porch widened to façade width, columns were introduced with an order of architecture, and dormers were placed on the side elevations.

In the first decade of the twentieth century, the suburban took on its most distinctive form, which can be found in most regions. The straight, closed gable was widened, so that the classical feeling expressed on the façade organization was more emphatic. The gable overhang and the gable itself became more decorative, and the entrance became more formal, using not only the usual Tuscan order but the Ionic as well. The porch was either full width or a veranda. Oval windows were applied to elevations, while bay windows, which had been present throughout the development of the cottage, continued to appear on façades and side elevations. The side-hall plan that had been traditional sometimes gave way to a centered entrance with a vestibule or hall. Overall, the suburban became sumptuous, a large, sometimes cubical structure that reflected colonial revival sensibility. The front Palladian window in the gable was often displayed in the dormers. Balustrades appeared on porch roofs, and secondary porches at the side or rear of the house helped spread the building out on the site.

The suburban cottage developed into a grand statement about what the cottage could become. One of the few full-blown colonials that did not imitate a historic form, throughout its development it remained a cottage.

WINDOWS:
SYMMETRICAL FENESTRATION, 1/1 MAJOR PATTERN, SOMETIMES BAY ON FAÇADE, PALLADIAN IN GABLE

PORCH:
WIDE, ACROSS FAÇADE, SOMETIMES VERANDA

COLUMNS:
IONIC, TUSCAN

ENTRANCE:
PANEL AND GLASS

WALLS:
CORNERBOARDS, SOMETIMES 2-STORY BAYS ON SIDE

2-STORY BAY

2-STORY BAY

VERANDA

GABLED COTTAGE: COLONIAL

6/1 PATTERN

NONFUNCTIONING SHUTTERS

PEDIMENT

TYPICAL FAÇADE

CHARACTERISTICS
2 STORIES,
3-BAY ORGANIZATION
CLADDING:
  CLAPBOARD,
  BRICK,
  SHINGLES
ROOF:
  GABLE,
  RIDGELINE
  PARALLEL TO
  STREET
CHIMNEY:
  END WALL
DORMERS:
  SOMETIMES
  GABLE
  DORMERS

COLONIAL COTTAGE

FROM 1870 TO 1940 SEVERAL COLONIAL REVIVAL houses developed; this section deals with two of them. The fervor for American culture that swept the country after the 1876 Centennial resulted in the revival of two house types, the New England eighteenth-century cottage of English medieval origins, and the Georgian. Well into the twentieth century the vernacular tradition included these in its inventory, as well as the Dutch gambrel, the so-called Cape Cod, and the large hipped and pedimented cottages with colonial motifs, which are all discussed in other sections.

When the entire country is taken into account, the Georgian style probably outnumbers the medieval. Both styles remained closely tied to the concept of the picturesque cottage. The colonial illustrated relied on a rationally organized façade and an interior plan that was well lighted by multi-paned windows, carried a three-bay front, and utilized a bit of Georgian millwork to ornament the entrance. The shutters were ornamental gestures toward the vernacular habit of using shutters for picturesque effects. The whole question of effects is difficult to factor out because of the eclectic use of Georgian, federal, and medieval details on different house forms. The interchangeability of parts was tied to the industrial production of architectural materials without any rules of decorum.

In large houses the colonial cottage maintains a central hall plan, but small models are characterized by a modern

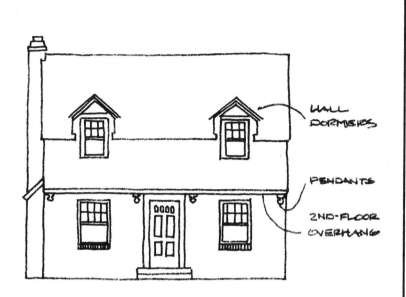

WALL DORMERS

PENDANTS

2ND-FLOOR OVERHANG

WINDOWS:
SYMMETRICAL FENESTRATION, DOUBLE-HUNG SASH, 6/1 MAJOR PATTERN

PORCH:
END-WALL PORCH, OR SUNROOM

ENTRANCE:
PORTICO, OR FLUSH DOOR ENTRANCE WITH PEDIMENT OR HOOD, PANEL DOOR, OR PANEL WITH LIGHTS DOOR, SOMETIMES SIDELIGHTS

WALLS:
NONFUNCTIONING SHUTTERS, SOMETIMES HISTORICAL DETAILS — LUNETTE, DENTILS, 2ND-FLOOR OVERHANG, PENDANTS

open plan. The addition of side porches, terraces, sunrooms, and the like are also concessions to modernity. The clean, relatively unadorned surfaces of these houses—despite their historical references to things like end-wall chimneys—and the precise alignment of elements, suggest modern as well as historical style.

The medieval type—which some refer to as a "garrison"—was built through the 1930s, and also reflects the rational, coherent order of the general colonial design. To carry the tradition forward, certain design elements were necessary: a second-story overhang that invoked the eighteenth-century New England house with an overhang and pendants. The house illustrated also carries wall dormers that curiously suggest the gables of New England vernacular houses and the dormers of the Georgian style. The medieval tradition usually included a massive interior chimney, but in time this was replaced by end-wall chimneys serving fireplaces and central heating furnaces. As in the Georgian type, vertical alignment of windows, symmetrical fenestration on all elevations, cross-ventilation, and flow-through space were important design elements in the modern colonial cottage. Cladding materials also varied slightly. Clapboard covers most colonial houses, whatever the type, but brick as well as wood and asbestos shingles are also used.

The colonial cottage has been a successful house form, serving single-family needs quite well. Most have family-oriented functional rooms such as the usual service rooms plus dens, fruit cellars in basements, and sleeping porches, while the orderly fronts give form to the streetscapes on which they are located. While most of these houses have little that is authentically colonial, there is something pragmatic and aesthetically pleasing about them.

GABLED COTTAGE: CAPE COD

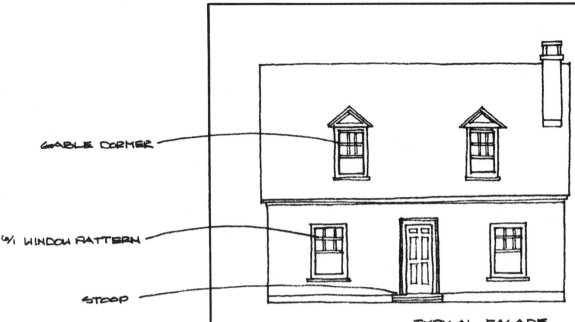

GABLE DORMER

6/1 WINDOW PATTERN

STOOP

TYPICAL FAÇADE

CAPE COD COTTAGE

CHARACTERISTICS
1½ STORIES,
COMPACT HOUSE
OFTEN HAD:
WIDE CLAPBOARD
OR SHINGLES,
WIDE GABLE
ROOF,
LARGE CHIMNEY,
GABLE DORMERS
ON FAÇADE,
SOMETIMES
SHED DORMER
ON BACK,
SYMMETRICAL
FENESTRATION,
6/6 OR 6/1
WINDOW PATTERN,
PROJECTING
VESTIBULE
OR STOOP,
COLONIAL
MOTIFS ON
ENTRANCE,
SOMETIMES
SHUTTERS

THE *CAPE COD* HOUSE HAS BEEN RECOGNIZED AS a unique vernacular type for almost 200 years but was not adopted by the industrial vernacular tradition until the 1920s, and even then it was referred to as a colonial cottage. Following Massachusetts custom, the early commercial Cape Cod was a compact house clad with shingles, featuring a small portico or pedimented entrance and a large interior central or end-wall chimney. Many models had a low gable on the façade, twin gable dormers, or a cutaway porch. The Cape Cod was produced and distributed in packages of integrated architectural elements. A major component of large subdivisions, the Cape Cod was often streamlined and abstracted until only the basic form, with narrower gables, remained. The cladding became clapboard or brick, as well as natural or man-made shingles. The chimney disappeared, and the entrance developed a projecting vestibule. The house was still sold as charming and cozy, but market forces made it a starter home.

PEDIMENT

PORTICO

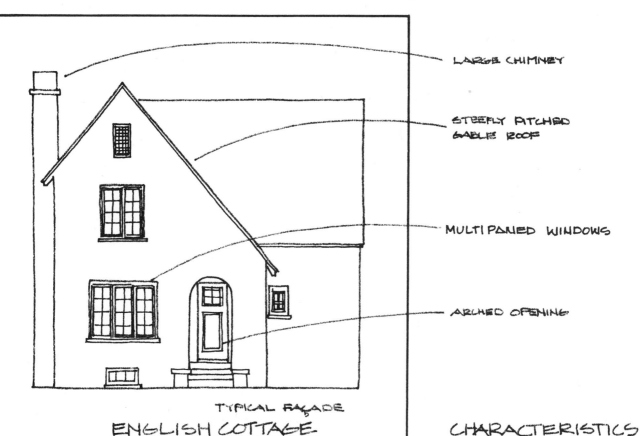

LARGE CHIMNEY

STEEPLY PITCHED GABLE ROOF

MULTI PANED WINDOWS

ARCHED OPENING

TYPICAL FAÇADE

ENGLISH COTTAGE

THE *ENGLISH COTTAGE* UNDERWENT A REVIVAL IN the first few decades of this century. This picturesque cottage featured asymmetrical massing of steeply pitched roofs, stucco walls with clean edges, unusual window patterns, tall chimneys, and English detailing—all calculated to produce a charming, moderately rustic design. On plan, rooms were often clustered around a hall, and room sizes and shapes differed so as to provide new spatial experiences and opportunities for built-in furniture, a window treatment, and perhaps access to a terrace or a porch. These different interior spaces often projected from the main body of the house. Specific detailing included brick trim around openings, the use of Tudor framing in gables, some changes in materials, clipped gables, and high-contrast coloration.

Not all English cottages were the same in form or intent. There were Tudor models in which the application of the dark wood framing thoroughly divided the walls into geometric units. The gables were broader, and the entire house was more volumetric. There were also would-be manor houses that eschewed ornament for large-scale geometry, bands of windows, and broad expanses of stucco—rambling houses, mostly architect-designed, that played only a marginal role in the vernacular tradition. The English cottage was built in most parts of the country, but particularly in northern climates; it was constructed close to the ground, yet high enough to promote its profile. A striking structure, it invited attention and implied that the occupants enjoyed a cultivated but pastoral life.

CHARACTERISTICS
2 STORIES,
ROOF MOST
IMPORTANT
ELEMENT,
CONTRASTING
ROOF LINES,
COMBINATIONS OF
SHORT OR LONG
STEEPLY PITCHED
GABLES
OFTEN HAD:
LARGE CHIMNEY,
MULTI PANED
SASH OR
CASEMENT
WINDOWS,
ARCHED ENTRY
OR DOOR SET
IN SMALL GABLE,
SOMETIMES
HALF-TIMBER
FRAMING
(2ND STORY)

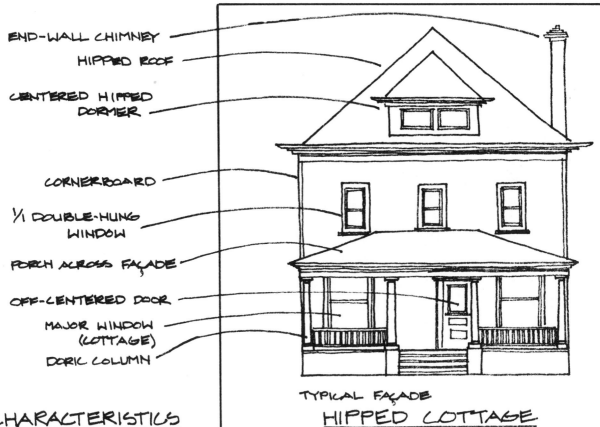

END-WALL CHIMNEY

HIPPED ROOF

CENTERED HIPPED DORMER

CORNERBOARD

1/1 DOUBLE-HUNG WINDOW

PORCH ACROSS FAÇADE

OFF-CENTERED DOOR

MAJOR WINDOW (COTTAGE)

DORIC COLUMN

TYPICAL FAÇADE
HIPPED COTTAGE

CHARACTERISTICS
2 STORIES,
3-BAY ORGANIZATION
CLADDING:
  CLAPBOARD
ROOF:
  HIPPED
CHIMNEY:
  1 END-WALL,
  BRICK
DORMER:
  CENTRAL HIPPED
WINDOWS:
  LARGE WINDOW ON
  1ST-FLOOR FAÇADE,
  1/1 DOUBLE-HUNG,
  VARIABLE
  FENESTRATION

THE *HIPPED COTTAGE* IS A GENERIC HOUSE TYPE that was built throughout most of the 1870–1940 period. It had the unique ability to be rendered in many styles, from Italianate to prairie, and could be adapted to most climatic conditions. This cottage was a classic box characterized by a large hipped roof, an almost square floor plan, and compact massing often cubical in shape. In many parts of the country it has been called a four-square. But no matter what its name or form, it is a substantial and dignified house.

Like all cottages, the hipped cottage is conceived as a four-sided building with changes in materials, fenestration, and ornamentation possible on all elevations. This approach to styling, when tied to the kind of siting employed for cottages, places the hipped cottage in the picturesque tradition. The hipped cottage seems to have been built as a speculation house throughout residential areas of cities, as a distinctive suburban house, as a double house, and as a rural house. It stands alone and is rarely built in rows on the same block.

In design, the hipped cottage pushes a large mass straight up from ground level and caps it with a pyramidal roof. The termination of the building is so precise that our attention is drawn back to the lower levels. The vertical thrust is countered by horizontal lines inherent in the cladding, in the long, low porch roof, and in the porch proper. Window placement accents both directions but, because of window groupings, the horizontal seems to dominate. On the other

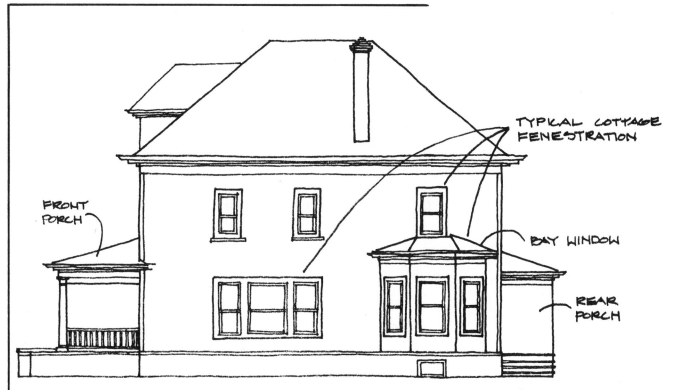

FRONT PORCH

TYPICAL COTTAGE FENESTRATION

BAY WINDOW

REAR PORCH

SIDE ELEVATION

hand, vertical accents derive from the chimney, corner-boards, porch columns, and vertical window alignments on some elevations.

The hipped cottage often served as an anchor for the development of neighborhoods. It was both historic and comtemporary, in that internal organization included compartmentalized spaces and some expression of inside-outside spatial continuity—open plan, as it came to be known—and the interior and exterior could employ historical ornamentation. As a focal point on any block, the hipped cottage could occupy a corner lot and set a tone for the remaining buildings, or it could be placed in midblock where other cottages could cluster around it.

PORCH:

EXTENDS ACROSS ENTIRE FAÇADE, OPEN RAIL WITH VERTICAL BALUSTERS

COLUMNS:

DORIC OR IONIC

ENTRANCE:

ASYMMETRICALLY LOCATED, PANEL AND GLASS DOOR

WALLS:

CORNERBOARDS OR PILASTERS CARRY A FASCIA OR ENTABLATURE, STONE, BRICK, CAST-CONCRETE FOUNDATION

HIPPED COTTAGE

TYPICAL PLAN
RECTANGULAR,
3 OR 4 ROOMS
DOWNSTAIRS,
3 OR 4 BEDROOMS
AND BATH
UPSTAIRS

VARIATIONS OF
HIPPED COTTAGES
CLADDING:
    BRICK,
    STUCCO,
    SHINGLES
ROOF:
    FLARED EAVES,
    BRACKETS
CHIMNEY:
    2 END-WALL
    OR INTERIOR
DORMERS:
    ON OTHER
    ELEVATIONS,
    LARGE DORMER
    ON FACADE.
WINDOWS:
    PAIRED
    OR TRIPLE,
    BAY, PALLADIAN
    OR ART GLASS

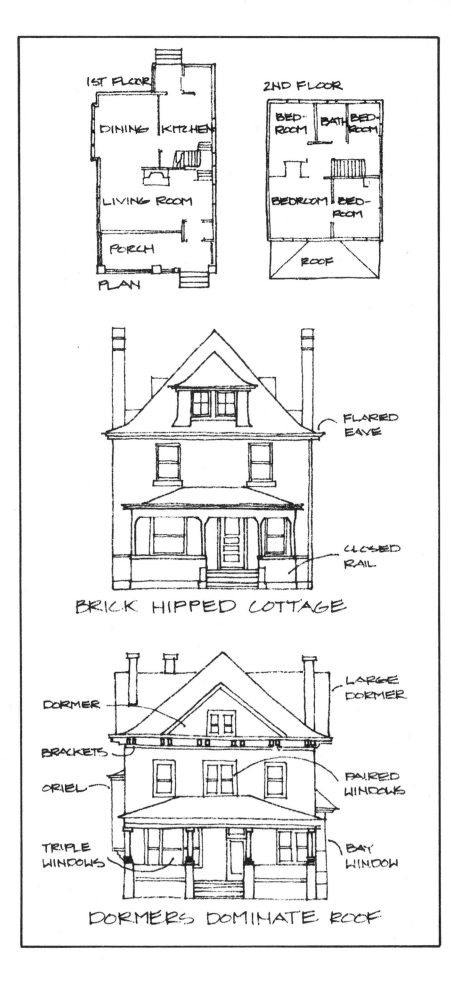

1ST FLOOR

2ND FLOOR

DINING   KITCHEN

LIVING ROOM

PORCH

PLAN

BED-ROOM   BATH   BED-ROOM

BEDROOM   BED-ROOM

ROOF

FLARED EAVE

CLOSED RAIL

BRICK HIPPED COTTAGE

DORMER

LARGE DORMER

BRACKETS

ORIEL

PAIRED WINDOWS

TRIPLE WINDOWS

BAY WINDOW

DORMERS DOMINATE ROOF

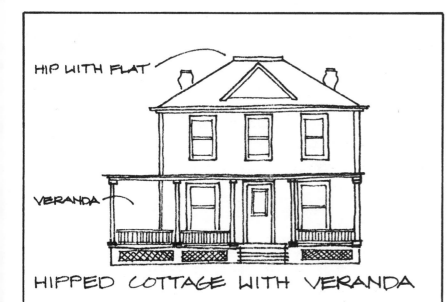

HIP WITH FLAT

VERANDA

HIPPED COTTAGE WITH VERANDA

VARIATIONS ON THE HIPPED COTTAGE INVOLVE the manipulation of major design elements. A change in materials affects the impact of the walls on overall design: for instance, the use of brick, stucco, or cement may give the building a more compact, even monolithic, quality. Other elements that lend themselves to change included the roof structure, which can be obscured by dormers or reduced by a flat, and the porch structure, which may be enlarged or made more formal. Formality itself is a clear variation, since symmetrical fenestration, an order of architecture, and closed porch rails combine to alter the design character of the cottage. The hipped cottage rarely moves toward informality or rusticity. Fine tuning on variations includes flared elements (eaves or walls); variety in chimney placement; changes in window groupings, so that double or triple windows replace the traditional single unit; multiple dormers; and a broader display of porch details.

PORCH:
STOPS SHORT OF FULL FAÇADE OR VERANDA

COLUMNS:
PANELED, POSTS, PEDESTALS AND COLUMNS

ENTRANCE:
ELONGATED OVAL OR RECTANGULAR LIGHT DOOR

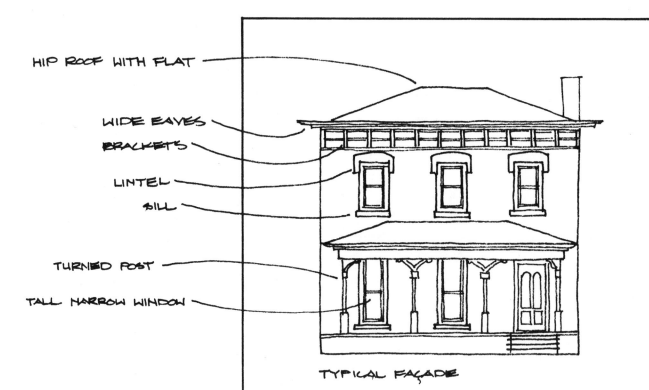

HIP ROOF WITH FLAT

WIDE EAVES

BRACKETS

LINTEL

SILL

TURNED POST

TALL NARROW WINDOW

TYPICAL FAÇADE

CHARACTERISTICS

2 STORIES,
3-BAY ORGANIZATION

CLADDING:

BRICK

ROOF:

HIP WITH FLAT
OR LOW PITCHED
HIP ROOF,
SOMETIMES A
CUPOLA OR
BELVEDERE,
LARGE BRACKETS
(OFTEN PAIRED)
WIDE EAVES

CHIMNEYS:

1 OR 2 END-WALL
OR INTERIOR

DORMERS:

NONE

ITALIANATE HIPPED COTTAGE

THE *ITALIANATE* VERSION OF THE HIPPED COT-
tage is one of the oldest subtypes of the period under study.
Italianate design predates and postdates the Civil War.
Early Italian styles tend toward the Tuscan, which usually
includes a pronounced tower. The vernacular hipped cottage
is more generally Italian. It has a strong vertical orientation
centered on vertical alignment between stories, including
multistory bay windows and elaborate design schemes on
the axis of the entrance. The roof profile is low, which reinforces the upward thrust of the façade, and many cottages
are topped by a belvedere, which helps to extend the building visually. The vernacular Italianate is an ornamented
style: it uses brackets or modillions and quoins to articulate
the edges of forms; moldings, pronounced lintels, and sills to
add texture and articulate the fenestration; and brackets,
pendants, and cut or turned pieces to ornament porches and
other entrances.

Many Italianate cottages are on narrow lots, and many
extend to a third story. Some of these carry a projecting bay
window that extends the interior space and adds distinction
to the façade. An ell plan was also popular in the Italianate.
The juncture of the ell was often engaged by a porch, and
occasionally by a modest tower. With time, porches got
larger as the ell form of the Italianate became linked with
the generic hipped cottage and finally disappeared in favor
of new styles.

WINDOWS:

TALL NARROW, SYMMETRICAL FENESTRATION, STONE LINTELS OR SURROUNDS, STONE SILLS, SOMETIMES PAIRED, CIRCLE-TOP OR BAY WINDOWS

PORCH:

OFTEN EXTENDS ACROSS FAÇADE

COLUMNS:

TURNED POSTS

ENTRANCE:

SINGLE OR PAIRED PANEL DOORS

WALLS:

SOMETIMES QUOINS, STRING COURSE

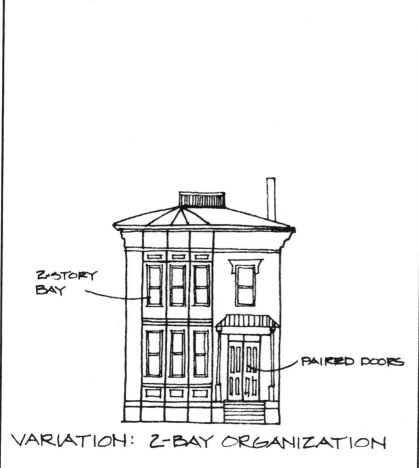

2-STORY BAY

PAIRED DOORS

VARIATION: 2-BAY ORGANIZATION

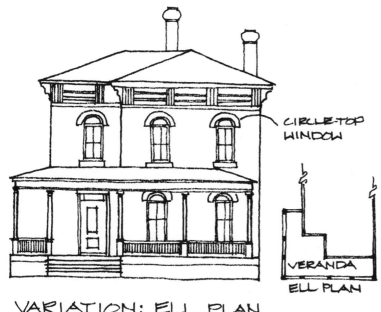

CIRCLE-TOP WINDOW

VERANDA

ELL PLAN

VARIATION: ELL PLAN AND VERANDA

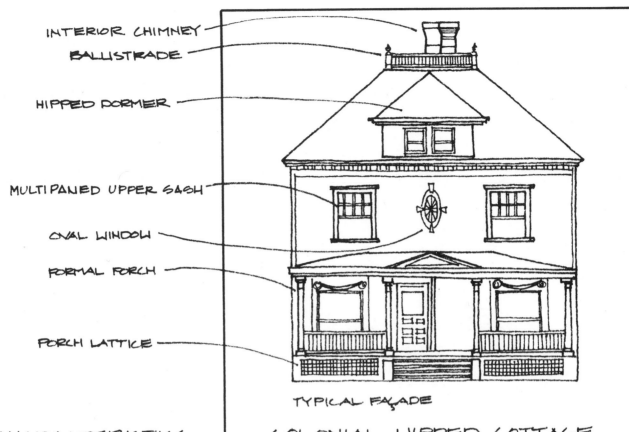

INTERIOR CHIMNEY

BALLISTRADE

HIPPED DORMER

MULTI PANED UPPER SASH

OVAL WINDOW

FORMAL PORCH

PORCH LATTICE

TYPICAL FAÇADE

COLONIAL HIPPED COTTAGE

CHARACTERISTICS
2 STORIES,
3-BAY ORGANIZATION,
ALMOST SQUARE,
ALMOST CUBICAL
CLADDING:
  CLAPBOARD,
  SOMETIMES
  SHINGLE
ROOF:
  HIPPED, OFTEN
  WITH FLAT AND
  BALLISTRADE
CHIMNEY:
  INTERIOR BRICK
  WITH ORNATE
  CAP
DORMER:
  HIPPED OR
  GABLE ON
  FAÇADE,
  SOMETIMES A
  PALLADIAN
  WINDOW

COLONIAL-STYLE HIPPED COTTAGES APPEARED before the end of the nineteenth century, but were especially popular during the first few decades of the twentieth. The overall shape and plan were closely related to the generic cottage. There is historical continuity in the use of a square plan and the cubical shape, but the real essence of this colonial revival lay in the application of colonial motifs to the basic form. The entire design became formal and, for the most part, restrained. The roof took on a flat with a balustrade, while chimney caps were vaguely colonial or Queen Anne. The roof carried a central hipped dormer. The façade received slightly different treatments on each level, the first floor being a wide, plain wall pierced by large cottage windows, by a paneled door with molding plants derived from historic patterns, and occasionally by sidelights. The porch was distinctly classical: the porch posts were columns, and most often the porch treatment included an order of architecture complete with a short pediment over the porch steps. The second-floor windows did not align with the first. Windows were indented toward the center, which often displayed an oval window on the center line. In a few cases, a second-floor door replaced the oval window for access to a balcony.

The corners of these houses usually carried a vertical board, whether a corner trim or a pilaster. The boards rose uninterrupted to the cornice line, where they met a wide fascia. Other cornice details included dentils or brackets on the eaves. Side elevations were less formal and more allied with traditional cottage arrangements, so that this building never lost its cottage heritage.

Two other versions of the colonial deserve mention. One has the same shape and plan as the primary model, but expands on the colonial vocabulary by including a Palladian window on the façade and by adding a portico—frequently, a two-story structure with large columns, an entablature, and a pediment.

The other version varies slightly in plan, in that it adds a circular form to the façade elevation. The circular shape is rarely a semicircle, but it is deep enough to serve as a bay window that may extend the full height of the façade. A few designs in this mode use twin bays. An extension of this kind of plan uses circular forms in the plan of the porch while leaving the façade walls flat.

Ornamentation and other details do not vary from the prototype, except that dormers may be more common on the portico and curved-front types than on the basic colonial cottage. The curved-front cottage seems most prevalent in New England, where the building's historic antecedents are located, providing a cultural as well as aesthetic connection.

WINDOWS:
SYMMETRICAL FENESTRATION, DOUBLE-HUNG, MULTI PANED UPPER SASH, 1 LIGHT LOWER SASH, PALLADIAN OR OVAL ACCENT

PORCH:
FORMAL WITH ORDER OF ARCHITECTURE, SOMETIMES BALCONY, 1-OR 2-STORY PORTICO

COLUMNS:
IONIC OR TUSCAN

WALLS:
SOMETIMES GIANT PILASTERS, QUOINS, CURVILINEAR BAYS, SHUTTERS, PORCH LATTICE DENTILS

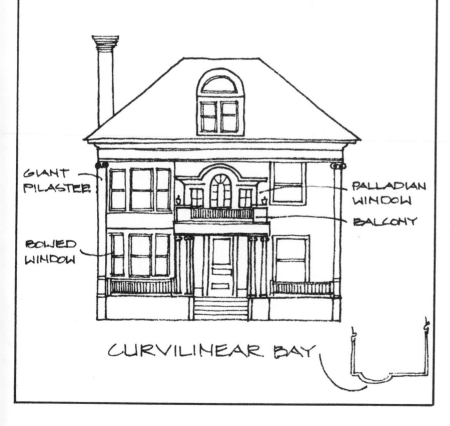

GIANT PILASTER

BOWED WINDOW

PALLADIAN WINDOW

BALCONY

CURVILINEAR BAY

CHANGE IN CLADDING BETWEEN FLOORS

PRAIRIE WINDOW

BELT COURSE BETWEEN FLOORS

SQUARE COLUMNS

CLOSED RAIL

TYPICAL FAÇADE

RECTILINEAR COTTAGE

CHARACTERISTICS

PLAIN, UNADORNED HIPPED COTTAGE, CUBIC SHAPE, SQUARE PLAN OFTEN HAD: OVERHANGING EAVES, SQUARE POSTS OR COLUMNS WITH PEDESTALS, BELT COURSE, CHANGE IN COLOR BETWEEN FLOORS, EXPOSED RAFTERS, PRAIRIE AND BUNGALOW WINDOWS

THE *RECTILINEAR* HIPPED COTTAGE WAS ESPE-
cially popular in the plains states. In the decade following 1910 this square-looking version of the hipped cottage
developed as an alternative to the Italianate and Queen
Anne styles. Eschewing ornamental details, the rectilinear
builder changed color at the upper level, changed materials,
used trim boards or belt courses that framed the walls into
panels, and modified window placement. The rectilinear was
a practical design that paralleled the development of the
prairie-style design. The first floor of the rectilinear cottage
contained social and service areas organized in an open
plan, while the second floor had the usual array of bedrooms
and a bath.

Specific design features include a low-pitched roof with a
hipped dormer on the façade side; a full-width or slightly
inset porch, most commonly with a closed rail; widely and
evenly spaced second-story windows; irregularly spaced
first-floor windows; and polychromy through the use of
materials. Porches are plain, or in an understated classical
style with Tuscan columns. Additional elements include a
bay window in a parlor or dining room; an end-wall chimney; changes in glazing pattern, with 6/1 and 1/1 being
popular; and changes in cladding. As for the latter, clapboard, shingles, brick, stucco, and cement are common, and
changes in materials usually take place three-quarters of the
way up the elevation, at about the window sill line. Cast-
concrete block is used in foundations as well as in porch
piers.

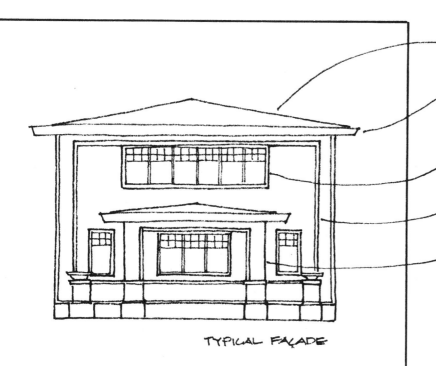

LOW PITCHED HIP ROOF

WIDE PROJECTING EAVES

HORIZONTAL BAND OF WINDOWS

DECORATIVE STRIPS

SIDE ENTRANCE

TYPICAL FAÇADE

PRAIRIE COTTAGE

THE *PRAIRIE-STYLE* HIPPED COTTAGE SEEMS TO have been both a natural outgrowth of the development of the hipped cottage, and an outright borrowing of prairie motifs. Like the four-square, the prairie found receptive builders and owners on the prairies and plains. Indeed, some of the literature of the period referred to this preference for the unconventional stucco house as a "popular Western tendency." The vernacular prairie cottage never abandoned the almost square plan and cubical shape of the prototype. However, it did have strong horizontal lines transmitted by its low roof and wide eaves. On the façade the porch roof and the banded windows reinforced the horizontal thrust of the main roof. The prairie cottage often had a stucco finish that gave it a monolithic quality, which even so was relieved by wood strips. Other prairie wall treatments included a type that used one kind of cladding on three-quarters of the elevations and a second cladding on the last quarter.

The prairie cottage had the most open plan of any of the hipped cottage subtypes. The continuous flow of space helped to break the boxlike character of the outer shell. Casement windows were part of the vocabulary for this house, as were double-hung windows in which only the upper half of the top sash had muntins.

The prairie cottage brought a change in the overall configuration of the hipped cottage, in that the wall planes were reasserted. The house was approached through planes— horizontals that extended the house form and verticals that hung from the horizontal elements. Traditional full-sized porches even became squared to the façade, so that they too described a planar system.

CHARACTERISTICS
2 STORIES,
RECTILINEAR LINES
OFTEN HAD:
STUCCO CLADDING,
LOW PITCHED HIP ROOF,
WIDE PROJECTING EAVES,
HORIZONTAL BAND OF WINDOWS,
SCREENED-IN OR ENCLOSED SUN PORCH,
SIDE ENTRANCE,
DECORATIVE WOOD STRIPS OF CONTRASTING COLOR,
BELT COURSE BETWEEN FLOORS

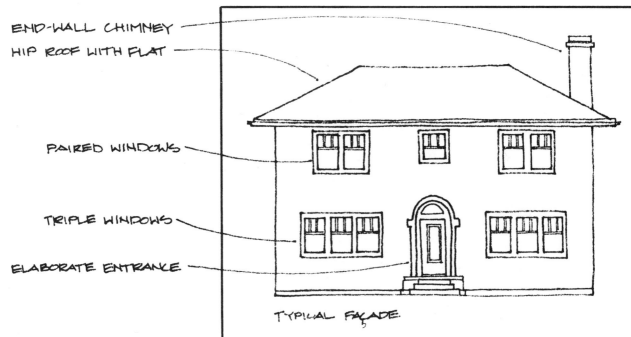

END-WALL CHIMNEY

HIP ROOF WITH FLAT

PAIRED WINDOWS

TRIPLE WINDOWS

ELABORATE ENTRANCE

TYPICAL FAÇADE

VILLA

CHARACTERISTICS

2 STORIES,
3-BAY ORGANIZATION,
RECTANGULAR,
LONG SIDE TOWARD
STREET

CLADDING:
　STUCCO

ROOF:
　HIP WITH FLAT,
　CLAY TILE ROOF
　OR SHINGLES
　WITH CRESTING

CHIMNEY:
　END-WALL

WINDOWS:
　SYMMETRICAL
　FENESTRATION,
　CASEMENT OR
　SASH,
　OFTEN PAIRED
　OR TRIPLE,
　OFTEN FRENCH
　DOORS AS
　WINDOWS

THE *VILLA* FORM OF THE HIPPED COTTAGE WAS the most formal and most historic of all the designs in this group. It abandoned the square and the cube for a rectangular shape that measured about 40 by 25 feet, with the long side facing the street. The villa developed from 1910 on, and early examples reflect prairie style influences on cottage design. By the 1920s the villa began to exhibit four design motifs: Italian, Spanish, French, and an eclectic type that is generally Mediterranean. By the 1930s a fifth type had appeared—an abstracted classical design featuring giant pilasters on the façade and the styling of the architect Paul Cret.

All this historicism brought a new vocabulary to the hipped cottage. The shape became a general palazzo that could display curvilinear elements such as round-headed entrance systems and arcades, while also featuring clay tiles for roofing, symmetrical fenestration, the placement of the sunroom and porches (which had shown up in the rectilinear style as dependencies to the main house), and the reassertion of the central entrance hall on plan. Ornaments for the villa included brackets, quoins, balconies with iron railings, shutters, ornamental rails above sunrooms or porches, canvas awnings, carved or cast ornament, and high-contrast paint schemes. In terms of color, villas were usually a pastel stucco with light or dark trim, depending on the base color, and the tile roofs were red. By the 1930s, however, many villas were brick or hollow-tile buildings painted white. As for siting, most villa types required a formal setting and approach, with plantings, terraces, and gardens to emphasize formal geometry.

BELT COURSE

QUOINS

DOOR MOLDINGS

SUN PORCH

BALCONY

MEDITERRANEAN ORNAMENTATION

The Spanish or Mediterranean styles most often introduced an arcade into the façade. Common arcade placements included the entrance, with from one to three arches, and the second-floor space above the entrance. Occasionally, arcades also provided a screen or side entrance to a porch or sunroom.

ENTRANCES:
ELABORATE AND FORMAL DOOR RECESSED SLIGHTLY FROM FAÇADE, SURROUNDED BY MOLDINGS, SOMETIMES A HOOD, PANEL DOOR

WALLS:
RELATIVELY FLAT, SOMETIMES QUOINS, PILASTERS, BELT COURSE, SUN PORCH, BALCONIES

ORNAMENT:
GENERALLY MEDITERRANEAN— WROUGHT IRON, CARTOUCHE, RUSTICATION, PRONOUNCED SILLS AND LINTELS, LATTICEWORK

GABLE DORMER

MANSARD ROOF
(FULL STORY HIGH)

LOW PITCHED
PORCH ROOF

PARALLEL
CORNICES

TYPICAL FAÇADE
MANSARD COTTAGE

CHARACTERISTICS

2 STORIES

CLADDING:
CLAPBOARD,
BRICK

ROOF:
MANSARD (FULL
STORY HIGH),
USUALLY
STRAIGHT-SIDED
OR CONVEX,
WOOD, SLATE, OR
COMPOSITION
SHINGLES,
SOMETIMES
CRESTING

DORMERS:
MULTIPLE
DORMERS

CHIMNEY:
INTERIOR,
TALL STACKS

THROUGHOUT 1870–80 THE COTTAGE WITH A MAN-
sard roof was referred to as a *French cottage*, and historians
link this cottage to the development of the Second Empire
style. In vernacular design the French cottage was less Second Empire than the design of high-style buildings, and it
was more generally French. One could argue that it was a
hybrid affair with Italianate features, and that over time it
absorbed other kinds of cottage detailing.

In its early history, the mansard cottage had Victorian details, in that much of the ornament around windows and
floors and along both cornice lines was heavy, with thick,
layered, wide board or masonry courses. Façade organization included a symmetrical two- or three-bay front that
might truncate to two windows at the roof level. The house
was two or three stories in height and usually had a side-
hall plan. Cladding was brick or clapboard. The unusual
shape of the mansard roof meant that the roof plane could
become another wall on the façade. In the straight-sided
mansard, the roof was prominent as a wall, whereas the
curved roof swept back from the façade and projected the
ever present dormers forward. The roof was dark in color
and covered with slate shingles that added texture and pattern to the façade design.

Some mansard cottages included a square tower. It seems
linked to the Italianate Tuscan villa with a tower. The
mansard tower repeated the roof shape, served as a main

entrance on the ground level, and lifted the rectangular façade skyward. Over time there was some shifting in placement, as the tower left its central position for an off-center or even a side placement.

By the 1880s the mansard cottage became even more "cottaged"; it began to lose its French renaissance–inspired lintels, sills, moldings, and quoins and took on general cottage detailing. Brackets got lighter, as did the trim around openings in the walls, while porches got larger and utilized turned and sawn manufactured materials. These were subtle changes, but the overall shift from a refined, rationalist sensibility to a picturesque one is evident in the extant buildings.

The mansard cottage was built throughout the country. With the exception of some areas in New England, where the house was built in rows of detached and double houses, the mansard was a single-family, detached house designed both in the grand manner—somewhat like an American chateau—and in the vernacular. In the former style the cottage seems arithmetical, yet when one adds up all the design elements and their detailing, the sum of these angles, segments of circles, and planes is not quite comprehensible. The vernacular, on the other hand, exploits the unusual shape, as if it were sliced off from a thick loaf of French bread.

WINDOWS:
TALL, NARROW, 2/2 OR 1/1 PATTERN, BAY WINDOWS COMMON

PORCH:
SMALL ENTRANCE PORCH, OR PORCH COVERS FAÇADE, COLUMNS, BRACKETS

ENTRANCE:
PANEL DOOR, SOMETIMES PAIRED, SOMETIMES HOOD OVER ENTRANCE

WALLS:
SOMETIMES HIGH FOUNDATION, BRACKETS IN EAVES, ELABORATE CORNICES

ROUND-HEADED WINDOWS

SEGMENTAL LINTEL

PAIRED DOOR

BAY WINDOW

VARIATION: 3 STORIES

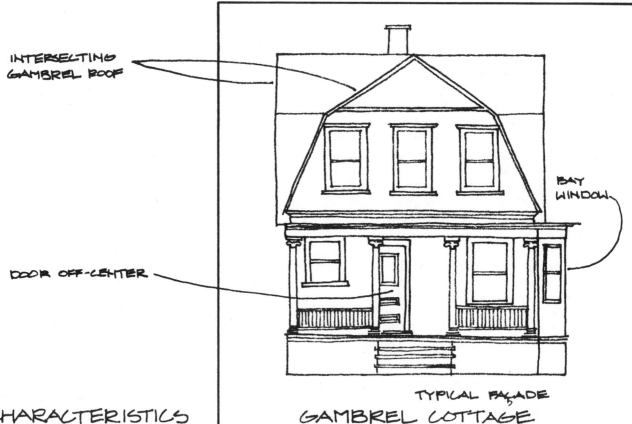

INTERSECTING GAMBREL ROOF

BAY WINDOW

DOOR OFF-CENTER

TYPICAL FAÇADE
GAMBREL COTTAGE

CHARACTERISTICS

2 STORIES

CLADDING:

CLAPBOARD, SHINGLE, COMBINATION- CLAPBOARD ON 1ST FLOOR, SHINGLES ON 2ND FLOOR

ROOF:

GAMBREL, GABLE END PERPENDICULAR TO STREET, OR INTERSECTING GAMBREL

CHIMNEY:

BRICK INTERIOR

DORMERS:

OFTEN GABLE DORMERS ON SIDE ELEVATIONS

THE GAMBREL ROOF HAS CONTRIBUTED A COTTAGE to the history of the vernacular house. Because of the shape and pitches of both sections of the roof, the gambrel encloses a great deal of second- or third-floor space. The house proper has the largest roof of the cottage types in which the roof is a principal design element. The shape of the roof is so forceful that it separates itself from the lower level, obliging builders to find ways to make sure that the roof did not overpower the entire structure. They did this by intersecting the roof, which broke the form down yet expanded the square footage. The intersection also produced cottage-type elevations where fenestration could be varied and changes in color and materials could be accommodated. These later changes in color and materials helped to layer the gambrel cottage. Clapboard lower stories and shingled upper stories were common. Clapboards contributed horizontal lines in the design. The cornice line and belt or string courses between floors also pulled the house away from the compaction implied by the roof.

While gambrel organization usually meant turning a gambrel gable end toward the street, some houses were built having a single gambrel with its ridge parallel to the street. In traditional façades the porch and entrance system are of two kinds: cutaway porches cut out from one side or across the width of the façade, or a projecting short porch with a low-pitched roof of its own. In the first instance the void of the porch helps to balance the large volume of the gambrel end wall, while in the second the lateral flow of the porch, reinforced by an open rail or a porch roof balustrade, lightens the front of this mass-oriented structure.

    Detailing on the gambrel cottage often attempts to diminish the volume and mass of the house. Common treatments include canted walls, especially at façade corners; a wide eave at the roof line which cuts the roof off from the wide body below; bay or oriel windows that break up the wide wall planes; and gable ornamentation that includes special windows, stickwork to help relieve or mask the wide gable, and usually more than one dormer.

GABLE:

    RETURNS OR PENT ROOF, CHANGES IN SHINGLE PATTERN, STICKWORK, PALLADIAN WINDOW, ELLIPTICAL WINDOW, PAIRED OR TRIPLE WINDOWS

WINDOWS:

    DOUBLE-HUNG SASH, 1/1 AND VARIETIES OF MULTIPLE UPPER LIGHTS, BAY OR ORIEL ON SIDE ELEVATIONS, SOMETIMES PAIRED OR TRIPLE WINDOWS ON 2ND-STORY FAÇADE

PORCH:

    ACROSS FACADE, SOMETIMES CUTAWAY PORCH

WALLS:

    HIGH-CONTRAST COLOR BETWEEN WALL AND TRIM

SHED DORMER

CUTAWAY PORCH

1½-STORY VARIATION

TRIPLE WINDOWS IN GABLE

PEDIMENT

PAIRED COLUMNS

2½-STORY VARIATION

END-WALL CHIMNEY

SHED DORMER ACROSS FAÇADE

6/6 WINDOWS

END-WALL PORCH

PANEL DOOR WITH SIDELIGHTS

TYPICAL FAÇADE

COLONIAL GAMBREL

CHARACTERISTICS

2 STORIES,
3 OR 5 BAYS

CLADDING:
WIDE CLAPBOARD, SOMETIMES BRICK VENEER ON 1ST FLOOR FAÇADE

ROOF:
GAMBREL, RIDGELINE PARALLEL TO STREET

CHIMNEY:
1 OR 2 END-WALL, BRICK OR STONE

DORMERS:
SHED ACROSS ENTIRE FAÇADE, SOMETIMES GAMBREL OR GABLE DORMERS

THE *COLONIAL GAMBREL COTTAGE* IS A SUBTYPE of the generic model. Throughout most of its history, which includes authentic eighteenth-century examples as well as several revival-style types, the house has been thought of as Dutch in origin and spirit. The revival style presented on these pages was popular during 1900–1940 and was referred to as Dutch colonial. The shape of the building was strongly dictated by the shape of the roof, which in the Dutch-Flemish tradition frequently had flared eaves. In many models the flare was wide enough to provide some shelter over the entrance. The roof ridge ran parallel to the street, so that the façade was available for a full design treatment. A three-bay front was common, but five-bay units can be found. The second-floor level was outlined by either a long shed dormer that covered most of the roof, or by two or three evenly spaced gable dormers. The dormers were repeated on the rear elevation. The entrance was understated, with only a hood or a pediment to mark the door and the shallow porch. Some pediments evolved into porticoes with slender columns. Fenestration was for the most part symmetrical on all elevations.

The main house often received an extension in the form of an open or enclosed porch, a sunroom, or even a pergola, to all of which there was access through French doors from inside. Although the porch was formally composed, it added a bit of informality to the overall design. An end-wall chimney in brick of stone completed the design. Clapboard was the dominant cladding material, but on the first-floor façade; brick-veneer and shingle treatments were also popular.

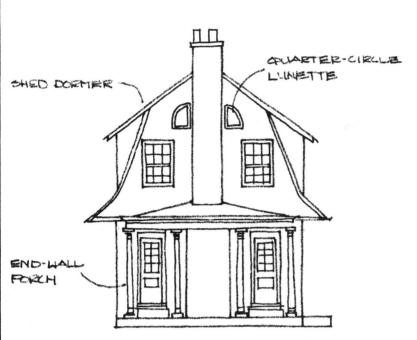

SHED DORMER

QUARTER-CIRCLE LUNETTE

END-WALL PORCH

SIDE ELEVATION

The colonial gambrel has often included elements of the Georgian style, which accounts for the use of orders of architecture (Tuscan) on entrances and porches, and the central hall plan that many of these cottages have. The alternative to a central hall was a modern open plan in which the entrance door opened directly into the living room. The use of classical columns was one of the few instances of ornamentation on these buildings. Accents included small lights or half lights bracketing the chimney stack in the gables, local stone foundations and chimneys, sidelights or a fanlight transom at the entrance door, and shutters.

All-in-all, the gambrel colonial was not a house that relied on small effects to carry the design. It was a large, commodious design with open space, a good relationship to its suburban site, plenty of room for family functions, and a strong, rationally and pragmatically designed façade. While it was not built in rows, individual units were built in a great number of subdivisions throughout the country.

WINDOWS:
MANY DOUBLE-HUNG SASH, MULTIPANED LIGHTS AS 6/1, 6/6, 9/1, QUARTER-CIRCLE LUNETTES IN GABLE END, OFTEN PAIRED OR TRIPLE ON 1ST-FLOOR FAÇADE

PORCH:
END-WALL PORCH OR SUNROOM, TUSCAN COLUMNS

ENTRANCE:
SMALL ENTRANCE PORCH, HOOD, ROOF, OVERHANG OR PORTICO, PANEL DOOR, SOMETIMES SIDELIGHTS OR FANLIGHTS, SOMETIMES BENCHES

WALLS:
OFTEN SHUTTERS, SOMETIMES STONE FOUNDATION

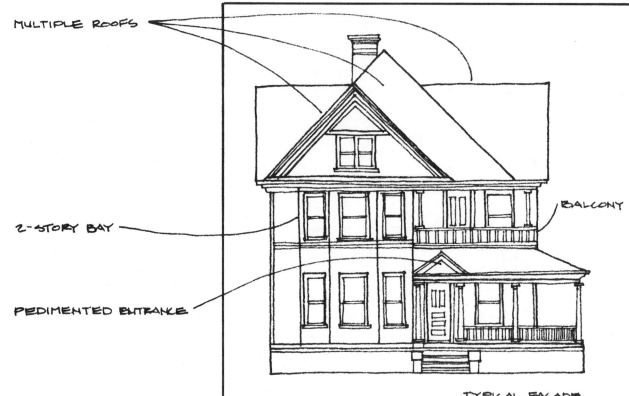

MULTIPLE ROOFS

2-STORY BAY

PEDIMENTED ENTRANCE

BALCONY

TYPICAL FAÇADE

ORGANIC COTTAGE

CHARACTERISTICS

1 2 STORIES,
ASYMMETRICAL
MASSING,
PROJECTING WINGS,
GABLES, BAYS,
INTERCONNECTED
INTERIOR AND
EXTERIOR SPACES

CLADDING:

CLAPBOARD
OR CLAPBOARD
AND SHINGLE
COMBINATIONS

ROOF:

MULTIPLE ROOF
FORMS,
STEEP PITCHES,
CENTRAL HIP
PREDOMINATES

THE YEARS 1875-90 WERE ONE OF THE MOST IN-
tense periods for the development of the American cottage.
Of major importance to the period was the Centennial cele-
bration of 1876 in Philadelphia, which led American designers, builders, and manufacturers to rediscover qualities
present in original colonial construction. Since the period
was still a part of the Victorian era, interest in ornamentation and vigorous massing was strong. Therefore much of
this period was devoted to evolving an original American
cottage plan from all these ingredients. Stylistic influences
that nourished the design dialogue were the Charles Eastlake style of ornamentation, the house forms of the Arts and
Craft style, and the so-called Queen Anne style derived from
the English medieval tradition through the eyes of another
English designer, Norman Shaw. There were also other Eu-
ropean influences, such as the French forms that Henry
Hobson Richardson utilized. Local influences occurred in the
form of American colonial building types and materials, and
the cottage tradition as developed from midcentury Gothic
cottages. The result was the short-lived but powerful shingle
style and various derivatives of Queen Anne.

At the heart of the entire movement—which ultimately
produced the modern American house—was a common design concept: the organic cottage. This cottage had a central
plan—a strong feeling for centrality through living halls,
circulation around a core, and tension between centrifugal
and centripetal forces. Common design characteristics were

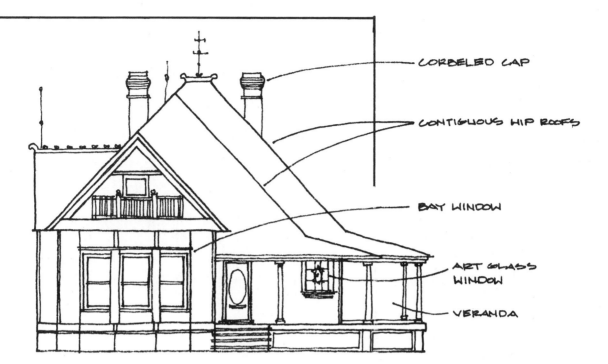

CORBELED CAP

CONTIGUOUS HIP ROOFS

BAY WINDOW

ART GLASS WINDOW

VERANDA

a tall center, in that the central plan was expressed through vertical thrust; asymmetrical massing; patterned textures on exterior surfaces; projecting gables and bays; interconnected interior and exterior spaces; and either a steep roof on the centripetal types or a low, close-to-the-ground roof in the centrifugal types. The modes of expression, then, were central plan/vertical expression or central plan/horizontal expression. In both cases there was considerable tension between the push toward the center and the pull away from it.

As in most American design, the design dialogue among these styles and organizing principles was more eclectic than pure. Thus, one finds Queen Anne motifs, on other cottage types. Similarly, the shingle style that gave us an original plan and form rarely appeared as a shingled building beyond the east coast, but the plan and form did appear in clapboard cottages and the lines—for instance, the dramatic sweep of the gable from the roof to near ground level—were used in several kinds of vernacular buildings.

The examples, covering almost fifty years of design, are arranged in general chronological order, starting with the stick style and concluding with what the popular journals referred to as a California cottage, but which was actually built on the southwest plains, on the prairies, and in border states of the south. Categorically, the central plan/vertical expression type included buildings constructed in the stick style, the Eastlake style, and the Queen Anne (and its derivative, the Princess Anne), while the central plan/horizontal expression type included the shingle style and the late Western cottage, the latter often balancing shingle and Queen Anne elements.

CHIMNEYS:
INTERIOR BRICK, CORBELED CAPS

DORMERS:
GABLE, SOMETIMES MULTIPLES

GABLES:
GABLE FINISH

WINDOWS:
VARIETY IN PLACEMENT AND GROUPING

PORCHES:
VERANDAS WITH TURNED POSTS AND BRACKETS OR TUSCAN COLUMNS WITH ENTABLATURE

ENTRANCES:
DOOR OFF-CENTER, PANEL AND GLASS

WALLS:
DIVIDED INTO PANELS, PATTERNED SURFACES

IN THE STICK
MANNER:

TALL
PROPORTIONS,
APPLIED
STICKWORK AS
EXPOSED
FRAMING AND
BRACING,
ORNATE GABLES,
PICTURESQUE
PROFILES

IN THE QUEEN
ANNE MANNER:

STRONG
SENSE OF
CENTRALITY,
PROJECTING
WINGS,
GABLES, BAYS,
OCCASIONAL
TOWER OR
TURRET,
MUCH ORNAMENT
IN EARLY
EXAMPLES,
LESS ORNAMENT
IN LATE
EXAMPLES,
MULTIPLE
CLADDINGS

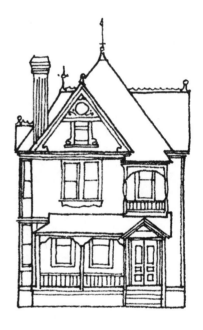

IN THE QUEEN
ANNE MANNER:

CENTRAL
CIRCULATION
CORE,
INSIDE-OUTSIDE
CONTINUITY,
LESS TURNED
AND SAWN
ORNAMENT

IN THE QUEEN ANNE MANNER:

CENTRAL HIP ROOF WITH GABLE PROJECTIONS, LESS ORNAMENTATION, MULTIPLE DORMERS, ENTRANCE PEDIMENT, CENTRAL RECEPTION HALL OR SIDE HALL PLAN

IN THE SHINGLE MANNER:

HIDDEN FRAMING, LARGE GEOMETRIC FORMS, EXTENDED ROOF LINES, WIDE GABLE OR GAMBREL ROOF, PARTIAL OR FULL SHINGLE CLADDING, FLARED WALLS

IN THE SHINGLE MANNER:

CLOSE TO THE GROUND, HORIZONTAL FLOW OF SPACE, SEMICIRCULAR WALL OR PORCH, TALL CENTRAL HIP ROOF, SHINGLE PANELS

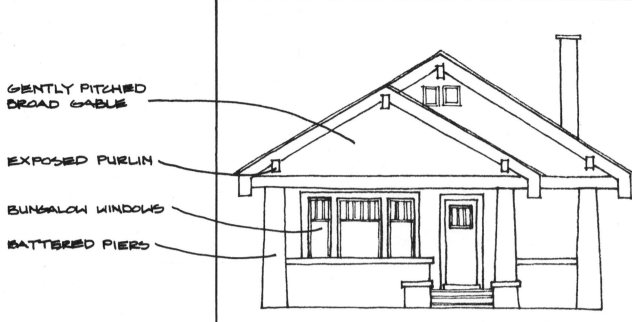

GENTLY PITCHED BROAD GABLE

EXPOSED PURLIN

BUNGALOW WINDOWS

BATTERED PIERS

TYPICAL FAÇADE

BUNGALOW

CHARACTERISTICS

1 STORY,
LOW HORIZONTAL
LINES,
6 ROOMS COMMON
CLADDING:
    CLAPBOARD
ROOFS:
    GENTLY PITCHED
    BROAD GABLES,
    LOWER GABLE
    COVERS PORCH,
    LARGE GABLE
    COVERS HOUSE,
    EXPOSED
    RAFTERS OR
    PURLINS,
    WIDE PROJECTING
    EAVES,
    HEAVY BARGE-
    BOARD
    SUPPORTED BY
    BRACKETS

THE *BUNGALOW* IS A UNIQUE HOUSE TYPE THAT borrowed house forms from other cultures and invested in American sensibility and American materials to produce an original and intelligent design. As built from 1895 to 1915— its first development period—the bungalow was known as the California bungalow. Because of the nature of the design and the kind of living which that design suggested, it was appropriate for this form to develop on the west coast. The bungalow plan, which reduces the distinction between outside and inside space, reflects the open, practical, outdoor living possible in California. During the first part of the twentieth century, Americans became more interested in casual living, in built-in storage, in compact arrangements with plenty of air and light, and in open plan and less complicated furnishings. The bungalow responded to those needs.

Stylistically the house type had an eclectic beginning, including Indian, Spanish, and Japanese influences, and it continued to incorporate sytlistic elements from other cultures and styles throughout its development. Thus the resulting American bungalow had plain models with clapboard or shingle cladding intended for vacation areas, and a Swiss chalet model for mountainous regions. It could be rustic, or clean and open in the manner of prairie houses, or clustered with patios or terraces in the Spanish colonial mode, or built up to approximate a cottage form. And it could be historied, as in the application of English cottage motifs to the basic bungalow form.

Being a ubiquitous house type, the bungalow did not have totally consistent design characteristics throughout the entire period of its growth and development. The first phase of

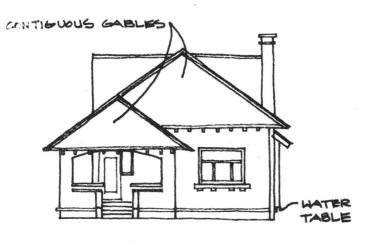

CONTIGUOUS GABLES

WATER TABLE

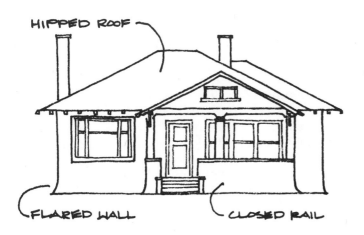

HIPPED ROOF

FLARED WALL

CLOSED RAIL

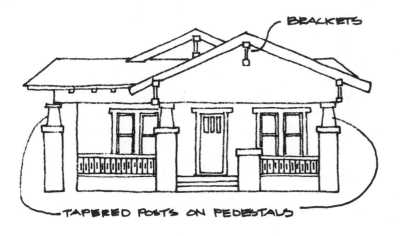

BRACKETS

TAPERED POSTS ON PEDESTALS

PORCH:
ENCLOSED, SCREENED, OR EXTENDED BY TERRACE, OFTEN PERGOLA OVER TERRACE

COLUMNS:
TAPERED POSTS ON PEDESTALS

WALLS:
FLARED, WATER TABLE

BUNGALOW

TYPICAL PLAN
LIVING ROOM
EXTENDS ACROSS
THE FRONT,
38' X 28' COMMON
DIMENSION

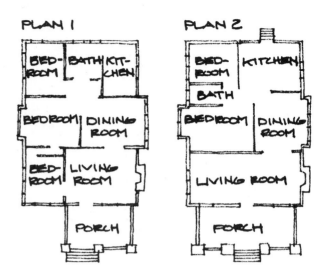

PLAN 1

PLAN 2

VARIATIONS

CLADDING:

SHINGLES,
STUCCO,
BRICK, OR
COMBINATION
OF MATERIALS

ROOFS:

GABLE TURNED
AWAY FROM
STREET OR
HIP ROOF

DORMERS:

SHED OR GABLE

GABLE:

STICKWORK
IN GABLE

WINDOWS:

MULTIPANED
RECTANGULAR
LIGHTS IN
UPPER SASH

that development, however, set the tone for the remaining phases. Throughout its early development the bungalow was best known as a low, small house that prototyped informal living, used natural materials, adapted well to sites, and relied on simplified design. The floor plan was spread out, necessitating a large foundation, long walls, and a large roof. The roof was both wide and projecting, and its shape was often repeated in the roof over the wide porch. Thus the house faced the street with contiguous and receding planes.

The shell of the bungalow was not always boxlike: the juncture of the porch with the main body produced a break in the box, as did a bay window and a rear porch. A more subtle refinement was effected by battering porch piers and walls, whose inclined edges broke the rectangle of the façade. Window placements tended to pull the house out along the horizontal, as did walls with large amounts of glass subdivided into panels of wood and glass. The broad groupings of glass contributed to the inside-outside continuity.

Bungalow designers were especially adept at generating floor-plan variations and roof forms that spoke to the plans. The roofs were often tied to establishing planes. In the illustrations, the edge of each roof and the ridge (if present) of a roof all become planes; reading bungalow design is, in part, a question of reading those successive planes. The planes are reinforced by windows and porch piers that help frame them. Other design variations include the alternation of mass and void on the façades—a push-pull effect that helps eliminate perception of the basic rectangle present in the plane. Ornamental variations include changes in gable motifs, window placement, and materials. This flexible vocabulary made it possible to build rows of bungalows without having to repeat forms on the same block.

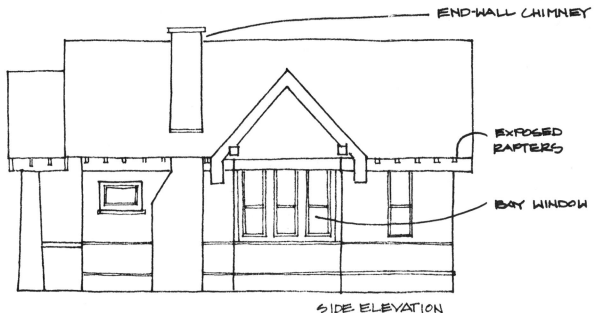

END-WALL CHIMNEY

EXPOSED RAFTERS

BAY WINDOW

SIDE ELEVATION

CHIMNEY:
LARGE END-WALL,
BRICK

DORMERS:
NONE

WINDOWS:
SASH,
PAIRED OR TRIPLE,
VERTICAL
DIVISIONS IN
UPPER SASH,
BAY ON ELEVATION

PORCH:
LARGE,
PROJECTED IN
FRONT OF HOUSE

COLUMNS:
BATTERED
PIERS COMMON

ENTRANCE:
SLAB DOOR
WITH LIGHTS,
CRAFTSMAN
DOOR

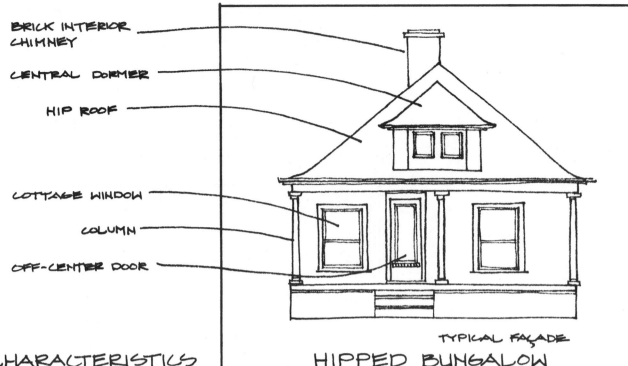

BRICK INTERIOR CHIMNEY

CENTRAL DORMER

HIP ROOF

COTTAGE WINDOW

COLUMN

OFF-CENTER DOOR

TYPICAL FAÇADE

HIPPED BUNGALOW

CHARACTERISTICS

1 STORY

CLADDING:
   CLAPBOARD

ROOF:
   HIPPED,
   FLARED EAVES
   COMMON,
   MAIN ROOF
   USUALLY
   COVERS FRONT
   PORCH

CHIMNEY:
   BRICK INTERIOR

DORMER:
   CENTRAL FRONT

WINDOWS:
   COTTAGE ON
   FAÇADE,
   1/1 DOUBLE-HUNG
   ON ELEVATIONS,
   SYMMETRICAL
   FENESTRATION

THE *HIPPED BUNGALOW* IS THE MOST CLASSICAL of bungalow designs. The low hip roof serves as a pediment for three or four columns that carry a restrained entablature. This temple-front building is relieved by a hipped dormer, an open porch rail, and pedestals for the columns. The structure is low to the ground and utilizes the full width of the façade for a porch. The bungalow is built with wood-frame construction, and clapboard cladding is most common. Other cladding materials include stucco, hollow concrete tile, cement block, and shingle in rustic or Craftsman-style bungalows.

A major alternative to the open-porch model encloses half the porch and adds a bay window, triple window, or large cottage window to the wall. Since the main roof almost always covers the porch area, the porch becomes a cutaway type, appearing as if carved out of the main house block.

The hipped bungalow has been popular in all regions of the country. In northern climates the roof is high and the porch may be cutaway or enclosed. In southern climates the roof is low, ventilators may replace dormers, and window placements facilitate cross-ventilation.

In all variations, ornamentation was a minor design consideration. Changes in glazing pattern, exposed rafters (a Craftsman motif), cast-concrete blocks with rock faces for the foundation or porch pedestals, and sidelights for the entrance were popular. Wall treatments included flared walls on the main house and/or porch, latticework, cornerboards, and a water table. Some hipped bungalows extended the porch as a separate element complete with its own roof.

PORCH:
    EXTENDS
    ACROSS
    FAÇADE,
    VARIATION:
    CUTAWAY
    PORCH
COLUMNS:
    TUSCAN,
    3 OR 4 SUPPORT
    PORCH,
    SOMETIMES
    PEDESTALS
    AND COLUMNS
WALLS:
    CORNERBOARDS,
    SOMETIMES
    FLARED WALLS,
    EXPOSED
    RAFTERS

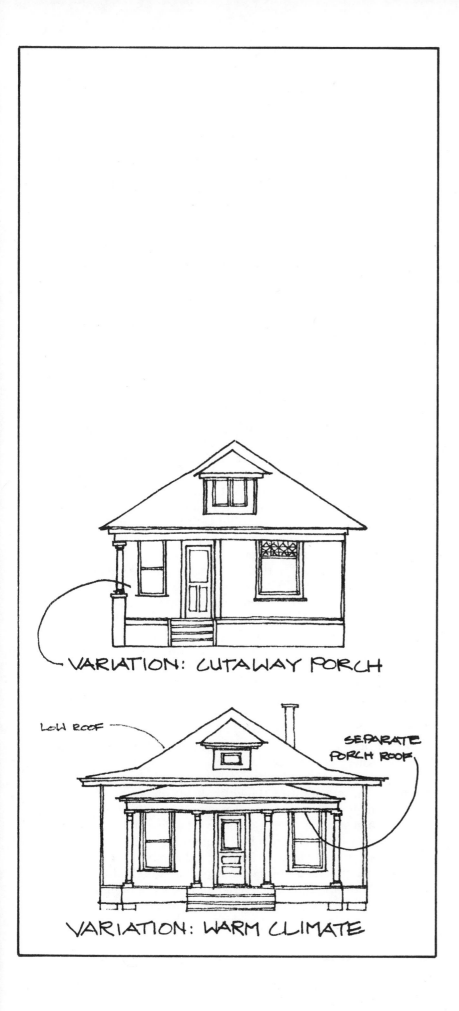

VARIATION: CUTAWAY PORCH

LOW ROOF

SEPARATE
PORCH ROOF

VARIATION: WARM CLIMATE

LARGE SHED DORMER

MAIN ROOF COVERS PORCH

SYMMETRICAL FENESTRATION

TYPICAL FAÇADE
BUNGALOW COTTAGE

CHARACTERISTICS

1½ STORY (THE ½ STORY RETAINS THE COMPACT BUNGALOW SHAPE), ALMOST SQUARE PLAN

CLADDING:
COMBINATION OF MATERIALS, VARIES BETWEEN 1ST AND 2ND FLOORS

ROOF:
BROAD GABLE, RIDGELINE PARALLEL TO STREET, ROOF COVERS PORCH

DORMERS:
SHED OR WIDE GABLE

CHIMNEY:
END-WALL COMMON

IN THE HISTORY OF THE AMERICAN HOUSE FORM, the term "cottage" covered most of what was built in the nineteenth century, and the term "bungalow"—sometimes wrongly applied—covered a good deal of what was built in the first half of the twentieth. It is not surprising that, in time, builders and designers also generated a building that combined attributes of both. While present-day critics refer to these as "bungaloid" forms, the period term *bungalow cottage* seems more appropriate.

The integration of both design modes can be seen on the various elevations. The façade—with the exception of the large central dormer—has bungalow traits. On most buildings the main roof covers the porch, which is wide and uses bungalow piers; on others there is a gable entrance area attached to a pergola. In all cases the entire roof line, the porch, and first-floor wall are close to the ground.

The major design change in the façade centers on the roof form, a straight gable that runs parallel to the street, and on the domination of the roof by a large hip or gable dormer. Bungalow details at the roof line are exposed purlins and rafters, and the chimney stacks that pierce the roof because of the wide overhang of the eaves.

Cottage treatment is especially noticeable on the side elevations, where additional height allows for cottage fenestration. The half story provides an opportunity to change materials; shingles were popular at the floor line. Other side elevation features include bay windows, a water table, and an occasional decorative element in the gable.

Overall, the bungalow cottage gave up the fluidity of horizontal movement in the layered gables of the bungalow for a compact form of simple and direct geometry. The form is lively, owing to the mix of motifs, yet the structure is solid,

DORMER

1/2 STORY

BAY ON ELEVATION SIDE ELEVATION

even reserved. Siting was usually a modest setback, so that the sweep of the roof and the big gable of the sides could be appreciated. A six- to eight-room house, the bungalow cottage came to be a staple of neighborhoods across the country from 1910 to 1940.

WINDOWS:
 BAY ON ELEVATION

PORCH:
 VARIETY OF BUNGALOW TREATMENTS

DOOR:
 PANEL AND GLASS, CRAFTSMAN

WALL:
 BRACKETS, EXPOSED RAFTERS, FOUNDATION MATERIAL DISTINCTIVE, TWO-TONE EFFECT FROM 1ST TO 2ND FLOOR

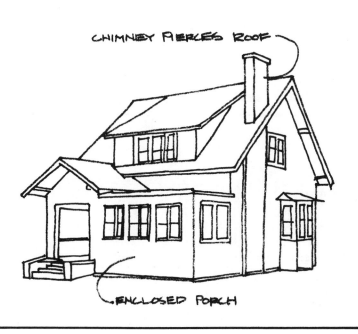

CHIMNEY PIERCES ROOF

ENCLOSED PORCH

CLIPPED GABLE

PORTICO

PAIRED WINDOWS
SYMMETRICALLY
PLACED

WATER TABLE

TYPICAL FAÇADE

PEDIMENTED BUNGALOW

CHARACTERISTICS
SMALL 1 STORY,
BROAD FRONT
EFFECT MAKES
IT LOOK LARGER
THAN IT IS
OFTEN HAD:

LOW ROOF
PARALLEL TO
STREET,
CLIPPED GABLE.

CHIMNEY,
PAIRED WINDOWS,
SMALL PORCH
WITH PEDIMENT
AND COLUMNS,
WATER TABLE

DURING THE 1920s ANOTHER VERSION OF THE BUN-galow began to appear. It was a five- or six-room house that had an intersecting gable roof, with the first gable parallel to the street, covering the two front rooms, and the second roof perpendicular to the street, covering the remaining rooms. Whatever the motif, the façade had an entrance pediment. In some cases the porch was small and served the entrance door with a hood or a small portico. Other versions extended the porch across the façade, with a pediment marking the entrance. Pediments were triangular or curvilinear. Pergolas were also used as a porch covering, and the pediment and pergola were joined. Occasionally the pergola would extend beyond the porch to become a porte-cochere.

While the majority of these houses was finished with clapboard, some had stucco or cement with pebble dash. Façade window treatments included cottage types, paired windows, French doors opening onto a porch or terrace, and bay windows. End-wall chimneys and side porches were also featured on these vaguely colonial bungalows.

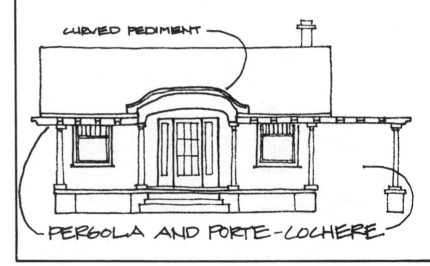

CURVED PEDIMENT

PERGOLA AND PORTE-COCHERE

2ND-STORY SECTION

MULTIPLE GABLES

GABLE MOTIF

TYPICAL FAÇADE

AIRPLANE BUNGALOW

THE *AIRPLANE BUNGALOW* IS ANOTHER TYPE
that emerged during the 1920s. The appellation "airplane"
seems to have been applied after this style appeared on the
market. This type was an attempt—modest at first—to extend the bungalow on the horizontal and accent the vertical.
The low gable roof forms are the key to the design. The gables are contiguous and successive as in other structures, but
the massing of roofs is quite different. Not only are roofs
built so that they grow out of each other on the façade, but
gables abut the main roof on the side elevations. Smaller
gables cover the second-floor sections. This kind of house
looks accretive, in that sections could have been added arbi-
trarily to the base structure, but that is not the case. All the
roof and frame sections are tightly integrated, and there is
nothing accidental about the design.

On plan, the airplane reflects the jigs and jogs in the
walls, and since these bungalows are larger than traditional
ones, a hallway appears on some plans. Nevertheless, most
of the interior spaces are open plan in organization.

Special exterior features of the airplane include thick, battered piers and porch columns, exposed purlins and rafters,
and combinations of claddings and gable motifs. The proportion of window to wall area is quite high, and windows
are grouped in imaginative combinations such as bands,
doubles, and triples, with wide cottage windows. Porches are
extensively developed and include multiple interior and exterior accesses to porch areas. In summary, the airplane
bungalow is a wide, sweeping, dynamic house that was
more successful in warm climates than in cold ones.

CHARACTERISTICS
1 STORY AND A
PARTIAL 2ND STORY
FOR BEDROOMS,
SUN PORCH,
SLEEPING PORCH,
BUNGALOW
CHARACTERISTICS,
BROAD HORIZONTAL
LINES
OFTEN HAD:
   LOW PITCHED
   GABLE ROOFS,
   OVERHANGING
   EAVES,
   GREAT PROPORTION
   OF WINDOWS TO
   WALL (COTTAGE,
   PAIRED, TRIPLE
   WINDOWS),
   LARGE DEEP
   PORCH ON 2 SIDES

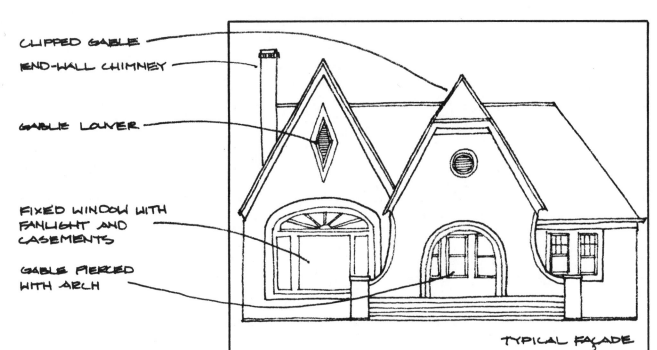

CLIPPED GABLE
END-WALL CHIMNEY
GABLE LOUVER
FIXED WINDOW WITH FANLIGHT AND CASEMENTS
GABLE PIERCED WITH ARCH

TYPICAL FAÇADE

ENGLISH BUNGALOW

DURING THE 1920s AND 1930s MANY BUILDERS turned to an alternative bungalow design, the *English bungalow*. The planes suggested by low gables were filled in, so solid walls were tied to the gables. The open gable gave way to mass in receding planes. The result was a compact brick or stucco house with successive gables and different motifs on each gable wall. The English bungalow included from one to three gables, a terrace usually on the street side, and an end-wall fireplace chimney. Gables were steep but not broad; one raking cornice of the gable often descended far below the wall line, even to ground level. Some gables served as screens behind which the entrance door was set, parallel to the street and hidden from view. Other features included varied window placement and size, combinations of cladding, a combination of roof forms (a hip on one end and clipped gable on the other), decorative louvers in the gables, arches, ornamental brickwork, and shingled roofs. All this produced a cozy five- or six-room house whose façade could look different from that of its neighbors.

CHARACTERISTICS

I STORY,
I OR 2 GABLES FACE STREET,
EACH GABLE ON A DIFFERENT PLANE

OFTEN HAD:

BRICK OR STUCCO CLADDING,
STEEPLY PITCHED INTERSECTING GABLES,
CLIPPED GABLE OR HIPPED ROOF,
GABLE CARRIED TO GROUND,
GABLE PIERCED WITH RECTANGLE OR ARCHED OPENING,
PAIRED OR TRIPLE WINDOWS,
DOOR NOT VISIBLE FROM STREET

ORNAMENTAL BRICKWORK

TERRACE

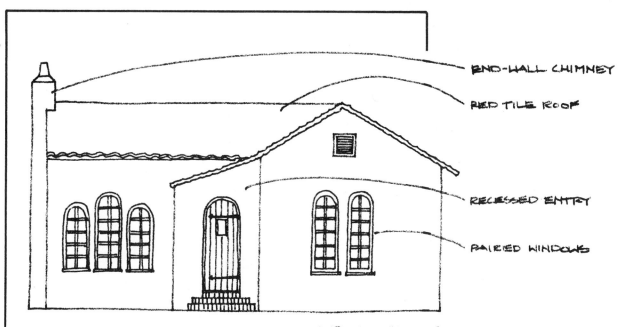

END-WALL CHIMNEY

RED TILE ROOF

RECESSED ENTRY

PAIRED WINDOWS

TYPICAL FAÇADE

SPANISH BUNGALOW

THE *SPANISH BUNGALOW*—LIKE SO MANY VARIA-
tions on the bungalow theme—developed after 1910. Geo-
graphically, it emerged in California, the southwest, and
Florida. Examples of the style may be found in other sections of the country, but they are not as numerous as in the
Sunbelt climates. Throughout its development the bungalow
has lent itself to the imposition of fronts on a basic plan.
The Spanish bungalow is related to the English style, in
that a gable plays an important role in façade design. The
gable may be triangular or curvilinear, and the gable portion often projects in front of the main body of the house.
Beyond this single gable, arches or even arcades organize
other sections of the façade.

In shape the Spanish bungalow is more rectangular than
other types. Terraces extend interior space, but generally the
form is more compact, and one is more aware of mass than
is usual in bungalows. The walls—usually stucco, although
painted cement was popular—play a large role in design. In
Spanish colonial examples the walls are planar. In south-
western types they are monolithic and sculptural. Indeed,
some of these designs appear to be blocks from which
arches, openings for fenestration, and the like have been
carved. Detailing follows a general Spanish vocabulary,
although Spanish colonial motifs proliferate, including exposed wood (especially the Spanish rafter, the *viga*),
wrought iron, red roofing tiles, terra cotta ornament, decorative columns, and polychromy.

Although the Spanish bungalow was often an eclectic design, there are examples of purer forms. For example, in
New Mexico there are pueblo styles—adobe houses in which
ornament is secondary, and natural materials and sculptural, somewhat organic forms predominate.

CHARACTERISTICS
1 STORY,
STUCCO
OFTEN HAD:
    LOW PITCHED
    RED TILE ROOF,
    END-WALL
    CHIMNEY,
    1 GABLE FACING
    THE STREET,
    ROUND-HEADED
    MULTIPANE,
    PAIRED OR TRIPLE
    WINDOWS ON
    FAÇADE,
    SMALL PORCH
    AND ADJOINING
    TERRACE,
    ROUND-HEADED
    V-JOINT DOOR,
    ROUND-HEADED
    OPENINGS,
    EXPOSED WOOD,
    IRONWORK

TWO FAMILY: SUBURBAN

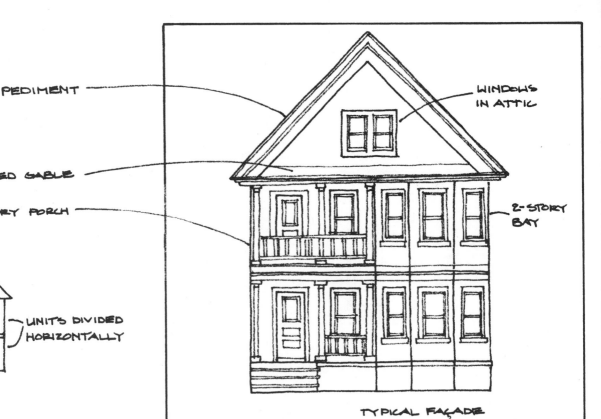

PEDIMENT

CLOSED GABLE

2-STORY PORCH

WINDOWS IN ATTIC

2-STORY BAY

UNITS DIVIDED HORIZONTALLY

TYPICAL FAÇADE

TWO-FAMILY SUBURBAN

DESIGN OF THE *TWO-FAMILY HOUSE* FOLLOWED design developments in cottages. The suburban two-family cottage employed large-scale geometric elements, such as a broad gable roof and a two-story, three-sided bay window that was answered by the formal porches. The façade divided into two "columns," the bay and the porches, topped by a pediment. Subsequent breakdowns of the large forms included five vertical bays—three in the bay window and two in the porch section—and a pair of centered windows in the gable that divided on center, making each side a mirror image of the other. Horizontal divisions were at the water table, the floor line between stories, and the cornice that closed the gable. The windows were placed at the same distance from the floor and ceiling on both levels, so that they looked like a band of evenly spaced windows. The massing of elements on the façade relied on the push-pull balance between the projecting bay window and the recessed porches. The porches were detailed with columns and open rails that helped activate the surface and provided opportunity for the play of light and shadow.

The two-family cottage, although not as ornamented as the single-family, was not without turned and sawn materials or Palladian windows or the columns and entablatures of classical treatments.

The two-family cottage suburban had an advantage over the double house in that it provided light on all sides and cross-ventilation. Both types were often built in the close-in suburbs, and many were grouped so as to generate their own streetscape and urbanism.

CHARACTERISTICS
UNITS SEPARATED HORIZONTALLY, SIDE HALL PLAN
OFTEN HAD:
CLAPBOARD OR SHINGLE CLADDING,
CLOSED GABLE PERPENDICULAR TO STREET,
PENT ROOF,
DECORATIVE SHINGLES IN GABLE,
WINDOWS IN ATTIC,
2-STORY BAY WINDOW ON FAÇADE,
PORCH ON BOTH LEVELS

HIP ROOF

DORMER

2-STORY BAY

STACKED PILASTER AND COLUMN

BAY WINDOW

UNITS SEPARATED HORIZONTALLY

TYPICAL FAÇADE

TWO-FAMILY HIPPED COTTAGE

THE *HIPPED COTTAGE TWO-FAMILY HOUSE* HAS some of the characteristics of the suburban type, in that the façade is classical and access to the second floor is through a side-hall stair. The organization of the façade also relies on the kind of classical design vocabulary used in colonial revival buildings. Both floors have an order of architecture, with the first-story columns under the second-floor pilasters. The second-floor entablature carries a fascia board around the house. The wide hip roof understates the temple front. The façade is divided into a large panel with two lights on the second story and a five-part composition on the first: entrance, three-sided bay window capped by a three-sided balustrade, and entrance. Overall, the façade has a horizontal emphasis that is echoed in the side elevations, which are long and broken only by a bay window on one side. The house is twice as long as it is wide.

The façade illustrated has another interesting cottage feature: it is quite distinctive in that it breaks the whole down into parts. The entrances, for instance, separate from each other; there is some ambiguity as to where they go. Except for the bay window, this façade might have been used on a double house. Despite this tendency to pull things apart, the design is still cohesive, and fits within the general design scheme of neighborhood cottages.

CHARACTERISTICS

2 STORIES,
SIDE HALL PLAN
OFTEN HAD:
CLAPBOARD
CLADDING,
HIP ROOF WITH
CENTRAL
DORMER,
2-STORY BAY
ON SIDE
ELEVATION,
1/1 DOUBLE-
HUNG WINDOWS,
SHALLOW PORCH
WITH COLUMNS
AND
ENTABLATURE

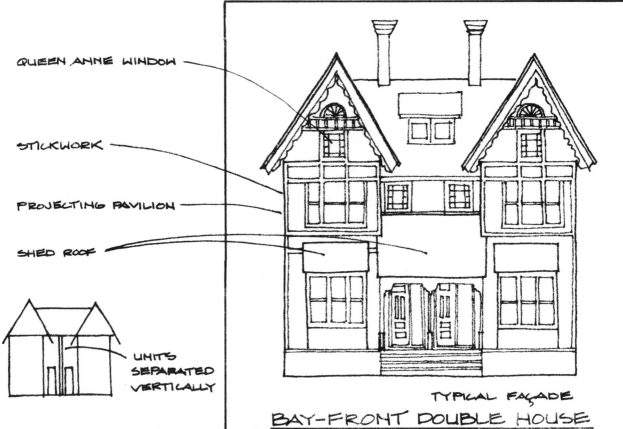

QUEEN ANNE WINDOW

STICKWORK

PROJECTING PAVILION

SHED ROOF

UNITS SEPARATED VERTICALLY

TYPICAL FAÇADE
BAY-FRONT DOUBLE HOUSE

CHARACTERISTICS
UNITS SEPARATED VERTICALLY (SIDE BY SIDE), SIDE HALL PLAN OFTEN HAD:

BRICK CLADDING, MULTIPLE ROOF FORMS, GABLE ORNAMENT, SYMMETRICAL FENESTRATION, 1/1 DOUBLE-HUNG WINDOWS, TURNED POSTS AND BRACKETS, STICKWORK DIVIDING WALLS INTO PANELS, ITALIANATE DETAILING

THE *BAY-FRONT DOUBLE HOUSE*, PRIMARILY A nineteenth-century building, was a two- or three-story structure with several roof options: a mansard roof, a gable roof with the ridge parallel to the street, or a flat roof and accompanying parapet. The primary design scheme required a full-height, usually three-sided bay window or pavilion on each end that flanked a double entrance. The bays terminated in their own roofs. Dormers were frequently built on these units to utilize attic space, especially on those with mansard roofs.

Stylistically, the bay-front was a side-hall-plan building with Italianate or picturesque detailing: pronounced lintels and sills, segmental arches or full-window surrounds with keystones, heavy brackets at the cornice line, an occasional wrought-iron balustrade or cresting, and a gable finish. The entrance system was often a steep stair leading to a small porch, or to a wider porch with its own roof and cottage-type roof supports. A number of these buildings had high foundations with almost full-size windows, implying that the basement level was living space. Those with high foundations wrapped the building with a water table.

The bay-fronts were often city buildings constructed individually or in clusters. They depended on their wide, tall bays and their roof lines for design focus. They were formidable when aligned with the same setback on both sides of a street. Bay-front double houses provided a broad, dense, yet rhythmic façade that suggested something about the difference between urban and suburban living.

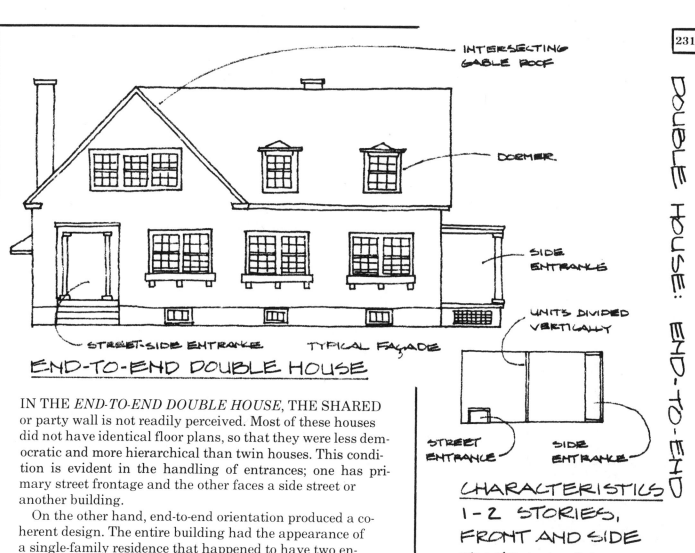

INTERSECTING GABLE ROOF

DORMER

SIDE ENTRANCE

UNITS DIVIDED VERTICALLY

STREET-SIDE ENTRANCE   TYPICAL FAÇADE

STREET ENTRANCE   SIDE ENTRANCE

END-TO-END DOUBLE HOUSE

IN THE *END-TO-END DOUBLE HOUSE*, THE SHARED or party wall is not readily perceived. Most of these houses did not have identical floor plans, so that they were less democratic and more hierarchical than twin houses. This condition is evident in the handling of entrances; one has primary street frontage and the other faces a side street or another building.

On the other hand, end-to-end orientation produced a coherent design. The entire building had the appearance of a single-family residence that happened to have two entrances. As such, it fit well into neighborhood settings.

Most end-to-end double houses were built in the twentieth century, and most were one- or one-and-a-half-story buildings. The bungalow was the primary form employed to create this kind of house. The use of materials and ornamentation followed the same patterns as established in the detached, single-family models of these structures. Fenestration was calculated to provide as equal lighting as possible so that symmetry, with variety in groupings, predominated.

CHARACTERISTICS

1-2 STORIES, FRONT AND SIDE ENTRANCES

OFTEN HAD:

BRICK OR CLAPBOARD SIDING, INTERSECTING GABLE, GAMBREL, OR LOW HIP ROOF, SMALL ENTRY PORCH ON STREET SIDE, PORCH ON SIDE, SYMMETRICAL FENESTRATION, DORMERS

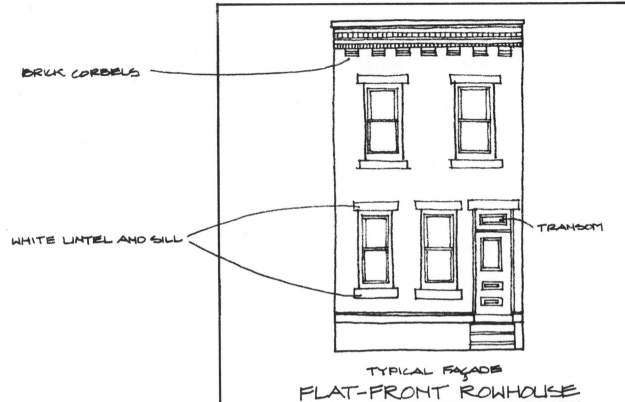

BRICK CORBELS

WHITE LINTEL AND SILL

TRANSOM

TYPICAL FAÇADE
FLAT-FRONT ROWHOUSE

CHARACTERISTICS
2 STORIES,
2- OR 3-BAY
ORGANIZATION,
NARROW,
BRICK
OFTEN HAD:
FLAT ROOF OR
VERY LOW
GABLE ROOF,
FLAT OR
SEGMENTAL
LINTELS,
1/1 MAJOR
WINDOW PATTERN
SOMETIMES:
CORNICE
DETAILING,
CORBELING,
SINGLE COTTAGE
WINDOW ON
GROUND LEVEL,
DORMER
ON ROOF

THE *FLAT-FRONT ROWHOUSE* IS THE OLDER OF THE two types in this section, predating the Civil War. After the war it was both an Italianate and a more generally classical house. Little attention was given to detail, and organization was kept simple—three bays on the ground level and two or three bays on the second level. The flat or gable roof carried back over the three rooms of each floor. Some houses had a kitchen or pantry space behind the last room, with its own shed roof.

On the façade the cornice, lintel, and sill lines—and the water table, if any—were opportunities for horizontal alignment. The cornice could be bracketed at the corners or across the cornice. The lintels and sills were brick, stone, or cement, and segmented or flat lintels and sills were often a high-contrast color such as white. By the twentieth century there were brick rowhouses with terra cotta ornament.

The flat-front rowhouse had a significant effect on many cities. The houses were inexpensive to build, and the scale was right for a quick buildup of city streets. For cultural or economic reasons, rowhouse districts tended to separate from other districts, so that in time they evolved their own style of living. Rowhouses could be adapted to local uses such as services or shops.

In some cases the rowhouse was an urban *shotgun*—a narrow two-story box—while in others it had a finely wrought front, a bay window on the front and back with quality features. Despite the fact that the flat-front rowhouse was usually built for mass consumption, it was capable of a wide range of applications.

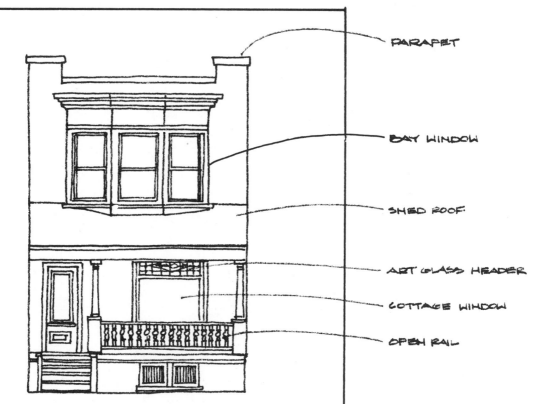

PARAPET

BAY WINDOW

SHED ROOF

ART GLASS HEADER

COTTAGE WINDOW

OPEN RAIL

TYPICAL FAÇADE
BAY-FRONT ROWHOUSE

THE *BAY-FRONT ROWHOUSE* WAS ONE OF THE LAST editions of this universal city house. Later nineteenth-century and early twentieth-century builders looked for ways to address the narrow façade. Most frequently they extended the house by means of a porch replacing the traditional stoop, and compressed the upper level with a three-sided oriel window. There were other variations in the window treatment on the second floor, but most motifs involved replacing the sash windows with an alternative form.

These developments evolved the house into a higher state—the so-called "swell front." The porch added formality or picturesque qualities to a house that had known modest formal organization and none of the picturesque. The bay window pulled the façade design toward the center—a direction with which it had not experimented before. The porch broadened the façade and pulled the interior back slightly from the street. To understand an entire rowhouse scheme, the spectator needs to draw back and view an entire block; then the rhythm of the repeated forms and elements becomes evident. The rowhouse gains design strength from association with its neighbors.

CHARACTERISTICS
2 STORIES,
BRICK
OFTEN HAD:
FLAT ROOF,
PARAPET OR
WIDE CORNICE,
BAY WINDOW
THAT SITS ON
SHED PORCH
ROOF,
SINGLE COTTAGE
WINDOW ON
1ST FLOOR,
PORCH WITH
COLUMNS AND
PEDESTALS
AND OPEN RAIL
SOMETIMES:
STONE
CLADDING,
ART GLASS
HEADER IN
COTTAGE
WINDOW

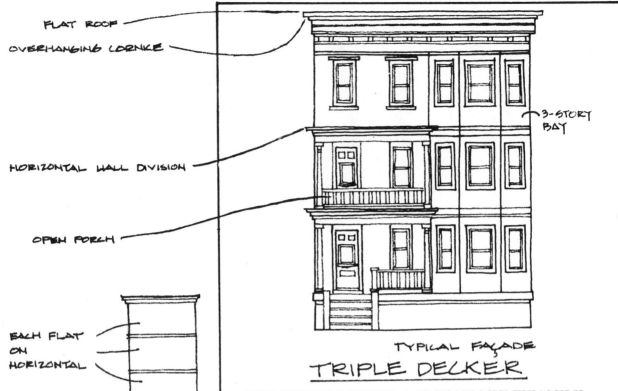

FLAT ROOF

OVERHANGING CORNICE

HORIZONTAL WALL DIVISION

OPEN PORCH

3-STORY BAY

EACH FLAT ON HORIZONTAL

TYPICAL FAÇADE

TRIPLE DECKER

CHARACTERISTICS

1 OR 2 3-STORY FRONT BAYS, SOMETIMES 3-STORY SIDE BAYS

OFTEN HAD:
CLAPBOARD CLADDING, FLAT ROOF, OVERHANGING CORNICE, REAR PORCHES, HORIZONTAL DIVISION OF WALLS

SOMETIMES HAD:
GABLE ROOF, OPEN PORCHES ON FRONT

THE *TRIPLE DECKER*, A UNIQUE MULTIFAMILY structure, originated in New England mill towns and cities. Constructed from about 1870 to 1920, the triple decker, could absorb cottage details even though it had outgrown the cottage scale. Most were long, rectangular buildings with the narrow side toward the street that provided three living spaces, one family to a floor. Most stacked one unit over the next, and ground-level motifs were repeated throughout an elevation. The main entrance, which might have an entrance porch, was on one side of the façade. Bay windows were common on either the façade or a side elevation. Roof treatments included flat roofs with an overhanging cornice, and gable-to-the-street roofs with a closed gable. Regardless of the façade porch treatment, most of these buildings had rear-access porches on all three levels.

There were several basic compositions for the façades. One type turned the corner into a tower that was round or three-sided; another utilized a single bay window and a flat section, or two bay windows flanking a central entrance; and still another stacked façade-wide open-railing porches that culminated in a pedimented gable. In general, detailing seemed to diminish in the triple decker, yet it was not without ornament: heavy cornices; porches with columns; elevations with horizontal divisions by means of trim boards that cut walls into panels, belt courses, or continuous sills or lintels; and overhanging eaves.

The triple decker was a clapboard or shingle building that provided the most multifamily living in a single-family context of all the multifamily types. Triple deckers were rarely elegant, but they were substantial, well-organized buildings that propelled the cottage design vocabulary into a less picturesque urban world.

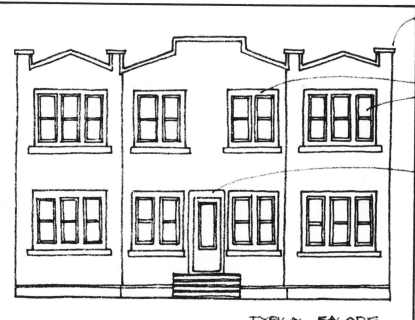

FLAT ROOF WITH PARAPET

DOUBLE AND TRIPLE WINDOWS

CENTRAL ENTRANCE

BAYS PROJECT PAST MAIN BUILDING

TYPICAL FAÇADE

FOUR-FAMILY BAY-FRONT

THE *FOUR-FAMILY HOUSE* IS THE LARGEST MULTI-family or apartment building to be discussed in this section. The *bay-front* type of "flats" building was a two-story rectangular structure. It combined the twin house and the two-family house, in that each side was often a mirror image of the other, but the four-family had two families per floor, each family having four or five rooms, a kitchen, and a bath.

Façade composition was the major statement with two kinds of organization: two bay windows, two stories in height, flanked a center section, or each corner had a projecting pavilion that was one room deep and one room wide, with a setback in the middle. Bays were rounded or three-sided. The center portion could be flat with some ornament around the entrance door, or an entrance porch might bridge the entire center. Porches were usually not very elaborate. The nonporch entrance generally had a decorative lintel, sidelights, or ornamental brickwork. In the projecting-pavilion type the setback was often a terrace and included plantings.

Fenestration was symmetrical, with both bays and pavilions adding more windows and light than usual to the façade. Roof composition included flat roofs with a parapet or gable, and clipped gable roofs on pavilions or bays with a flat or gable over the main body, possibly even a mansard or a large hip roof. Other details were stucco and half-timber stickwork, corbeling, roof eaves with dentils or brackets, walls with shingles or clapboard siding, and decorative sills or lintels.

These multifamily units increased population density while maintaining neighborhood scale. Each "house" often served as a starter for the incoming city population; residents enjoyed the same amenities of neighborhood living, with access to work and services, as single-family units.

CHARACTERISTICS
2 STORY,
EACH FLAT ON HORIZONTAL,
CENTRAL ENTRANCE FLANKED BY BAYS OR PAVILIONS
OFTEN HAD:
FLAT OR INTERSECTING GABLE ROOF,
MULTIPLE WINDOW GROUPINGS,
1/1 MAJOR WINDOW PATTERN,
LATERAL DIVISIONS OF FAÇADE WALL

BALLUSTRADE

QUOINS

BALCONY

2-STORY PORTICO

PORTICO PROJECTS FROM BUILDING

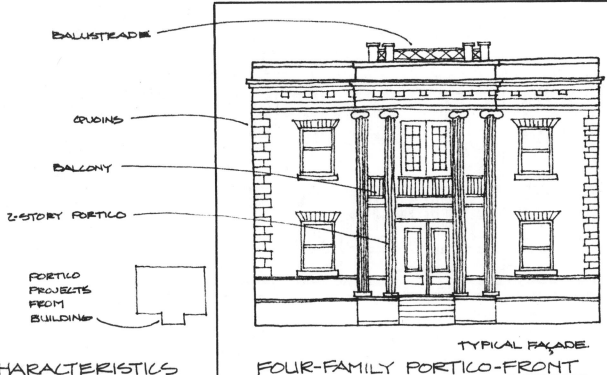

TYPICAL FAÇADE.

FOUR-FAMILY PORTICO-FRONT

CHARACTERISTICS
2 STORIES,
LARGE 2-STORY
PROJECTING
PORTICO
OFTEN HAD:
BRICK CLADDING,
FLAT ROOF WITH
WIDE CORNICE
AND PARAPET,
TWIN BAYS ON
FRONT,
1ST-FLOOR
PORCH,
2ND-FLOOR
BALCONY,
4 COLUMNS,
VARIED ORDERS,
CENTRAL
ENTRANCE

STYLISTICALLY, THE *PORTICO-FRONT* WAS THE most deliberately historical of the four-family types. The portico itself was the dominant feature, being invariably two stories in height and carrying an entablature. The orders of architecture were varied, including Doric, Tuscan, Ionic, and Corinthian. The large portico was attached to flat-front buildings or set between flanking bays or pavilions. Portico composition included four columns evenly spaced or paired, with a wide center space for the entrance; most columns sat on blocks on a shallow porch. The second-floor porch was usually railed and served as a balcony for second-floor residents. The entablature was full but usually eclectic, using moldings and ornament not true to the order. Plain architraves and friezes were popular, and the cornice line carried dentils and projected from the entablature. Some moldings and the entire cornice were often carried around the building. Some of these fronts placed a low pediment on center, in line with the entrance, as a gesture toward the full temple front. Entablatures without a pediment substituted a balustrade.

To enhance the portico on the front, more elaborate designs might place a pilaster behind each column, use quoins on the corners, place decorative lintels or sills on the façade, or employ a water table, rustication, and ornament around the entrance door. The remainder of the design was in the same mode as the bay-front building. Ironically, the portico-front extended colonial and classical revival design vocabularies to buildings more in scale with classical buildings than were most cottages, creating what might be called a colonial-Roman look. In any event, they dressed an urban building and encouraged a particular kind of urbanity.

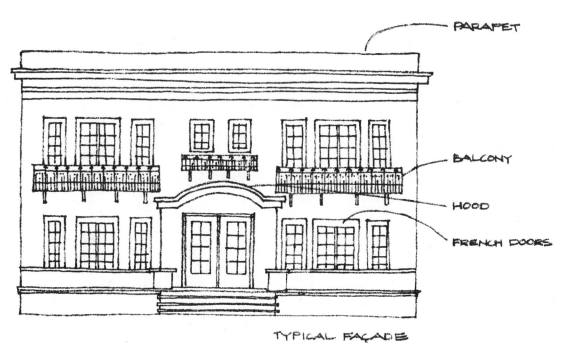

PARAPET

BALCONY

HOOD

FRENCH DOORS

TYPICAL FAÇADE

FOUR-FAMILY VILLA

THE *VILLA* STYLE OF BUILDING WAS THE LAST IN the hipped cottage line. It had a well-organized façade derived from the Italian and Spanish-style villa in single-family houses. The walls were greatly influenced by the symmetrical fenestration and the central entrance, which led to a long vestibule. The roof forms were either flat across the entire structure, or had a gable parallel to the street with corner pediments on the front section and a flat roof on the remainder. Floor plans in the villas were similar to the other types—four- or five-room flats, side by side.

In design these structures seemed to compensate greatly for having a windowless wall: the number of windows and the variety of window size and shape increased greatly. Window types included French doors to a balcony, fixed windows of cottage size, paired and triple windows, and the odd single window used to light a special-purpose space like the bath.

The entrance received attention: it might have an arch, a canopy, a pediment, or an elaborate hood to note its location and set a tone for the façade. Gable roofs often had brightly colored clay tiles, and flat roofs might have a parapet or cornice around the entire building. Surface treatments were usually brick or stucco on frame, hollow tile, block, or concrete walls. Some of the villas had entrance porches or terraces on the ground level.

Since the villa style echoed single-family design, it did not intrude on neighborhoods. With its general Mediterranean flavor, it opened the neighborhood design dialogue, or perhaps ended it, because the Italian and Spanish types began to fade after 1940.

CHARACTERISTICS

2 STORIES, RECTANGULAR SHAPE, RELATIVELY FLAT FRONT

OFTEN HAD:

BRICK WALLS, FLAT ROOF WITH PARAPET OR GABLE ROOF WITH TILE, FRENCH DOORS, MULTIPLE WINDOW GROUPINGS, ENTRANCE WITH ARCH, CANOPY, PEDIMENT, OR HOOD

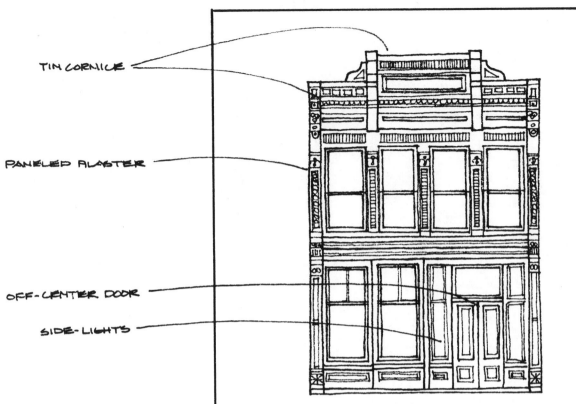

TIN CORNICE

PANELED PILASTER

OFF-CENTER DOOR

SIDE-LIGHTS

TYPICAL FAÇADE
IRON-FRONT

CHARACTERISTICS

1-3 STORIES,
3-5-BAY
ORGANIZATION,
CLASSICAL
DETAILING
OFTEN HAD:
BRICK AND
IRON CLADDING,
FLAT ROOF
WITH PARAPET,
4 COLUMNS,
DECORATIVE
PILASTERS
SOMETIMES:
ENTRANCE
OFF-CENTER
OR RECESSED

THE *IRON-FRONT* STORE WAS BUILT IN ALL GEO-graphical areas, the technology needed to produce iron architectural materials being almost as transportable as the materials. The mold makers had a predilection for classical details, so that most iron-front stores have at least a pair of plain pilasters at the corners or a set of stacked half columns with an entablature. Ironwork was integrated with pressed or stamped tinwork. While the iron posts and beams framed the façade, tin pieces were used for lintels or surrounds around the windows and for the large, bracketed, molding-heavy cornice. All metal pieces were painted to prevent rust.

The iron-front shown represents a page from the Mesker & Brothers catalog of 1881. While more fanciful than what most builders or owners chose to buy, the work illustrates the design concept. The ground level has a straightforward design with corner pilasters framing the display windows and entrance. On the second level, iron pilasters with ornamental panels divide the façade into four equal bays, and the entire structure is topped off with a series of moldings and fascia culminating in the bracketed sign band. The heavy use of ornament on the upper level and the elaborate cornice were to convince the owner that the textured wall and the distinctive profile would identify the store. Iron-front classical-motif stores lost popularity in the twentieth century, but the order, occasional elegance, and rich tapestry they gave to districts—especially those near the rails and rivers—were significant.

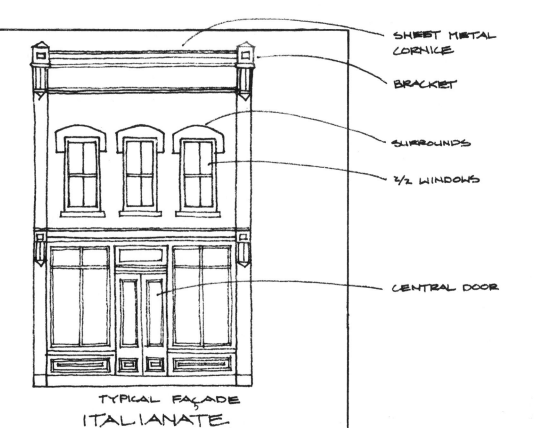

SHEET METAL CORNICE

BRACKET

SURROUNDS

2/2 WINDOWS

CENTRAL DOOR

TYPICAL FAÇADE
ITALIANATE

IN THE ITALIANATE STOREFRONT/POPULAR DURing the 1870s and 1880s, the window treatment (which included the shape and size of the window and the lintel or sill), the cornice line, and the corners of the building offered the most opportunities for detail from the limited design possibilities. Windows were generally long and narrow, and lintels and sills were of metal, brick, stone, or cement. Lintels were visually heavy units, segmented or rounded. Metal pieces had ornamented surfaces. The cornice was most often metal and had an entablature organization—architrave, frieze, and cornice—with heavy brackets at the corners and lighter, perhaps paired, brackets across the cornice. Façade designs that divided the first floor from the second had an ornamented beam or surface moldings that capped the display windows. The corners of buildings could be quoined in brick or stone, or pilasters or half columns might mark the edges and frame the lower level. It was also common to stack the upright elements on top of one another.

Italianate detailing could be accomplished through brick, iron-front, or wood construction, and the material affected the use of detail. Wood and metal offered the best opportunities for ornament. Brickwork tended to be limited to the cornice, although segmented lintels were popular. Other details included decorative anchor irons, rosettes or other floral motifs, and elaborate capitals on the pilasters. In the evolution of commercial fronts, the Italianate was one of the first successful historic styles built from manufactured materials. It set a precedent and a design standard that is still evident in the great number of Italianate upper stories in business districts throughout the country.

CHARACTERISTICS
2-3 STORIES
OFTEN HAD:
BRICK CLADDING OR IRON FRONT, FLAT ROOF, DECORATIVE CORNICE OF WOOD, BRICK, SHEET METAL, TALL NARROW WINDOWS WITH SEGMENTAL ARCH, MASONRY OR STAMPED METAL SURROUNDS, LINTELS, AND SILLS, DECORATIVE PILASTERS

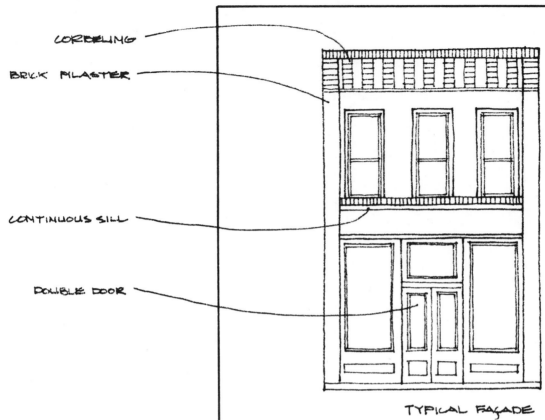

CORBELING

BRICK PILASTER

CONTINUOUS SILL

DOUBLE DOOR

TYPICAL FAÇADE
BRICK-FRONT

CHARACTERISTICS
**1-3 STORIES,
3-5-BAY
ORGANIZATION
CLADDING:
BRICK
ROOF:
FLAT WITH
PARAPET
CORNICE:
TIN BRACKETS,
DENTILS,
MOLDINGS,
PEDIMENTS
BRICKWORK-
CORBELING,
DENTILS,
GEOMETRIC
PATTERNS
FRIEZE:
DECORATIVE
BRICKWORK**

THE *BRICK-FRONT* STORE WAS BUILT AS A SINGLE building or in groups with party walls up to a block in length. In vernacular design, it was the most popular storefront for the longest time. Such buildings varied in height from one to three stories, but their plans were quite similar. Two- and three-story structures had ground-level store facilities, with storage or an apartment living space on the second or third floor. Access was from the street through a separate entrance or through the store. Single-story buildings offered no space for store owners or renters to live in, and they were not often built alone, but rather as a series of stores along a portion of a block tied together by cornices or other horizontal elements.

Brick-front organization resulted from the interaction of elements on the grid that underscored the front. Display space was conventional, whether the entrance was on- or off-center. The large windows framed by the building's corners and the panel of brick between floors dominated the lower level. These stores were often narrow and deep, and the windows were a source of light as well as an invitation to inspect goods. The upper levels had more options, including single or double oriel windows, panels of brickwork, brick friezes and cornices featuring corbeled or otherwise arranged brick, tin cornices with elaborate patterns, parapet walls of various profiles, decorative lintels or sills (especially continuous types that linked windows), and string courses or sections of belt courses that divided the wall laterally.

Despite the breadth of these choices, much of the façade's design centered on the overall framing of the shape: the structural system, post and beam, as suggested by the edges; the large lateral panels; and the cornice. The cornice functioned as a cap under which other elements were arranged and balanced. Most design systems, therefore, were a blend of large elements and more delicate detailing. This was still true when the brick-front was expanded to five or six bays.

WINDOWS:
DISPLAY WINDOWS WITH TRANSOMS, SOMETIMES ROUND-HEADED WINDOWS, SOMETIMES CANTED ORIELS ON 2ND FLOOR, SEGMENTAL LINTELS AND PEDIMENTS COMMON, CONTINUOUS LINTELS AND SILLS

ENTRANCE:
RECESSED, SINGLE OR DOUBLE PANEL AND GLASS DOORS

WALLS:
PILASTERS, STRING COURSES, RECESSED BRICK PANELS, PARTY WALLS BETWEEN BUILDINGS

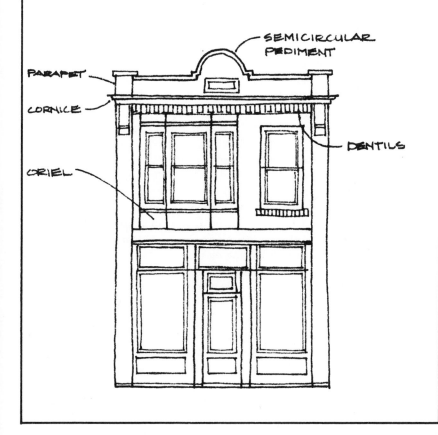

SEMICIRCULAR PEDIMENT

PARAPET

CORNICE

ORIEL

DENTILS

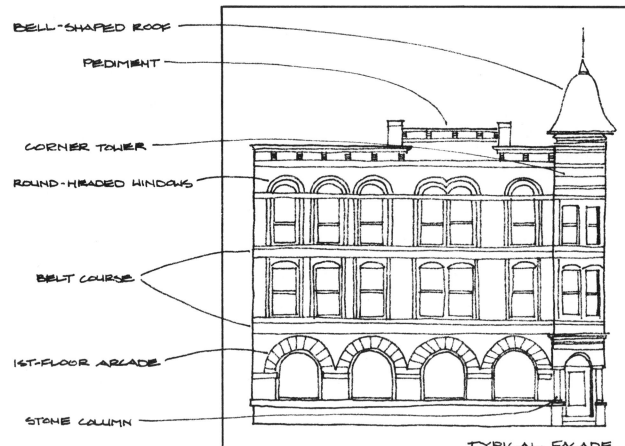

BELL-SHAPED ROOF

PEDIMENT

CORNER TOWER

ROUND-HEADED WINDOWS

BELT COURSE

1ST-FLOOR ARCADE

STONE COLUMN

TYPICAL FAÇADE

ARCADED BLOCK

CHARACTERISTICS
2-4 STORIES,
CORNER BUILDING
CLADDING:
  BRICK
ROOF:
  FLAT WITH
  PARAPET
CORNER
TREATMENTS:
  TOWER, OFTEN
  WITH SPIRE OR
  CANTED CORNER
  ENTRANCE

FROM THE LAST QUARTER OF THE NINETEENTH century right down to the present, much attention has been paid to the corner commercial building, particularly one marking the edge or the heart of a business district. The *arcaded block* was just such a building. It was intended to be an imposing building with a strong overall shape, solid massing, and firm lines on both its elevations. It was rarely uniform in size, for one elevation was often larger than the other, and one might have been designed somewhat differently from the other. As a corner property, the arcaded business block had a rich design vocabulary stemming from the history of business-block development after the Civil War and the introduction of a new sensibility. High-style architects such as H.H. Richardson and Louis Sullivan had demonstrated how an elevation could be integrated through the use of arches, round-headed elements, or arcades. The curvilinear elements were usually linked, which helped to break the wall away from domination by vertical bays. The new look presented windows in bands or clusters of light. This kind of design often gave a lighter feeling to portions of the wall and at the same time focused the design on the intersection of the walls. That corner often culminated in a tower that rose from a recessed or canted ground-level entrance.

Vertical accents or strict divisions of the elevations did

not disappear from business-block design. Many upright elements such as half columns or pilasters helped to organize the walls. Some of the linking between arched units took place within these vertical bays, even to the point of stacking window groups over one another.

Stylistically the arcaded block was an eclectic combination of classical and picturesque interests. The corner tower, tall chimney stacks, and occasional upper-level oriel window were cottage motifs often associated with Queen Anne design. Broad arches of stone blocks were part of the Romanesque revival vocabulary, while elaborate cornices with brackets or dentils were part of the general nineteenth-century design system.

Most arcaded blocks made distinctions between ground-level and upper level design schemes, owing in part to the location of storefronts within the block, and use of arches or arcades in the design. For example, a corner block might employ an arch that spanned each vertical bay on ground level yet broke down into paired windows on the second floor. The paired windows might be headed by a single arch or by two arches sized to the windows. In the Romanesque style, arches meeting at the corner often met on a column of stone with an alternative material like granite. Other ground-level detailing included rustication and a water table of large stone blocks.

The arcaded block was one of the strongest design statements of all vernacular building types and styles. It maintained its position in business districts throughout the 1870–1940 period. Symbolically it was a reminder of the importance of business in town and small-city life. Its scale was residential and its motifs visually related to neighborhoods. The arcaded block was an anchor for the commercial district and evidence of the power of industrially produced design materials.

CORNICE:
DECORATIVE BRICK-CORBELING, BRACKETS, DENTILS, SOMETIMES A PEDIMENT ON AN ELEVATION

FRIEZE:
DIFFERENT COLOR OR TEXTURE

WINDOWS:
1/1 DOUBLE-HUNG IN UPPER STORIES, CONTINUOUS LINTELS AND SILLS, LINTELS OF CONTRASTING COLOR

COLUMNS:
SOMETIMES PILASTERS

ENTRANCE:
IN CORNER, SOMETIMES LARGE STONE ARCH

WALLS:
ARCADED ON UPPER OR LOWER STORY

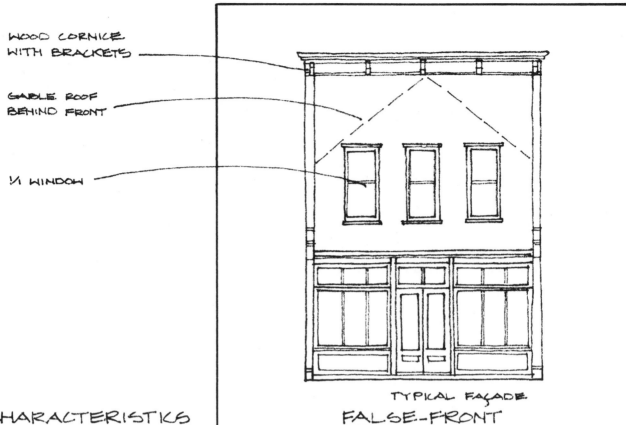

WOOD CORNICE WITH BRACKETS

GABLE ROOF BEHIND FRONT

½ WINDOW

TYPICAL FAÇADE
FALSE-FRONT

CHARACTERISTICS
1-2 STORIES,
2- OR 3-BAY
ORGANIZATION,
WOOD FRAME
CLADDING:
  CLAPBOARD,
  SOMETIMES
  BRICK OR
  BOARD AND
  BATTEN
ROOF:
  GABLE COVERS
  MAIN BUILDING,
  FRONT DOES
  NOT CONFORM
  TO ROOF
  SHAPE

THE *FALSE-FRONT* COMMERCIAL BUILDING HAS been associated with the settlement of the west, but false-front buildings were in fact built in upstate New York as well as in Iowa, Texas, Colorado, and Wyoming. The false-front has been associated with stores, and there is no doubt that the one- and two-story storefront is the most common of extant vernacular commercial buildings. This kind of building was used for services, small hotels, and as a meeting hall for social and fraternal organizations.

From a design point of view, the false-front simply extends the façade, so that the building seems larger than it is. The false portion extends the façade vertically and horizontally so that the roof over the main body—most often a gable or flat roof—remains hidden from view. The illusion was useful in suggesting an interesting profile when one could not afford to build a large enough building, or when town developers wanted to convey an image of progress and prosperity. On one-story buildings the false portion does not extend much beyond the apex of the gable; the extra section of wall provides ornamentation, with an elaborate cornice built on the front, or functions as a signboard. In most cases the false front has been integrated into the façade so that cornerboards, columns, or pilasters are carried up the front; panel divisions align with display windows below, and centered pediments align with the entrance. This integration is more evident on two-story fronts, whether they screen a half story or extend a second-story wall.

False-front commercial buildings did not create illusions

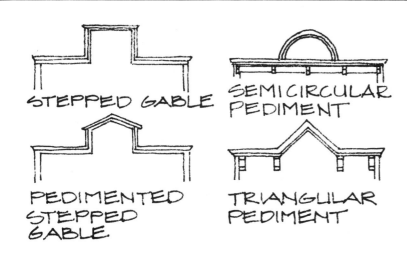

STEPPED GABLE

SEMICIRCULAR PEDIMENT

PEDIMENTED STEPPED GABLE

TRIANGULAR PEDIMENT

that fooled the citizenry but provided symbolic evidence of the general civilizing process. The fronts were orderly, partly because their lot sizes were similar , and because the design relationships among them were proportional. The stores helped to create enclosure and gave the sense of a developing center, even if the development proved transitory. The false-front often got replaced by or incorporated into brick buildings. It maintained the scale of the original town site, so that a community was momentarily held together by size, shape, and materials.

CORNICE:

BRACKETS, WOOD, BRICK, SHEET METAL TYPES - SIMPLE FLAT UNDECORATED, SEMICIRCULAR, TRIANGULAR, STEPPED GABLE

WINDOWS:

SYMMETRICAL FENESTRATION, 1/1 OR 2/2 PATTERN IN 2ND STORY

PORCH:

SOMETIMES PLAIN PORCH WITH SHED ROOF

ENTRANCE:

OFTEN RECESSED, SINGLE OR PAIRED PANEL AND GLASS DOORS

WALLS:

CORNERBOARDS

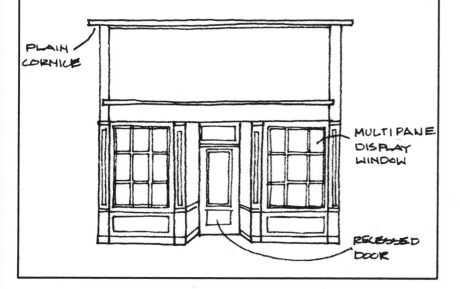

PLAIN CORNICE

MULTIPANE DISPLAY WINDOW

RECESSED DOOR

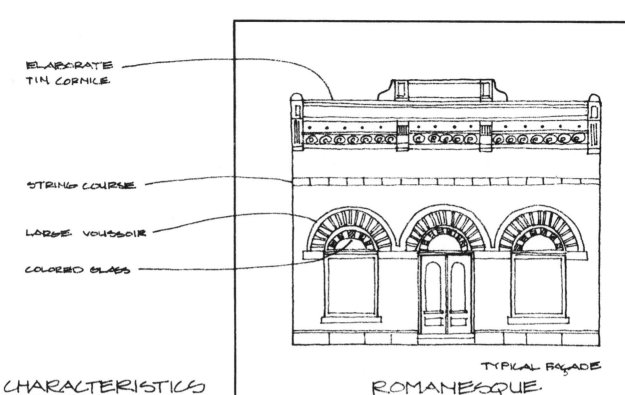

ELABORATE
TIN CORNICE

STRING COURSE

LARGE VOUSSOIR

COLORED GLASS

TYPICAL FAÇADE

ROMANESQUE

CHARACTERISTICS

1-2 STORIES IN
STONE,
2-3 STORIES IN
BRICK
OFTEN HAD:
FLAT ROOF
WITH PARAPET,
LARGE ROUND-
HEADED
WINDOWS,
LARGE LUNETTE
WINDOWS,
DEEP RECESSES
IN WALLS,
HEAVY VOUSSOIRS,
ARCADED
ENTRANCES
SOMETIMES:
ART OR
COLORED GLASS,
CANTED CORNER
ENTRANCE,
POLISHED
GRANITE
COLUMN AT
CORNER

THE *ROMANESQUE* COMMERCIAL STYLE WAS NOT as widespread as the Italianate. Nor was the style so easily accomplished in vernacular building, since it was often combined with what is now called Queen Anne detailing. The Romanesque was a picturesque mode of expression. At its most ambitious level, the vernacular Romanesque used coursed, rock-faced sandstone blocks with round-arch windows and a low, wide, arched entrance. Emphasis was on surface texture and the rhythm of the arches or arcades. Other Romanesque elements could include a corner entrance marked by a single thick granite column from which an arch sprung, and a corner tower. Romanesque buildings were also designed in stone and brick, one material serving as trim for the other, while other buildings were done entirely in brick. Brick changed the design somewhat, in that the rough surface was gone, so builders compensated with elaborate (Queen Anne) corbeled brick cornices, or brick arcades and arches with moldings surrounding the curved members. Both brick and stone buildings might have tin cornices. Fenestration varied by floor level: the first-floor windows might be larger than the second and be tied together by arches, or the second floor might use an alternative window such as a large-scale lunette divided by heavy mullions. Art glass or small, square panes of colored glass also appeared in Romanesque design.

Romanesque was popular for banks and public buildings, but storefronts and corner business blocks—especially in brick—were also Romanesque. Substantial, low, and heavy, the buildings implied security and commitment to purpose. A good number of them had corner sites, so as to anchor a business block.

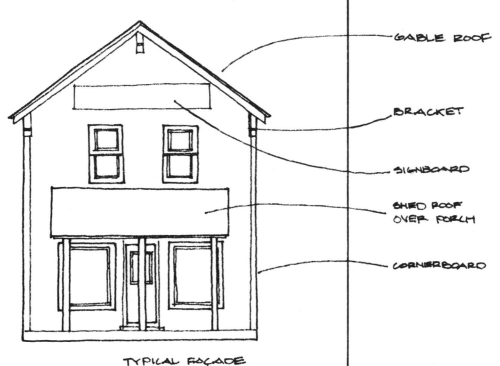

GABLE ROOF

BRACKET

SIGNBOARD

SHED ROOF OVER PORCH

CORNERBOARD

TYPICAL FAÇADE
GABLE-FRONT

WHILE A GOOD NUMBER OF COMMERCIAL BUILD-ing types have been designated for urban settings, the *gable-front* store was most often a small-town or rural building. This frame structure, usually clad in clapboard, served as a general store, hardware or small implements store, grocery, or feed store. Some gable-front stores were used like brick-fronts, the upper level providing living space for the owner.

In design the gable-front was a simple, direct, unadorned building with an assortment of windows—modest display windows on the ground level, but traditional double-hung sash windows in other locations. The straight gable roof and the end-wall gable defined the form, and most elements reinforced that shape. Fenestration was symmetrical, with the entrance on center with the apex of the gable. Most elevations carried no horizontal division between floors, and corners were delineated by narrow corner boards. A shed roof or awning covered the entrance area. Decoration was limited to brackets in the gable, a large signboard on the façade advertising the name of the store, and other boards advertising specific products. Occasionally the gable was clipped, or a gable ornament, or a change of materials such as shingles, was added. The gable-front was an important building; sometimes the post office was part of the store. The gable-front represented the distribution system in the econ-omy and linked outlying areas with commercial develop-ments. Its shape and scale tied it to its location. Locally it was often a center for social activity, service, and information.

CHARACTERISTICS

1-2 STORIES,
FRAME,
GABLE ROOF

OFTEN HAD:
DISPLAY WINDOWS,
½ DOUBLE-HUNG SASH WINDOWS ON 2ND STORY,
SIGNBOARD,
CORNERBOARDS

SOMETIMES:
PORCH

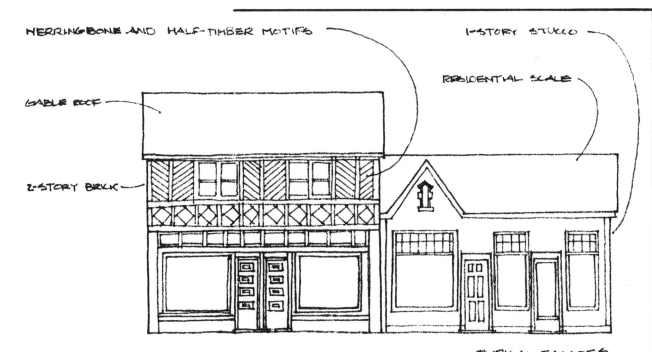

HERRINGBONE AND HALF-TIMBER MOTIFS

1-STORY STUCCO

RESIDENTIAL SCALE

GABLE ROOF

2-STORY BRICK

TYPICAL FAÇADES

CHARACTERISTICS

1 OR 2 STORIES,
DETACHED OR
GROUPED,
RESIDENTIAL
SCALE
OFTEN HAD:
BRICK OR
STUCCO
CLADDING,
GABLE,
INTERSECTING
GABLE, OR
STEPPED
PARAPET ROOF,
RECESSED
ENTRANCE WITH
HOOD OR
GABLE ROOF,
BRICKWORK
ORNAMENTATION
ON WALLS,
HALF-TIMBER
MOTIFS
ON WALLS

ARTISTIC FRONT

AS NEIGHBORHOODS BECAME SETTLED AND filled up with cottages, bungalows, and multifamily buildings, the increase in population and automobiles gave rise to a new kind of secondary business district. It was located within walking distance or within mass transit connections of a neighborhood or on the boundary between two neighborhoods where access by car was necessary. This kind of enterprise was a grouping of stores that offered a wide variety of goods and services. The stores were usually physically connected, so that utilities and façade treatments could be integrated. The major period for this development seems to have been the 1920s, although there were examples of shopping areas built before and long after that decade. They were referred to as *artistic designs*, based on their unusual appearances, which derived from the use of architectural details as attention-getting devices.

The artistic front went directly to the cottage design vocabulary to create intersecting roof forms, gable fronts, stucco and Tudor-trim gables, and historical profiles all bound in clusters, so that individual details could be perceived as belonging to a particular store. Thus each business separated itself from the others, yet still belonged to the group. In part, the artistic front attested to the power of the cottage-based neighborhood and to the successful use of industrially produced materials as a basis for design. Designers and builders alike had no difficulty in applying the housing vocabulary to commercial building. Occasionally these fronts were built as individual businesses (gas stations, florist shops, photography studios) and looked very much like cottages. Symbolically they clearly identified with the local residents and made owners appear sensitive to neighborhood design values.

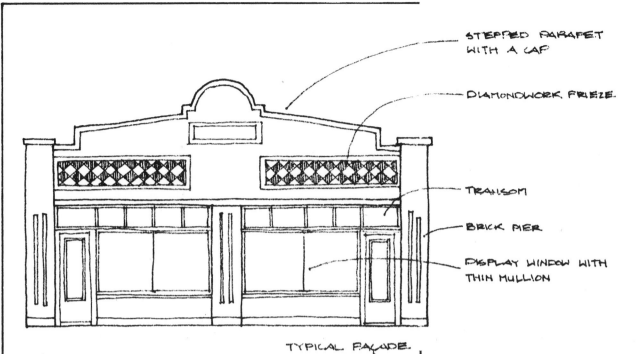

STEPPED PARAPET WITH A CAP

DIAMONDWORK FRIEZE.

TRANSOM

BRICK PIER

DISPLAY WINDOW WITH THIN MULLION

TYPICAL FAÇADE.

MODERN BROAD-FRONT

COMMERCIAL BUILDING PROTOTYPES DID NOT change basic organization and design until modern materials and design encouraged the change. One modern building was the double-width storefront, which has been labeled the *modern broad-front*. This building was both a neighborhood and a central business district building, although in the business districts it was frequently built on a side street. The broad-front embraced two stores or one wide store within one span. Steel beams and columns made this possible. It was most often a low one-story structure that could be twice as deep as it was wide.

The façade design reinforced the openness of the building's face. Two thick piers anchored the edges and held a brick panel that was usually subdivided. Display windows were partitioned into panels of glass with thin mullions, which helped broaden the front, and were topped by a series of continuous transom lights forming a band or clearstory. The open front could have an intermediary column on the façade and carry that back through the building to support the roof. Very often this column was on axis with a decorative treatment on the parapet wall. Ornamentation was simple, with brickwork panels or edges or terra cotta panels or copings around the edges. The broad-front was a linear building. Thin lines bound it together, and it sat lightly on its site. It moved away from the dual-purpose nineteenth-century store, in that it had no living space at all. The broad-front looked as commercially efficient as it was intended to be. Adaptable, it could house various kinds of enterprises. Though it had a few historical details as links to the past, it was originally—and today remains—a modern building.

CHARACTERISTICS
1 STORY,
SINGLE BUILDINGS
OR MULTIPLE
GROUPINGS
OFTEN HAD:
BRICK
CLADDING
(SOMETIMES
SKINTLED
BRICK),
FLAT ROOF
WITH SHALLOW
STEPPED
PARAPET,
DECORATIVE
BRICKWORK
(DIAMONDWORK,
CHECKERWORK,
HIGH-CONTRAST
COLORS),
BRICK PIERS,
TERRA COTTA,
CAST STONE
OR CEMENT
ORNAMENTATION

CHARACTERISTICS

CLADDING:

CLAPBOARD

ROOF:

GABLE

STEEPLE:

TOWER - OFTEN SQUARE, PIERCED WITH WINDOW OR LOUVER, LANTERN - LOUVERED, MOST USED AS BELFRY SPIRE - 4 OR 6 - SIDED, TERMINATES IN CROSS OR FINIAL

WINDOWS:

ROUND - HEADED OR GOTHIC

ENTRANCE:

DOOR IN CENTER OF STEEPLE, PAIRED DOORS COMMON, SOMETIMES HOOD OR ROOF OVER DOOR

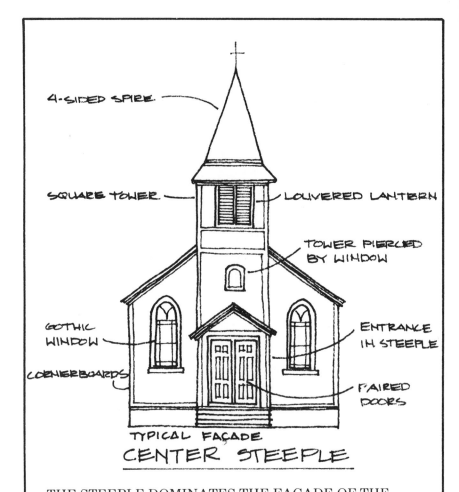

4-SIDED SPIRE

SQUARE TOWER

LOUVERED LANTERN

TOWER PIERCED BY WINDOW

GOTHIC WINDOW

ENTRANCE IN STEEPLE

CORNERBOARDS

PAIRED DOORS

TYPICAL FAÇADE
CENTER STEEPLE

THE STEEPLE DOMINATES THE FACADE OF THE *center steeple* church. The entire organization builds toward the steeple, including the gable roof, which helps pull the façade skyward. Designs with higher porches may align the windows and doors to broaden the elevation. Fenestration is symmetrical. Ornamentation is light; most walls and tower portions are framed by cornerboards and fascia. In steeple design the tower is about half the height of the entire structure, which leaves the lantern and spire in equal proportions to the tower. The tower may be built into the wall or stand separate from it. When the tower projects from the façade, it often serves as a vestibule. Despite its vertical accent, this type of church is earthbound, directly accessible, and orderly.

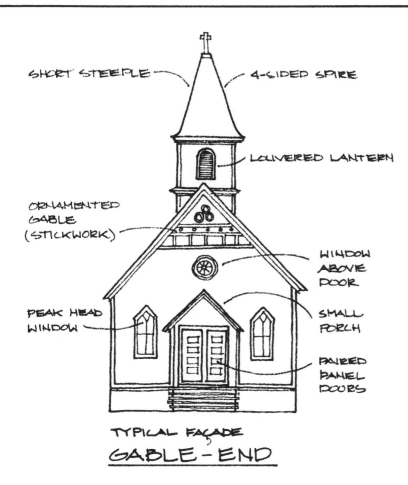

SHORT STEEPLE

4-SIDED SPIRE

LOUVERED LANTERN

ORNAMENTED GABLE (STICKWORK)

WINDOW ABOVE DOOR

PEAK HEAD WINDOW

SMALL PORCH

PAIRED PANEL DOORS

TYPICAL FAÇADE
GABLE-END

AS INDICATED BY ITS NAME, THE *GABLE-END* church exposes a broad gable to the street, the façade being subdivided into a few simple forms. Three-bay organization—window-entrance-window—is most common. Since. the scale of these buildings is often residential, it is not surprising to find residential gable ornament on their façades. The ornamentation scheme includes shingles that divide the gable visually from the rest of the wall, stickwork at the head of the gable, and brackets at the eaves. The small tower, steeple, and spire are rarely taller than the façade itself.

There is a two-story version of the gable-end that may not carry any other design element. A large, broad gable rises sharply to the full height, and the wall is pierced by windows, usually stained glass. The entrance is built on the center axis of the façade. This kind of building may not have any tower on the roof nor any other intersecting sections. The side elevations may feature large windows to light the broad central space.

CLADDING:
CLAPBOARD
ROOF:
GABLE
STEEPLE:
SHORT OR NONE AT ALL, LANTERN AND SPIRE SET BEHIND GABLE, LANTERN - LOUVERED FOR BELFRY, SPIRE-4-SIDED MOST COMMON
GABLE:
ORNAMENTED WITH SHINGLES, BRACKETS, STICKWORK MOTIFS, SOMETIMES CLIPPED GABLE, SOMETIMES BOXED RETURNS
WINDOWS:
0-2 ON FAÇADE, POINTED OR PEAKED HEADS, WINDOW ABOVE DOOR ON CENTER AXIS
ENTRANCE:
SMALL PORCH, HOOD OR GABLE ROOF OVER DOOR, PAIRED PANEL DOORS
WALLS:
3-BAY ORGANIZATION

CHARACTERISTICS

CLADDING:

CLAPBOARD

ROOF:

INTERSECTING GABLE ROOF

STEEPLE:

AT THE ELL, TOWER-SERVES AS ENTRANCE, LANTERN- EXPOSED BELFRY, SPIRE- 4-SIDED WITH FINIAL

GABLE:

WIDE BARGEBOARDS, SHINGLES, STICKWORK

WINDOWS:

PEAK HEAD OR GOTHIC, PAIRED OR TRIPLE

ENTRANCE:

STEEP, SMALL PORCH, TOWER AS VESTIBULE

WALLS:

ELABORATE WEST WALL- MULTIPLE WINDOWS, PRONOUNCED MULLIONS

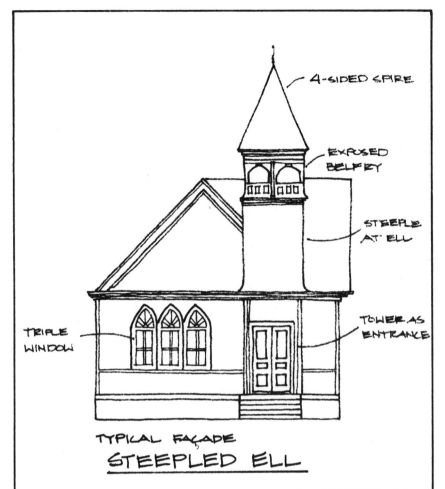

TYPICAL FAÇADE
STEEPLED ELL

THE *STEEPLED ELL* HAS A DIFFERENT DESIGN FROM other gable-end types. It utilizes larger design elements and bolder massing. The gables themselves are wide, and each section can be built as high as two stories. With this kind of configuration, the design consists of large geometric pieces. Even the trim boards are cut to emphasize the geometry: many are wide boards painted a color complementary to the wall, so that the trim outlines and frames entire sections.

At the ell the tower may stand alone or be built partially into the wall. Vertically, the tower and lantern are about the same height as the gable on the façade, with the spire about one third the height of the tower and lantern combined. Steepled ells with high-style intentions often have boxed buttresses at the corners of the tower and along the nave, with surrounds about the doors and windows. Such designs imitate historical masonry construction.

The steepled ell was not a heavily ornamented building. Decorative effects were limited to color (whether paint or in the cladding), some trim work, the tower, and the windows. For the latter, stained glass was often used in the gable ends.

Most churches with façade steeples rely on picturesque visual effects and accordingly are located in rural, suburban, or older residential settings where corner-lot or open-space siting is possible.

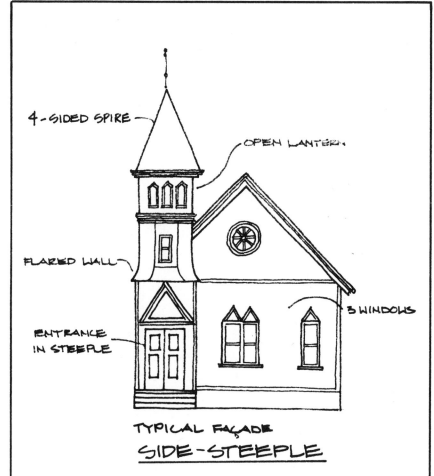

4-SIDED SPIRE

OPEN LANTERN

FLARED WALL

ENTRANCE IN STEEPLE

3 WINDOWS

TYPICAL FAÇADE
SIDE-STEEPLE

THE PLACEMENT OF THE STEEPLE TO THE *SIDE* REquires a bolder window treatment on the façade in order to balance the design. A grouping of windows or a large window with subdivisions is quite common. Other elements that contribute to the unification of the design seem to stem from the power of the gable to focus on simple geometric shapes, many of which can be echoed in the steeple. In churches that have north-south as well as east-west gables, gable-end treatments may vary. North-south gables may also reflect modest transepts; however, transepts are not standard on vernacular churches, as most employ deep, wide naves.

In tower design there is horizontal division of the entire structure, and a breakdown from three to five distinct sections is common. Tower placement varies, but few are freestanding. Most towers mitigate the joining of the tower and gable, regardless of whether the tower is built into or stands next to the body of the building.

The use of ornament on these buildings is restrained, but shingle work and stickwork are common in gables, as are cornerboards and other molding plants that divide walls into panels. The side-steeple church is a holistically conceived building with few divisions among the constituent design elements and emphasis on containing all elements within the gable's embrace.

CLADDING:
CLAPBOARD, BRICK, OR BOARD AND BATTEN

ROOF:
STRAIGHT GABLE

STEEPLE:
SERVES AS ENTRANCE, LANTERN - OFTEN OPEN BELFRY, SPIRE - 4- OR 6- SIDED, SHINGLED

WINDOWS:
PEAK HEAD OR POINTED ARCH, SYMMETRICAL FENESTRATION, 3 WINDOWS COMMON

ENTRANCE:
FEW STEPS, SMALL PORCH, DOUBLE DOOR, MANY HAVE NO PORCH ROOF OR HOOD. TOWER BASE SERVES AS VESTIBULE

WALLS:
HORIZONTAL DIVISIONS

CHURCH: TWIN TOWERS

CHARACTERISTICS

CLADDING:

CLAPBOARD OR BRICK

ROOF:

STRAIGHT GABLE

STEEPLE:

2 TWIN TOWERS - SQUARE, PROJECTING FROM FAÇADE, LANTERN - SQUARE OR 6-SIDED, SHINGLED

WINDOWS

GOTHIC-HEAD OR ROUND - HEADED SYMMETRICAL FENESTRATION, ORNAMENTED WEST WALL WINDOW

ENTRANCE:

CENTRAL OR IN TOWERS, HIGH STEP, SMALL PORCH, WING WALLS

WALLS:

HORIZONTAL AND VERTICAL DIVISIONS

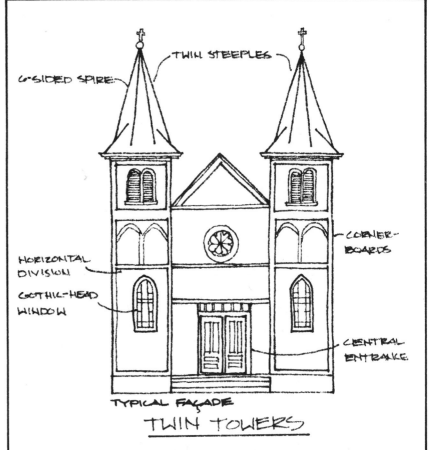

6-SIDED SPIRE

TWIN STEEPLES

HORIZONTAL DIVISION

GOTHIC-HEAD WINDOW

CORNER-BOARDS

CENTRAL ENTRANCE

TYPICAL FAÇADE

TWIN TOWERS

THE *TWIN-TOWER* CHURCH—THE MOST ELABOrate of all—seeks to enhance the west wall. The towers dominate the whole scheme, but towers and wall are integrated through proportional vertical and horizontal elements. For example, the width of the wall may be one-and-a-half or two times the width of a tower, and sections of the wall and tower may align through string courses and cornices. These churches reflect historical treatments of façades and accordingly have special windows, moldings, and other accents.

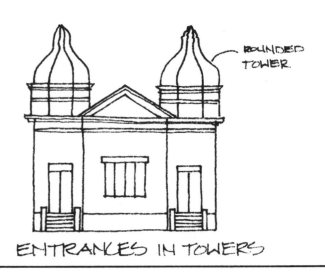

ROUNDED TOWER

ENTRANCES IN TOWERS

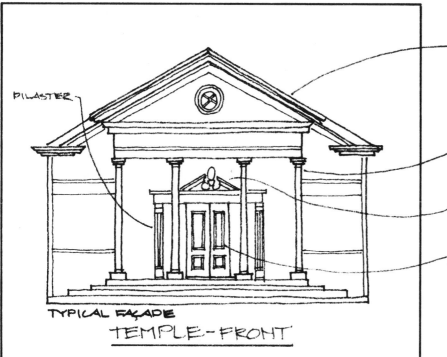

PILASTER

PROJECTING PORTICO

4 COLUMNS, TWO STORIES HIGH

BROKEN PEDIMENT

DOUBLE DOOR

TYPICAL FAÇADE

TEMPLE-FRONT

IN *TEMPLE-FRONT* CHURCHES A LARGE PORTICO projects from the façade. Although the portico derives from historic architecture, the use of orders is not extensive; Tuscan seems the most popular. The portico is frequently tall enough to obscure the roof and the main body of the church, but the side aisles of the nave often project beyond the width of the portico. This arrangement sets up an echo of pediment forms: the raking cornice of the pediment is repeated on the roof of the nave, so that the two forms establish parallel planes. To tie the planes to the same structure, the second cornice—that of the nave roof—may incorporate a return, so that the building's lines move back toward the center.

The focus of this kind of design is on orderly, rational design; a great deal of wall space is given over to windows in order to admit large quantities of light. Light, of course, is symbolically associated with rationality and the power of reason. The walls exhibit little division since the fenestration is the primary organizer of the side elevations, just as the portico is the prime mover of the façade. There is little ornamentation on these buildings. With the emphasis on rational order, even the entablatures are plain. Occasionally one finds an urn or a carved piece in the broken pediment over the entrance door.

CHARACTERISTICS

CLADDING:
  CLAPBOARD
  OR BRICK

ROOF:
  CONTIGUOUS
  GABLES

WINDOWS:
  RECTANGULAR
  SASH,
  MANY LIGHTS,
  SYMMETRICAL
  FENESTRATION

PORCH:
  WIDE AND DEEP,
  LOW STEPS,
  PORTICO PROJECTS
  FROM MAIN BODY,
  2-4 COLUMNS,
  FULL PEDIMENT

ENTRANCE:
  DOUBLE DOORS
  WITH PEDIMENT
  FLANKED BY
  PILASTERS

Bibliography

PATTERN BOOKS AND TRADE CATALOGS

Alladin Plan of Industrial Housing. Bay City, Mich.: The Aladdin Co., 1920.

All American Homes. Los Angeles: E. W. Stillwell and Co., 1927.

Architectural Designs Issued by the T. W. Harvey Lumber Co. Chicago: T. W. Harvey Lumber Co., 1889.

Badger, Daniel D. *Illustrations of Iron Architecture*. 1865; Reprint of *Badger's Illustrated Catalogue of Cast-Iron Architecture*. New York: Dover, 1981.

Better Built Homes, Volume VI. Clinton, Iowa: Curtis Companies, Inc., 1921.

Better Built Homes, Volume VII. Clinton, Iowa: Curtis Companies, Inc., 1920.

Bicknell's Village Builder and Supplement. 1872; Reprint of Watkins Glen, N.Y.: The American Life Foundation and Study Institute, 1976.

Bilt Well Millwork, for Every Home of Comfort. Dubuque, Iowa: Carr, Ryder and Adams Co., 1921.

The Building Brick Association of America. *One Hundred Bungalows*. Boston: Rogers and Manson, 1912.

Bungalowcraft: New English Bungalows. Los Angeles: The Bungalowcraft Co., 1930.

Cement Houses and Private Garages with Constructive Details. Building Age Series, No. 5. New York: David Williams Co., 1912.

Comstock, William Phillips. *Bungalows, Camps and Mountain Houses*. New York: The William T. Comstock Co., 1908.

Ellis, Mary Heard, and Raymond Everett. *The Planning of Simple Homes*. Austin: University of Texas, 1916.

Embury, Aymar II. *The Dutch Colonial House*. New York: McBride, Nast and Co., 1913.

Gibson, Louis H. *Convenient Houses with Fifty Plans for the Housekeeper*. New York: Thomas Y. Crowell and Co., 1889.

Gowing, Frederick H. *Building Plans for Bungalows, Cottages and Other Medium Cost Homes*. Boston: Frederick H. Gowing, 1922.

Holly, Henry Hudson. *Modern Dwellings in Town and Country*. New York: Harper and Brothers, 1878.

Home Plans. Madison, Wis.: Marling Lumber Co., 1925.

Homes for Workmen. New Orleans: Southern Pine Association, 1919.

Homes of Today. Chicago: Sears, Roebuck and Co., 1931.

Illustrated Catalog, 1911–12, Carr and Adams Co. Des Moines: Carr and Adams Co., 1912.

Keith's Plan Book Inexpensive Homes. Minneapolis: Keith Corporation, 1928.

Keith's Twenty Wonder Houses. Minneapolis: M. L. Keith, n.d.

Late Victorian Architectural Details. Combined Book of Sash, Doors, Blinds, Mouldings, Etc. 1898; Reprint of Watkins Glen, N.Y.: The American Life Foundation and Study Institute, 1978.

Lent, Frank T. *Sound Sense in Suburban Architecture*. New York: W. T. Comstock, 1895.

Lindstrom, J. W. *Bungalows*. Minneapolis: J. W. Lindstrom, 1922.

_____. *Cottages and Semi-Bungalows*. Minneapolis: J. W. Lindstrom, 1922.

_____. *Two Story Homes*. Minneapolis: J. W. Lindstrom, 1922.

Low-Cost Houses with Constructive Details. Carpentry and Building Series, No. 2. New York: David Williams Co., 1907.

Millwork Catalog No. 121. Fond Du Lac, Wis.: Moore and Galloway Lumber Co., 1900.

Modern Dwellings with Constructive Details. Carpentry and Building Series, No. 3. New York: David Williams Co., 1907.

Modern Homes. New Orleans: Southern Pine Association, 1921.

Pacific Universal Catalog of Sash, Doors, Millwork, Art Glass, and Odd Work. Charles K. Spaulding Logging Co., 1923.

Palliser's Model Homes. 1878; rpt. Felton, Calif.: Glenwood Publishers, 1972.

Pedersen, Jens. *Practical Homes*. St. Paul: Brown, Blodgett and Sperry Co., 1922.

Saxton, Glen L. *The Plan Book of American Dwellings*. Minneapolis: Glen L. Saxton, 1914.

Saylor, Henry H. *Bungalows*. 2nd ed. New York: McBride, Nast and Co., 1913.

Schumacher, W. H. *A New Book of Distinctive Houses*. Oklahoma City: Distinctive Books Publishers, 1938.

Shopell, Robert W. *How to Build, Furnish, and Decorate*. New York: Cooperative Building Plan Association, 1883.

Stickley, Gustav. *Craftsman Homes*. New York: The Craftsman Publishing Co., 1909.

_____. *More Craftsman Homes*. New York: The Craftsman Publishing Co., 1912.

Suburban Homes with Constructive Details. Building Age Series, No. 4. New York: David Williams Co., 1912.

Two-Family and Twin Houses. New York: William T. Comstock, 1908.

Universal Millwork Design Book No. 20. Dubuque, Iowa: Universal Catalogue Bureau, 1920.

Victorian Architecture. Reprint of A. J. Bicknell, *Detail, Cottage and Constructive Architecture*, 1873, and William T. Comstock, *Modern Architectural Designs and Details*, 1881. Watkins Glenn, N.Y.: The American Life Foundation and Study Institute, 1979.

The Vitrolite Company (catalog). Chicago: The Vitrolite Co., 1927.

Von Holst, Hermann Valentin. *Modern American Homes.* 1913; Reprint of *Country and Suburban Homes of the Prairie School Period.* New York: Dover, 1982.

Whitehead, Russell F. *Good Houses: Typical Historic Architectural Styles for Modern Wood-Built Homes.* St. Paul: Weyerhouser Forest Products, 1922.

Wooden and Brick Buildings with Details. New York: A. J. Bicknell and Co., 1875.

HISTORIC SURVEYS AND REHABILITATION GUIDES

The Buildings of Biloxi: An Architectural Survey. Biloxi, Miss.: City of Biloxi, 1976.

Bunting, Bainbridge, and Robert H. Nylander. *Report Four: Old Cambridge.* Survey of Architectural History in Cambridge. Cambridge, Mass.: Cambridge Historical Commission, 1973.

The Burlington Book. By the Historic Preservation Program, Department of History, University of Vermont. Burlington, Vt.: University of Vermont Historic Preservation Program, 1980.

Charles City, Iowa: A Historic Inventory. Charles City, Iowa: City of Charles City, 1976.

Cheyenne Landmarks. Cheyenne, Wy.: Laramie County Chapter, Wyoming State Historical Society, 1976.

Downing, Antoinette F., Elisabeth MacDougall, and Eleanor Pearson. *Report Two: Mid-Cambridge.* Survey of Architectural History in Cambridge. Cambridge, Mass.: Cambridge Historical Commission, 1967.

Early Cheyenne Homes: 1880–1890. Cheyenne, Wy.: Laramie County Chapter, Wyoming State Historical Society, 1975.

Field Guide to Historic Sites Survey in South Dakota. Vermillion, S. Dak.: Historical Preservation Center, 1982.

Gebhard, David, et al. *A Guide to Architecture in San Francisco and Northern California.* 2nd ed. Santa Barbara: Peregrine Smith, Inc., 1973.

Goeldner, Paul. *Utah Catalog—Historic American Buildings Survey.* Salt Lake City: Utah Heritage Foundation, 1969.

Goins, Charles R., and John W. Morris. *Oklahoma Homes Past and Present.* Norman, Okla.: University of Oklahoma Press, 1980.

Heimsath, Clovis. *Pioneer Texas Buildings: A Geometry Lesson.* Austin: University of Texas Press, 1968.

Henderson, Arn, Frank Parman, and Dortha Henderson.
Architecture in Oklahoma: Landmark & Vernacular.
Norman, Okla.: Point Riders Press, 1978.

Heritage Preservation Associates, Inc. *Building Kenosha.*
Kenosha, Wis.: City of Kenosha, Department of Community Development, 1982.

. *Historic Janesville: An Architectural History of
Janesville, Wisconsin.* Janesville, Wis.: City of Janesville,
Department of Community Development, 1982.

Hoffstot, Barbara D. *Landmark Architecture of Palm
Beach.* Pittsburgh: Ober Park Associates, Inc., 1980.

Howard, Cynthia. *Your House in the Streetcar Suburb.* Medford, Mass.: City of Medford Department of Community
Development, 1979.

Indianapolis Architecture. Indianapolis: Indiana Architectural Foundation, 1975.

Krim, Arthur J. *Report Five: Northwest Cambridge.* Survey
of Architectural History in Cambridge. Cambridge, Mass.:
Cambridge Historical Commission, 1977.

Lafore, Laurence. *American Classic.* Iowa City: Iowa State
Historical Department, 1975.

Legner, Linda. *City House: A Guide to Renovating Older
Chicago-Area Houses.* Chicago: Commission on Chicago
Historical and Architectural Landmarks, 1979.

Linley, John. *Architecture of Middle Georgia.* Athens, Ga.:
University of Georgia Press, 1972.

Nineteenth Century Houses in Lawrence, Kansas. Lawrence: University of Kansas Museum of Art, 1968.

Omaha City Architecture. Omaha, Nebr.: Landmarks, Inc.,
and the Junior League of Omaha, Inc., 1977.

Pearson, Arnold, and Esther Pearson. *Early Churches of
Washington State.* Seattle: University of Washington
Press, 1980.

Peat, Wilbur D. *Indiana Houses of the Nineteenth Century.*
Indianapolis: Indiana Historical Society, 1962.

Pitts, Carolyn, Michael Fish, Hugh J. McCauley, and Trina
Vaux. *The Cape May Handbook.* Philadelphia: The Athanaeum of Philadelphia, 1977.

Preservation Guidelines. Trenton, N.J.: City of Trenton Department of Housing, 1979.

Preserving Waukesha's Past. Waukesha, Wis.: City of
Waukesha, 1982.

Proctor, Mary, and Bill Matuszeski. *Gritty Cities.* Philadelphia: Temple University Press, 1978.

*Rehab Right: How to Rehabilitate Your Oakland House
without Sacrificing Architectural Assets.* Oakland, Calif.:
City of Oakland Planning Department, 1978.

Reiff, Daniel D. *Architecture in Fredonia, 1811–1972.* Fredonia, N. Y.: The Michael C. Rockefeller Arts Center Gallery
and State University College, 1972.

Report Three: Cambridgeport. Survey of Architectural History in Cambridge. Cambridge, Mass.: Cambridge Historical Commission, 1971.

Saint Anthony Falls Rediscovered. Minneapolis: Minneapolis Riverfront Development Coordination Board, 1980.

Schwartz, Helen. *The New Jersey House*. New Brunswick, N. J.: Rutgers University Press, 1983.

Shank, Wesley I. *The Iowa Catalog: Historic American Buildings Survey*. Iowa City: University of Iowa Press, 1979.

Sherwood, Bruce T., ed. *On the Mountain, in the Valley: Catskills Architecture, 1750-1920*. Hobart, N. Y.: The Catskill Center for Conservation and Development, Inc., 1977.

Shivers, Natalie. *Those Old Placid Rows*. Baltimore: Maclay and Associates, 1981.

The Shotgun House. Louisville: Preservation Alliance of Louisville and Jefferson County, Inc., 1980.

Sommer, Lawrence J. *The Heritage of Dubuque*. Dubuque, Iowa: The First National Bank of Dubuque, 1975.

Stoehr, C. Eric. *Bonanza Victorian*. Albuquerque: University of New Mexico Press, 1975.

Thomas, George E., and Carl Doebley. *Cape May, Queen of the Seaside Resorts*. Philadelphia: The Art Alliance Press, 1976.

Tulsa Art Deco: An Architectural Era, 1925-1942. Tulsa, Okla.: The Junior League of Tulsa, Inc., 1980.

Wilson, Richard Guy, and Sidney K. Robinson. *The Prairie School in Iowa*. Ames, Iowa: The Iowa State University Press, 1977.

Woodbridge, Sally B., and Roger Montgomery. *A Guide to Architecture in Washington State*. Seattle: University of Washington Press, 1980.

MONOGRAPHS AND ARTICLES

Garvin, James L. "Mail-Order House Plans and American Victorian Architecture." *Winterthur Portfolio* 16 (1981): 309-34.

Grow, Lawrence, ed. *Old House Plans*. New York: Universe Books, 1978.

Harvey, Thomas. "Mail-Order Architecture in the Twenties." *Landscape* 25, No. 3 (1981): 1-9.

Hirshorn, Paul, and Steven Izenour. *White Towers*. Cambridge, Mass.: MIT Press, 1979.

Lancaster, Clay. "The American Bungalow." *The Art Bulletin* 40 (Sept. 1958): 239-53.

National Trust for Historic Preservation, Tony P. Wrenn, and Elizabeth D. Mulloy. *America's Forgotten Architecture*. New York: Pantheon Books, 1976.

Pillsbury, Richard. "Patterns in the Folk and Vernacular House Forms of the Pennsylvania Culture Region." *Pioneer America* 9, No. 1 (July 1977): 12-31.

Rapoport, Amos. "An Approach to Vernacular Design." In James Marston Fitch. *Shelter: Models of Native Ingenuity*. Katonah, N.Y.: The Katonah Gallery, 1982, pp. 43-48.

———. *House Form and Culture*. Englewood Cliffs, N.J.: Prentice-Hall, 1969.

"Some California Bungalows." *The Architectural Record* 18 (Sept. 1905): 217–23.

Stillwell, E. W. "What Is a Genuine Bungalow?" *Keith's Magazine*, April 1916, pp. 273–91.

Vieyra, Daniel I. *"Fill 'er Up."* New York: Collier Macmillan Publishers, 1979.

Warner, Sam B., Jr. *Streetcar Suburbs: The Process of Growth in Boston.* Cambridge, Mass.: Harvard University Press and M.I.T. Press, 1962.

Winter, Robert. *The California Bungalow.* Los Angeles: Hennessey & Ingalls, Inc. 1980.

HANDBOOKS AND DICTIONARIES

Blumenson, John J.-G. *Identifying American Architecture.* Nashville: American Association for State and Local History, 1977.

Burke, Arthur E., J. Ralph Dalzell, and Gilbert Townsend. *Architectural Building Trades Dictionary.* Chicago: American Technical Society, 1950.

Fleming, John, Hugh Honour, and Nikolaus Pevsner. *The Penguin Dictionary of Architecture.* Baltimore: Penguin Books, 1966.

Foley, Mary Mix. *The American House.* New York: Harper Colophon Books, 1980.

Gwilt, Joseph. *Encyclopedia of Architecture.* Aberdeen: Aberdeen University Press, 1912.

Hammett, Ralph W. *Architecture in the United States.* New York: John Wiley and Sons, 1976.

Harris, Cyril M., ed. *Historic Architecture Sourcebook.* New York: McGraw-Hill Book Co., 1977.

Lloyd, William B. *Millwork: Principles and Practices.* Chicago: Cahners Publishing Co. and The National Woodwork Manufacturers Assoc., Inc., 1966.

Moss, Roger. *Century of Color, 1820–1920.* Watkins Glenn, N. Y.: The American Life Foundation and Study Institute, 1981.

Rifkind, Carole. *A Field Guide to American Architecture.* New York: New American Library, 1980.

Saylor, Henry H. *Dictionary of Architecture.* New York: John Wiley and Sons, 1952.

Scott, John S. *The Penguin Dictionary of Building.* New York: Penguin Books, 1964.

Sturgis, Russell. *A Dictionary of Architecture and Building.* New York: Macmillan Co., 1902.

Walker, Lester. *American Shelter.* Woodstock, N. Y.: Overlook Press, 1981.

Whiffen, Marcus. *American Architecture since 1780.* Cambridge, Mass.: M.I.T. Press, 1969.

Whiton, Sherrill. *Elements of Interior Design and Decoration.* Philadelphia: J. B. Lippincott Co., 1951.

INDEX